The Other Latin@

Camino del Sol
A Latina and Latino Literary Series

The Other Latin@

Writing Against a Singular Identity

Edited by
Blas Falconer and Lorraine M. López

THE UNIVERSITY OF ARIZONA PRESS | TUCSON

The University of Arizona Press
© 2011 The Arizona Board of Regents

www.uapress.arizona.edu

Library of Congress Cataloging-in-Publication Data
The other Latino : writing against a singular identity / edited by Blas Falconer
and Lorraine M. López.
    p. cm. — (Camino del sol)
  Includes bibliographical references.
  ISBN 978-0-8165-2867-7 (pbk.)
    1. American literature—Hispanic American authors—History and criticism.
2. Identity (Philosophical concept) in literature. 3. Stereotypes (Social psychol-
ogy) in literature. 4. Characters and characteristics in literature. 5. Hispanic
Americans—Intellectual life. I. Falconer, Blas. II. López, Lorraine, 1956–
  PS153.H56O74 2011
  810.9'868073—dc23
                             2011034940

Publication of this book is made possible in part by the proceeds of a permanent
endowment created with the assistance of a Challenge Grant from the National
Endowment for the Humanities, a federal agency.

Contents

Foreword   vii
William Luis

Acknowledgments   xi

Introduction   1
Blas Falconer and Lorraine M. López

1   The Long Road Home   9
Lisa D. Chávez

2   Latina Enough   15
Stephanie Elizondo Griest

3   Love, Prejudice, and Latinidad   21
Carla Trujillo

4   Coyotes   27
Alex Espinoza

5   A Latinidad Litmus Test   33
Teresa Dovalpage

6   When We Were Spanish   39
Lorraine M. López

7   My Word Hunger   47
Judith Ortiz Cofer

8   Jotonovela   53
Erasmo Guerra

9   Island of Bones   61
Joy Castro

10   Aesthetics and Theme: Time and Place
(with an afterword on Polemics)   69
Steven Cordova

11   What We Write About When We Write About Gangs   75
Daniel Chacón

12   Latte No! Notes on a (Late) Latino Awakening   85
Urayoán Noel

13   "I Don't Write About Cuba"   91
Helena Mesa

14   The Child in the House   99
Gina Franco

15 A Meditation on the Experience and Aesthetics of the Other Rican 107
    Blas Falconer
16 Curative Poetics   113
    Maria Melendez
17 Chola de los Hinterlands   119
    Carmen Giménez Smith
18 My Emily Gore: Freudian Obsessions, Biculturalism, and
        Autobiographical Poetry   123
    Peter Ramos
19 Fringe Poetics   131
    Gabe Gomez
20 La Página Roja   137
    Lucha Corpi
21 Afterword   145
    William Luis

    Bibliography   155
    About the Contributors   157

Foreword

WILLIAM LUIS

A cursory reading of the essays gathered here (and in other Latino works) shows that Latino literature tends to narrate a familiar and personal experience, mainly from a first-person perspective. The author provides insight into the life of the protagonist, who has undergone a significant experience or come to terms with a particular moment in the past. Read together, these stories lay the foundation for a collective memory—I would argue a necessary one—that documents the lives of Latinos in the United States, because history, whether written in the United States or in Spanish-speaking countries, has omitted their customs from any official discourse. US history has not recorded in a systematic manner their experiences as part of a long-standing tradition that can be traced to an expanding nation with continental aspiration. In the nineteenth century, such aspirations are represented by the annexation of parts of Florida as early as 1810, the Treaty of Guadalupe-Hidalgo of 1848, the arrival of Cubans and Puerto Ricans in New York and other US cities during the first half of the century, and the Spanish American War at its end. For better or worse, literature has assumed the responsibility of filling in that void. It describes the rich Latino experience, with varying ways of life, accents, cuisines, music, religions, customs, and cultures; in cities, suburbs, and countryside; in states with large populations but also those as sparsely populated as Alaska; all essential components of US history and society. These same factors necessarily impact the histories of their cultures of origin. Literature, I argue, antecedes history, politics, philosophy, theory, and literary criticism.

For Latinos, writing is a journey to the past, undertaken in order to gain greater understanding of who we are, where we came from, and what we have become—necessary information for answering questions about our present concept of identity. By and large, a young protagonist refers to a moment of an awakening consciousness that allows the author to explore, reflect, and understand the past in relation to the present. The other persona, the innocent one, fascinates and intrigues us; he/she lives in a sacred and protected moment before the fall, prior to damnation. If we take into account certain historical and cultural forces, the past could have been different from, perhaps worse than, what it was; even, at its worst, marked by the absence of writing. But the past also helps us to understand and even justify the present. Writing allows us to search for and uncover how the world around us could have reflected a different reality of life after the fall. So, literature negotiates a way of coming to terms with a reality present in the past that we did not fully understand at the time we lived that moment in time. We are mesmerized by our blindness, innocence, and wants, for writing represents an indispensable tool for uncovering the past.

While this structure may be commonplace for many writers, for Latinos it has become an obsession of sorts, not only because it says something about who we are but also because it provides information about our communities, thus allowing us to share and understand the varied Latino experiences, the similarities and differences that exist among all the Latino groups, linked to each other like a desiring-machine.[1]

Latino literature creates a collective memory and lays the foundation for a narrative that is social, cultural, racial, linguistic, and historical, and one not available in official texts. As a collective project, this book documents more than just an individual voice or perspective. On the contrary, it conveys different ways of speaking, walking, acting, thinking, and writing; that is, the cultural traits of a growing and expanding population that has been and will continue to be a part of the United States. As Latinos, we are curious to know how our lives are similar but also different from others who look like us or like someone in our family; how our place of origin or residence makes us distinct; and how each of us has been impacted by the dominant US culture. We want to know how each of us has navigated the murky waters of the so-called American Dream. How did we achieve success? What types of adversities did we face? How did we overcome them? Could it have been different? There is ample evidence, and the media constantly tells the same tired story, of those who failed. However, there are untold stories of the many who survived. Each experience is different yet familiar. In some respects, there is a desire or responsibility, if we wish to share our lives with each other, to better understand who we are as communities of Latinos in the broad sense of the word.

Only a handful of books, movies, and television programs—from both high and low culture—represent Latinos or certain aspects of the Latino experience, and the images that are propagated, like those of the African American community, are more often than not caricatures. The dominant society pressures Latinos to abandon our sense of identity and accept a commercialized version of the people they perceive us to be, as promoted by the mass media. And those with black or dark complexions have to withstand a stronger reaction, one more difficult to overcome and with lasting effects. The broader term Latino, that is, "the other Latino," as used not in Spanish but as an integral part of the US culture, allows for the desiring-machine to be connected to other Latinos who may be similar to and yet different from us, for Chicanos to connect to Cubans, to Salvadorians, and so on. For Latino identity is not singular but plural. It is not only how people see you, but how you see and consider yourself, at times regardless of origin or family, place of birth, or upbringing. Identity is a machine that connects to another machine; it is a process without a beginning or an end.

Like the writers in this collection, I am "the other Latino" or another Latino. Though my father was from Guangzhou, China, and my mother from Caibarién, Cuba, I was born and raised in New York City. As a child I had the visible markers of a "foreigner" at a time in which identity became a mandate for some and an act of resistance for others. In the Lower East Side of the Manhattan of my childhood—or as many Nuyoricans have come to know it,

Loisaida—the school forms, which reflect the manner of thinking of local government officials, demanded students to identify themselves as either white, black (I believe that back then the operative term was "negro"), or Puerto Rican, something that puzzles me to this day, since Puerto Rican is not a race. It did show, however, the insistence on classifying non-whites into perceived racial categories. Without an "identifiable" community, I became the perpetual outsider or, as Tato Laviera has termed this, "Nideaquínideallá." While I attempted to navigate through the different types of cultures, many of my friends stayed within their own ethnic or linguistic groups. Still, most of my time was spent with my Puerto Rican and African American and later my Chinese pals, though each group only accepted the side of me that reinforced its interest or sense of identity. When I was with my Puerto Rican friends, we sometimes talked about Puerto Rican and Hispanic cultures in Spanish but mainly we spoke in English; with my African American buddies, we were drawn to the culture associated with our dark skins; with my Chinese neighbors, we shared an Asian background and traditions, in which martial arts played an important role; and with my Jewish, Polish, and Italian schoolmates, we discussed school and other pertinent matters that were of interest to all of us. Little did I know that each group had a profound influence on me and that, as the "other Latino," all of the communities impacted my identity and writing. When I looked back, I did not feel comfortable accepting one identity over another but felt the need to embrace all of my multiple identities. I continue to ask myself, why must we limit ourselves to one identity and choose one over another? Is it not possible for many of us to have more than one way of expressing who we are?

Note

1. The desiring-machine is a concept that I define and elaborate upon in the Afterword to this book.

Acknowledgments

We would like to thank the contributors, who inspire us to think beyond conventional categories in Latino literature. Critic William Luis deserves special thanks for writing the Foreword and the Afterword. We are also grateful to Matthew Baker, our graduate student assistant whose proofreading skills greatly benefited this work. Finally, we would like to recognize the University of Arizona Press for its support of this project and for its commitment to publishing books that address concerns of diversity.

The Other Latin@

Introduction

BLAS FALCONER AND LORRAINE M. LÓPEZ

All Latinos share some Latin American heritage. Apart from this, there is no essential or singular trait of Latino identity. Nonetheless, in the United States, Latinos or Hispanics are often viewed as a monolithic and homogeneous group. Of course, this is an impossibly narrow categorization, an imaginary space for filing diverse people in a singular slot for purposes of fast access and easy comprehension. Many Latinos are likewise complicit in constructing this fictive categorization in order to create the illusion of solidarity, the myth of unanimity that promises national political power. From such reductive and oversimplified ideas of cultural identity, the Latino writer often appears on the scene as a mediator, translator, or insider ethnographer bearing literary artifacts from the native culture to enlighten and entertain members of the dominant culture. He or she often succumbs to the pressure to support the illusion of cultural cohesion despite multiple variations that challenge, counter, and flat out deny the assertions of sameness that are necessary for promoting even the feasibility of such a spokesperson. Still other Latino writers and many literary theorists resist essentializing myths of Latino cultural identity while somehow clinging to the notion of a clearly recognizable Latino experience presented through literature.

The preeminent Chicana author and theorist, the late Gloria Anzaldúa, is best known for resisting reductive, essentialist cultural narratives. In *Borderlands/ La Frontera: The New Mestiza*, Anzaldúa states, "I, a mestiza, must continually walk out of one culture and into another, because I am in all cultures at the same time." As such, she portrays her experience of culture as what critic Yvonne Yabro-Bejarano terms "a constantly shifting process or activity of breaking down binary dualisms." Although Anzaldúa's objective is to take apart paradigms in the process of decolonizing the self, her own writing often evokes comparatives that reinforce cultural essence with allusions to the Chicano people being "indigenous like corn" and similar to "the chile colorado." Despite the fact that many Latino authors struggle against being confused with Latin American writers and resist the concomitant expectation to manufacture magical realism, Anzaldúa further claims that US Latinos and Latin Americans share a "common culture."

In an essay titled "On Finding a Latino Voice," the Dominican American author Julia Alvarez likewise articulates an inherent cultural bond between herself and William Carlos Williams, a poet born of a Puerto Rican mother and a North American father. In another piece titled "Democracy and Literature," Cuban American writer Pablo Medina derides Alvarez's claim to a "deep unconscious ethnic connection" to Williams as sentimentality, as "kitsch." Medina goes on to assert that Williams is "as quintessentially and unhyphenatedly American" as Whitman, stating that Williams "is a poet whose work transcends nationality and ethnicity and affects us on a human level." By such reasoning, writing that essentializes cultural experience is incapable of transcending its categorization, to speak beyond and outside of its own definition of self. Medina's essay argues against "the tyranny of the adjective" or our national "predilection for labeling" people. He complains that "too many critics and editors tend to rely on labels because they make easier what is, essentially, a very difficult task: the evaluation of literature." To exemplify this, Medina recounts a time a book review editor declined to assign a novel of his to a reviewer because it proved difficult to find someone to do "that kind of book" without explaining or even knowing anything about the kind of book Medina had written beyond the fact that he, a Cuban American, had written it.

While Medina reacts against the constraints of cultural labeling and its impact on literary production and promotion, essayist Richard Rodriguez eschews the term *Latino* itself, questioning its preferred political correctness. "In fact," Rodriguez writes, "*Latino* commits Latin American to Iberian memory as surely as does *Hispanic*." He states his preference for Hispanic over Latino thusly: "To call oneself Hispanic is to admit a relationship to Latin America in English. Soy Hispanic is a brown assertion." And author Sandra Cisneros has reportedly turned on her heel to stride out of bookstores with sections labeled *Hispanic*. "The term Hispanic makes my skin crawl," Cisneros says. "It's a very colonistic term, a disrespectful term, a term imposed on us without asking what we wanted to call ourselves." Because the word was coined for census purposes during the Nixon administration, Cisneros believes that the dominant culture affixed this label as a way of erasing Latino identity. Diversity within the cultural group complicates even the simple act of referring to ourselves appropriately, and in Medina's case, this raises the question of whether we should be called anything at all.

Such contradiction and dissent testifies to the undeniable diversity within this cultural diversity, especially among those engaged in production of this literature. This sampling of conflicting positions and beliefs compels the question: How can we treat US Latino literary production as a definable corpus while allowing for multiple and shifting identities and perspectives along with the ongoing transformation of Latino culture? This interrogatory shapes our project in collecting these essays. While we seek to engage literary works by Latino writers as a recognizable opus in which varied pieces are linked by shared experiences specific to culture, we also believe it is our responsibility to defy the limitations that categorization imposes on production of creative work and especially to dismantle stereotypes concerning cultural identity. Clearly the stereotype spells death to the imagination by shrinking all possibilities into one. Generalizations encourage us to stop considering what can be, in favor of using a stereotype shorthand as a way to stop thinking. They dehumanize people by divesting them of individuality and replacing it with facile categorization and dismissive judgment.

The impulse to define and neatly categorize the Latino experience not only shapes the way that Latino literature is understood; it influences what is available to us, what is acceptable to publishers, and what is read in the classroom. In her essay, "Island of Bones," Joy Castro begins, "Anthologies don't mention us." By us, she means those Cubans who immigrated to the United States before the so-called first wave in 1959: the lower classes and the economic refugees as opposed to the professional and upper-class political exiles whose experiences dominate and define Cuban American narratives. The anthologies also tend to exclude authors like Teresa Dovalpage, who grew up in postrevolutionary Cuba and immigrated to the United States after marrying a missionary when she was thirty. By writing books in both Spanish and English, she straddles two cultural groups as a Latin American and as a Latina writer.

Judith Ortiz Cofer similarly describes her experience of exclusion and consequent feelings of shame for being unable to write and speak fluently in Spanish by recalling her panicked response when asked to present a paper in her native tongue. "A puerto-riqueña who will not write or give a talk in her native language," she writes. "¡Que vergüenza!" Ortiz Cofer's meditation on language mourns the loss of her first language, Spanish, as a signifier of the lost realm of childhood and familial intimacy, a closed door that cracks open now and again, never to swing wide the way it once did. Other authors, including Lisa D. Chávez, Stephanie Elizondo Griest, and Lorraine M. López, also confess a linguistic limitation—the lack of Spanish—that has always compromised a full sense of belonging to this monolithic cultural group. Apart from some connection to Latin American culture, nothing defines Latino identity more in mainstream consciousness than the Spanish language.

The immigrant experience, though, is a close runner-up. Many Chicanos—who comprise the largest group of Latinos, outnumbering all other groups combined, doubled—descend from Hispanics who resided in what is now the mainland United States before Jamestown was established. Nevertheless, the common assumption that Latinos comprise an immigrant culture prevails. A recent review of a novel that spans a century and a half in the lives of native Hispanics and indigenous Hopi and Pueblo characters oddly lauds the Latina author for "yet another take on the immigrant experience." Authors Carla Trujillo and Lorraine M. López address the persistence of this assumption about Latino identity in their contributions to this collection; the former probes the prejudice emanating from native Chicanos toward those who have emigrated recently from Mexico, suggesting that there are at least as many ways to be Chicano as there are to be Latino.

If the aforementioned literary anthologies are designed around common experiences and themes, then Latino texts, attempting to reflect the diversity in America and American literature, ironically run the risk of excluding those authors who do not fit neatly into the parameters outlined by scholars and editors. Furthermore, if educators at all levels are unfamiliar with this literature, they will likely seek out what is widely available or look for recognizable (i.e., stereotypic) tropes, themes, and props in selecting texts for teaching the growing number of Latino students in their classes. In all cases, the idea of "that kind of book," as expressed by the editor referred to by Pablo Medina, speaks to the notion that the well-established authors and the widely available texts perform an especially implausible synecdoche, in which the anomalously successful part represents the whole of Latino literature, encouraging scholars, editors, and educators in the false belief that they have done due diligence to this great and sprawling corpus of literature by covering one or two pieces by the most well-known Latino authors.

In an effort to challenge notions of a singular and essentialized cultural identity, to redefine this corpus of literary production accordingly, and to complement existing scholarship on Latino literature, we invited writers whose work diverges from expected cultural narratives to consider how their unique experiences relate to recurring themes in their work and shape their aesthetic concerns. We invited prose writers and poets, men and women, straight and gay, writers of different races and experiences. We invited Chicanos and Puerto Ricans, Dominican Americans and Cuban Americans, as well as those who have connections to other, less represented Latin American countries. They are unique because of the themes they raise in their books and the way they approach writing. Together, these authors reflect the richness of the Latino community and the growing body of Latino literature.

Several contributors focus primarily on experiences that challenge what many perceive to be a Latino "narrative." For example, in her essay, "The Long Road Home," Lisa D. Chávez describes growing up with her Norwegian American mother far from a close-knit Latino community. She writes, "There simply weren't many Latina/os in Alaska then; despite my last name, I melted quickly into being seen as 'Native,' and that formed my identity." Stephanie Elizondo Griest also examines her bicultural identity to consider how "passing" in elementary school led to the initial privileging of her Euro-American heritage and later plagued her with guilt: "As absurd as it sounds, I actually started wishing that my skin was darker, my accent thicker, so that I could endure the discrimination that befell real Mexicans." Early on in "Coyotes," Alex Espinoza dismisses the notion of a common narrative: "Growing up Mexican and poor is one thing, but growing up Mexican, poor, and disabled was something else entirely." Urayoán Noel, too, rejects a fixed definition, stating, "My own Latino awakening came late. Or rather, it's still happening. Like this city. This brain. This heart." Each author tells his or her unique story, but they all debunk assumptions about Latinos to reflect, among other things, a variety of racial, geographic, cultural, and social-class backgrounds.

These stories complicate our understanding of themes commonly found in Latino literature. In his essay, Steven Cordova recognizes that Latino poems often include a "cast of characters . . . made up of the speaker's family and immediate community. His or her community is, in the final effect, characterized by its ethnicity." Cordova's identity, family, and community are defined by his ethnicity, but also, he writes, "[by] an acceptance of another part of myself—my sexuality, my gayness, my HIV status." Similarly, Blas Falconer draws a connection between his Puerto Rican ethnicity and sexual orientation. Both marked him as an outsider within the mainstream and straight community. In drawing this connection, he calls the essentialist notion of machismo into question. In "Jotonovela," Erasmo Guerra further counters the stoic machismo ideal by revealing how his personal life is inextricably bound to his writing life; dramatic breakups and reconciliations with men inspire him in his role as an "exaderado," an embellisher who draws inspiration from the heartbreak that shapes his work and his identity.

"When I think of Cuban American poetry," Helena Mesa writes, "I think of identity politics. I think about political poetry draped in an elegiac tone . . . . I think about narratives that capture a sense of displacement and exile, that often rock the speaker between the two shores of loss and longing." However, when Mesa writes about Cuba, she doesn't do so out of nostalgia. Cuba, for her, has become, she says, "a portrait of my father, particularly my desire to comfort a loss that I do not possess." The exile narrative, for Mesa, has become a device for considering more personal themes.

In "What We Write About When We Write About Gangs," Daniel Chacón places the "Latino" theme of violence into a larger context to explain how it emerges in his fiction. In doing so, he defends a theme that has lost favor in recent years as well as the risks inherent in generating what can appear, by satisfying the residual mainstream expectation that Chicano culture is synonymous with gang culture, as essentialist literature. As such, Chacón claims the freedom to choose his material rather than have it dictated by concerns over political correctness. As mentioned, Carla Trujillo similarly handles intra-cultural conflict by moving beyond the broadly defined subject of Latino oppression to examine how other forms of prejudice exist within the Latino community. These nuances allow readers to draw connections between those texts that do fall within the dominant narratives and those that do not.

Almost all of the book's essays address the many stylistic choices that Latinos make to articulate these varied experiences or themes, but some challenge writers to explore new means of writing. Lucha Corpi, for example, encourages writers to try their hand at crime fiction. In spite of its formulaic nature, Corpi argues that crime fiction "reveals the injustices of which we have been the victims but also the flaws and the contradictions we carry within us as individuals and as a people." For Corpi, an activist in the Chicano Movement, detective fiction is the ideal vehicle for her to explore the discontinuities of the past and how these discontinuities influence the construction of self in this post-nationalist moment. Peter Ramos, influenced by the Confessional poets as well as the Modernists, agrees. As he explores how his Latino identity—which he attempted to suppress—manifested in his poems, Ramos writes, "One way then to make poetry out of our rich, occasionally confusing heterogeneous backgrounds is to be open to all the artistic influences that are available, regardless of where they come from, and to explore those parts of the self that are not quite clear, yet insist somehow."

Others, such as Gabe Gomez and Carmen Giménez Smith, encourage new methods of expression. While Giménez Smith considers what would happen if more Latino writers moved away from "traditional narrative identity poetry," Gomez urges writers "to push and seek to reinvent [literature] that will ultimately reclaim the understanding of the Latina/o experience in America." Yet some, like Gina Franco in her lyric essay, "The Child in the House," ask not how but if Latino writers can overcome the obstacles that stand in their way. Maria Melendez maintains her faith in poetry's capacity to remedy: "Cures for numbness, for despair, for disconnection—they're what I'm after much of the time, going about my business with words." The contributors remind us that Latino literature resists definition, and that much fiction and poetry falls outside of any list of narratives, themes, and tropes.

Scholar and critic William Luis, in his Afterword on Latino identity, confronts the limitations of cultural definition through equating Latinos and Latino literature to a desiring-machine, a dynamic system linked to other mechanisms that create an often-interrupted flux of desire. Such a metaphor aptly and reasonably privileges the fluid and dynamic quality of cultural identity over a checklist of defining traits. While complicating Luis's own construct of the Latino writer's identity—as one who is connected to people with Latin American or Hispanic heritage but who is "born or raised and educated in the United States and write[s] mainly in English"—the analogy recognizes the disruption of this identity by Hispanic writing produced by writers "born or raised and educated in a Spanish-speaking country," and grapples with identifying writers who are born in this country but migrate to Latin America only to return to the States and write predominantly in Spanish. From an academic perspective, this kinetic system captures a vital aspect of the complexity portrayed in the essays collected here.

Our book's title reflects the idea that the Other is one who appears not to belong to a particular group due to fundamental difference. A group—identified by nation, race, culture, or gender—views itself and is viewed by other groups as possessing certain normative and recognizable characteristics and behaviors. As a consequence, an individual lacking in these definitive traits is perceived as the Other, often relegated to a liminal space outside of the privileges and protection of group affiliation. While the outsider can be taken for the Other, the outsider's status is different, since those outside the group entertain the possibility of self-definition in opposition to the group or of being absorbed into another coalition. The Other, while too perceptibly connected to the target group to be incorporated elsewhere, is profoundly different, missing critical traits that identify the group. The Other Latino exists, then, as a subset apart from the larger cultural collective defined by aforementioned essentializing characteristics until such time that these traits no longer define Latinidad.

This book not only investigates reactions against cultural essentialism. It also seeks to dismantle an absurdly narrow definition of this wide and sprawling collective of individuals by honoring the diversity within this diversity: the right—as Gloria Anzaldúa says—"to carve and chisel" our own distinct and varied identities, to crawl out from under the umbra of ethnic writer, predictable performer of the same old dance to the same old tune, churning out charmingly harmless tales deploying the usual cultural signifiers—the wise abuela, the chaotic barrio, the ubiquitous helpings of rice and beans—with inconsequential sprinklings of Spanish added like exotic spice to make it ethnic. Only when we honor the multiplicity of voices in our cultural group can we honor the artistic spirit that drives us to create, as our first complex and original creation must be the self.

1

The Long Road Home
LISA D. CHÁVEZ

I want . . . an accounting with all three cultures—white, Mexican, Indian. I want the freedom to carve and chisel my own face, to staunch the bleeding with ashes, to fashion my own gods out of my entrails. And if going home is denied me then I will have to stand and claim my space, making a new culture—una cultura mestiza.

—Gloria Anzaldúa, *Borderlands/La Frontera*

Where I grew up there are glaciers wider than highways, and the aurora swoop and swirl in the winter sky, loops and ribbons of green, blue, and red. Where I grew up winter's brief sun makes riches of snow—light refracting on ice crystals, making fields of sapphires and diamonds. That lazy sun barely rises in winter, and in summer it can't stop shining—hours of light and summer frenzy. Where I grew up there are grizzly bears and moose, wolves and salmon.

Where I grew up there is white and more white: ice-paved roads, and snow falling on snow. Sometimes it seemed everything was white, even the people.

Where I grew up, in Alaska, there were not many people like me.

There were people that looked like me, Alaska Natives, people who were Athabascan or Tlingit or Yupik. We were superficially similar: brown skin, dark hair, high cheekbones. There simply weren't many Latina/os in Alaska then; despite my last name, I melted quickly into being seen as "Native," and that formed my identity.

There was one Chicano at my high school, and he was a Chavez too. He was handsome, somewhat popular, lighter skinned than I, and we never spoke. It was instant avoidance—perhaps he had discovered what I had learned: here no one had opinions about Latinos, positive or negative, and a Spanish surname did not bring the sort of stigma it might have in southern California in the seventies, so he was free to re-create himself, his skin color and facial features affording him an entry into whiteness I did not have. I knew some things about him: that he, like me, was originally from California; that we were the same age and had arrived in Alaska in the same year—1975. Mostly I knew what I saw once—someone asked him if I was his sister, and he recoiled as if slapped. No! People asked me the same question, and I had the same answer, though perhaps not the same expression. No. We never spoke, two Chicanos adrift in the great white north.

Our identity shapes our art indelibly, whether it is something we write about or something we avoid. I have always written about the strange

borderland I found myself in: a Chicana born in Los Angeles but raised by an
Anglo mother in Fairbanks, Alaska, where I was always seen as Alaska Native—
Indian—regardless of my last name, regardless of my attempts to explain my
mixed heritage. Entirely mestiza, a word and idea I was decades away from
encountering.

I grew up far from my Chicano father and grandparents back in southern
California. Far from the cousins in New Mexico that I would not meet for years.
Far from tortillas and refried beans—okay, not true—I ate those all the time. But
far from most expected markers of Latinidad. I talk about this with my friends
who also grew up away from the hubs of Latino identity in the United States,
far from LA or Miami, Chicago or New York. We have no poems about abuelas
or tortillas, no poems about coquís or rice and beans; we have eschewed the
details that provide the typical Latin flavor. My poems are about identity, yes,
but when I wrote about race and racism, I wrote about the Native people I grew
up around, who accepted me unconditionally and easily, and who helped me
survive and shape my identity in the face of a profound white racism. Even my
images are not those of the typical Latina—if there is such a thing. My images
are drawn from the landscape I loved: fireweed and river ice, ptarmigan and
black spruce, and the breathtaking cold of fifty below zero.

Alaska is a beautiful place, but harsh and unforgiving. Where I grew up,
we watched gruesome films in school on the effects of frostbite, and everyone
was told to keep emergency supplies in their cars: blankets, an extra parka and
boots, food, matches. An accident on a road far from town could mean more
than inconvenience in those days before cell phones—it could mean death if
you weren't prepared. If you weren't tough. Long before white people came to
Alaska, the Athabascan people of the interior called spring the starving season,
and many died after those long cold winters. In those days long past, people in
Alaska lived a hard, marginal existence, barely surviving. It was like that for me
too—so compelling and beloved that I felt like I'd amputated a limb when I left
for good; for years I thought of myself as in exile. And yet, harsh, so harsh. I
wrote of all of it: the cruel beauty of that hard, isolated place.

It's caused confusion, my mixed identity. In Alaska, sometimes people
tried to speak to me in Athabascan or in Yupik. Once I left Alaska—to graduate school in Tempe, Arizona—I was in a world where my looks and last name
were read differently. I was suddenly thrust into the world of Latina/os. And just
as quickly thrust out, for I didn't speak Spanish and had few ties to the culture
of my father. It happened every time I met another Latino at ASU: there was a
quick exchange in Spanish—with me saying, sorry, I don't speak Spanish—and
then the person would glance away from me. It made me feel odd, inauthentic,
dismissed. In Alaska, people were quick to welcome me into the group—the
Native people, as I said, accepted me without question as a "lower-forty-eight
Indian" and didn't care that I didn't know which tribe, exactly, my father's family came from. I even had a friend from Mexico, who quickly recognized me as
part of the Mexican diaspora, and who spent an entire semester educating me
on the great Mexican writers—Fuentes and Paz and Rulfo—before he went back

to Mexico City. This ease was not the case in Arizona. I was too pocha for the Chicanos, and too detribalized for the Dine', the only Native people I met. Or rather, just not Dine'.

So I took my education elsewhere. I had begun shaping my identity as a woman of color in Alaska, reading everything I could find on race, reading African American writers who addressed the color line in fierce and eloquent poetry and prose. It felt right to call myself a woman of color—for I knew I was not seen as white, a fact driven home one afternoon in Mesa, Arizona, when a man shouted out to my white husband, "Couldn't you find a white woman?" I read Audre Lorde, and met her one memorable afternoon not too long before she died. I remember feeling awkward—I'm not black, and I'm not Latino or Native enough, what am I?—and was utterly comforted by her generous hug and warrior woman advice: women of color need to stick together, regardless of racial or ethnic background. I read Lucille Clifton and Toni Morrison and June Jordan. It would be years before I discovered my own: Gloria Anzaldúa, who gave a name to my identity with her discussion of mestisaje, and Sandra Cisneros, whose rhythms and play slipped into my own poems. In the meantime, I learned to be a strong woman of color.

And I wrote. I wrote about Alaska and race and gender and class. And I realized that the idea of authenticity that I had worried about—the little voice that told me that if I could not produce a tribal designation, I was not really Indian, and if I couldn't speak Spanish, I was not Mexican—that little voice was just another kind of insecurity I could let go of. There is no one way to be Latina. My writing is true to my experiences as a mestiza in this country and thus authentic, whether it contains the obvious markers of ethnicity or not.

Just as I can't tease out the parts of me that are Indio, Hispano, even Anglo (the terms in use here in New Mexico), I can't really tease out where this or that part of my writing comes from. It comes from everywhere—who I am, what I read, what I experience, what I think and dream. The conquistadores birthed a new race in Mexico through conquest and rape, and I am a product of that, though generations removed from Mexico. And I am American, from a country that is in itself a mestisaje, a mix (however it tries to elide that fact). It is hard to pull out particular threads and say this is Latino, this is not. And that word itself, Latino, which I prefer to Hispanic, is only a made-up category. Because what do Dominicans have to do with Mexicans have to do with Cubans? We share—at some point in our family lines—a language, but we come from places with wildly different histories. Some of us are more conversant in that history than others. My way of being Latina is not the same as it is for someone who is Puerto Rican and grew up in New York. Nor is it the same for someone who grew up in LA in the same barrio my father lived in.

I often felt outside what was labeled Latina/o because of my background and because of the subjects I write about. What speaks to me most as a writer, or has, tends to be more "Indian," a word just as invented and vexed as Latina/o or Hispanic. I grew up studying and discussing Native issues—sovereignty, land claims, subsistence hunting rights. I read Native literature, and I even tried to learn to speak Koyukon Athabascan. I have always felt very connected to place, to land, and to my ancestors—even before I knew who they were. Much of my second book, *In an Angry Season* (University of Arizona Press, 2001), developed as I was taking classes in the conflicted history of Native relations with the US government, and my research and obsessions show up in the historical poems in that book. Of course, none of these things are uniquely Native; neither would they make me or anyone else Indian if we were not. They are simply interests, influences; I have read enough theory to dismiss the idea of an essential ethnic or racial core.

I thought my interests and background set me apart, but now I see that what I write about ties me to some of the earliest writers of the Chicano literary movement. I consider myself to be a political writer, and my poems are very often motivated by anger and a desire for justice. I write out of my identity as a woman of color in a white world. I write out of a desire to bear witness. I wrote poems about historical events, such as people of color on display at the World's Fairs, because I couldn't believe that more people don't know about these things. I want history—our complicated and bloody American history—to be known. I long ago learned that I am better at telling stories than I am at anything else, so I try to tell the stories I never learned about in history books. I want justice, even for those long dead, and telling these stories gives me a sense of rewriting history, if only in a very small way. It is in these ways that I am actually very much connected to a tradition of Latina/o political writing and testimonio.

What also compels me as a writer is the ways in which we are similar—the ways that our individual histories echo the histories of other individuals and other ethnic and racial groups. As Gloria Anzaldúa states, "before the Chicano can have unity with Native Americans and other groups, we need to know the history of their struggle and they need to know ours . . . each of us must know our Indian líneage, our afro-mestisaje, our history of resistance." It seems to me that it is only by recognizing the ways we are similar—and by still celebrating our diversity—that we can move forward as a people and as a country. We need to hear each other's stories.

By the time my second book was published, I was comfortable in my identity as a woman of color, even comfortable being a Latina, though a non-Spanish-speaking one. I'd been in classes with Latinas from all over and finally understood some of the diversity hiding behind that word. I'd met black Latinas and white ones from the Dominican Republic; Puerto Ricans and Cubans dark and light; Mexicans that looked like me—Indio—and those that were as fair as my Anglo mother. I felt secure in my mestisaje. So when my book was accepted and I was asked if it should in the Latina/o series or the Native series, I was actually a bit puzzled. How could I choose? I remember talking it over with a Native writer who felt the book should absolutely go in Sun Tracks, because so many of the poems were rooted in the history of conflict between the US government and Native people. But someone else wanted to know my tribal affiliation, and I couldn't produce it, and so I ended up classified by my last name: Chávez, and thus became a Latina writer.

There was a certain irony in all of that. The book was out for a little over a year before I moved to New Mexico and found my Native roots. One summer afternoon, I was standing on the steps of the National Hispanic Cultural Center in Albuquerque, a lovely place that manages to completely elide the Indio side of most Chicana/os and certainly most New Mexicans by focusing heavily on the Spanish. A man approached me—handsome, fair skinned—güero, I guess—and said he thought he was my cousin. I didn't recognize his name, but I knew virtually nothing of my father's family, so this didn't surprise me. But mi primo, Samuel, did surprise me. He took me to his office and showed me a family tree of my grandmother's side of the family, the Padillas. A map of my family, a key to the puzzle of my identity. My history, suddenly, on paper. And thus I learned that my family was from Los Padillas, south of Albuquerque, adjacent to Isleta Pueblo. And yes, my cousin told me, we have relatives at Isleta Pueblo. My family tree spread before me, neatly labeled courtesy of the Spanish obsession with degrees of race, an obsession the United States and the Germans would much later share. My cousin had listed the names and terms he'd found on birth and death and tax records (for so I imagine his research). I saw it again and again: mestiza, mestizo, coyote, puro indio, puro indio. That last appeared again and again, and while the most recent ancestors were mostly from Isleta, as we went back further in time, there were others: Mescalero, Tarahumara. I marveled over this and told my cousin how my father had said we had no Indian blood, a claim I had never believed.

"Of course," my cousin replied. "They all say that. All the old Hispanos here claim that. But look at them. Look at you. It's written in our faces."

"But everyone's Spanish, of course," I joked.

Samuel laughed. He shuffled through papers and pointed to a final distant name. "This was as far back as I could go," he said.

I don't remember the name now, though it was a man's name, nor do I remember the date, except that I was surprised by how early it was: the first half of the 1600s. That was as far back as we could trace the Padilla line, to a long-dead man born in Mexico City. No one came from Spain.

And there it was, on paper too, finally, the mystery of my Indianness, the looks that have somehow surfaced in me from an ancestor long dead. I look more Indian than anyone in my family, am darker than most too, in spite of my Anglo mother.

When I moved to New Mexico, I was moving home and moving into an old old story. I admit I don't see my cousins much, being too unused to being part of a big Hispanic family. But I do visit my ancestors. I have pictures of them on my altar, and I offer them food and drink and talk with them. I spend time in the old cemetery in Los Padillas, looking at the names and dates of people related to me. One day I met a man there who looks after the small cemetery; we talked, and he asked if I had people buried there. "Yes," I said. "My grandmother was a Padilla, though she was not buried here."

He smiled. "I'm a Padilla too, on my mother's side. We're probably cousins."

We probably are.

So now I live in the mountains of New Mexico, the only place I have loved since I left Alaska, and I know that the landscape I see every day is not so dissimilar to the one, generation after generation, that my ancestors knew. Now I breathe in high mountain air, scented with juniper and piñón, and the sky is as blue as the feathers of the scrub jay whose screeches break the afternoon quiet. Now I am surrounded by people who look like me, who may even be related to me. I don't have to spell out my last name or listen to it mispronounced—everyone knows it—even the mayor shares it, and my eye doctor alone has twelve patients named Lisa Chavez. I have moved from being the "other" Latina to being very rooted in a particular place and history, in a place where all the parts of my ancestry—Native, Latino, Anglo—have shaped an entire state. After a long journey, unguided by signposts, I've found my way home.

2

Latina Enough
Stephanie Elizondo Griest

Our reading class had too many students, our teacher announced one day in third grade. We needed to split in two. One by one, she started sending the bulk of the Mexican kids to one side of the room and the white kids to the other. When she got to me, she peered over the rims of her glasses. "What are you, Stephanie? Hispanic or white?"

I had no answer. Both? Neither? Either? My mother's roots dwell beneath the pueblos of northern Mexico; my father's are buried in the Kansas prairie. I had inherited her olive skin and caterpillar eyebrows, but his indigo eyes.

In South Texas, however, you are either one or the other. Scanning the classroom for an answer, I noticed my best friend Melida standing with the brown kids. "I'm Hispanic," I announced. The teacher nodded and I joined the Mexicans. A few minutes later, a new teacher arrived and led us to another room, where she passed around a primer and asked us to read aloud. That's when I realized the difference between the other students and me. Most of them spoke Spanish at home, so they stumbled over the strange English words, pronouncing "yes" like "jess" and "chair" like "share." I had the opposite problem: I spoke fluently in our English-only classroom but stuttered at my abuela's. My mom had faced so much ridicule for her Spanish accent growing up, she never used her native tongue at home. Mexico was only 150 miles away, but I could barely say baño.

When my turn came to read, I sat up straight and enunciated loud and clear. The teacher watched me curiously. After class ended, I told her that I wanted to be "where the smart kids are." She agreed and I joined the white students the following day.

From that day forward, whenever anyone asked what color I was, I quickly said white. Clearly, it was the way to be: everyone on TV was white, the characters in my *Highlights Magazine* were white, the singers on Casey Kasem's *American Top 40* were white (or black). White people even populated my books: there were bratty little sisters who baked baby dolls into birthday cakes; *Sweet Valley High* twins who roared around California in convertibles; girls named Deenie who rubbed their Special Places with a washcloth until they got a Special Feeling. (I sat in the bathtub for hours, trying to find this Special Place. Was it that spot behind my elbow? Or just beneath my toe?)

True, I often wondered when somebody's primo was going to roar onto the scene in a low-rider. And how come nobody ever ate tamales or cracked piñatas or shopped for empanadas at H-E-B? But I took no offense at these absences. White people's stories just seemed worthier of being told. And so

I grew closer to Grandma Griest in Kansas, who resembled the feisty Jewish grandmothers in my books more than Abuela Elizondo, who lived on a ranch thirty miles out of town. I used to beg Grandma for stories about life on the prairie as she baked me vats of macaroni and cheese. She regaled me with the adventures of my great-great-Uncle Jake, a hobo who saw America with his legs dangling over the edge of a freight train. When I wound up across the kitchen counter from Abuelita hand-rolling tortillas, however, I'd sit in silence—and not just because of the language barrier. I simply couldn't fathom that she had anything interesting to say. I'd watch her flip the masa on the comal and wish she'd whip up something like *Are-You-There-God-It's-Me-Margaret*'s grandma would instead. Like matzo ball soup. I'd never tried this dish before, but it sounded like mini-meatballs floating in cheese sauce.

I switched back to being Mexican my senior year in high school. I was thumbing through the college scholarship bin in the Career Center when my guidance counselor called me into her office and asked a familiar question: "What are you, Stephanie? Hispanic or white?"

Before I could respond, she hinted that my SAT scores weren't high enough for funding if I was considered white. If I was Hispanic, she predicted, doors would swing open. "Think about it," she said.

I did for about three seconds, then changed the little *W* on my transcript to a big fat *H*. Suddenly, I qualified for dozens more scholarships. I applied for them all, and acceptance letters poured in. Not only was my freshman year at the University of Texas at Austin fully funded, I received free tutoring, a faculty adviser, and a student mentor, plus invitations to myriad clubs and mixers. It was exciting—until I started meeting the other Latino scholarship recipients. Some were the children of migrant farm workers. A few had spent summers picking sugar beets themselves. Their skin was brown, and they had undergone hardships because of it. Even our experiences at UT differed dramatically. They told lonely stories of walking into classrooms and realizing they were the only person of color. Of being asked to speak on behalf of "their people" during group discussions. Of dirty looks and derogatory remarks.

It dawned on me that—because of my racially ambiguous appearance—I had reaped only the benefits of being a minority and none of the drawbacks. Guilt overwhelmed me. Had I snatched away scholarships from a real Latino out there? If so, what should I do? Give back the money I received? Take out a loan? Transfer to a cheaper school?

"Hell no!" my mom snapped when I called to ask. My scholarship, she explained, was ancestral payback for all the adversity our family had endured.

Although this made karmic sense, I decided to at least try to resemble the *H* emblazoned on my transcripts. So I decorated my dorm walls (and myself) with images of Frida Kahlo and the Virgen de Guadalupe. Enrolled in Chicano politics classes. Devoured Latino literature. Got a job at the Admissions Office and fought to increase minority enrollment. Drank margaritas. Fell in love with a Colombian who smuggled emeralds (bad idea). Changed my white-bread middle name (Ann) to my mother's maiden name (Elizondo) and made everyone use it. I even set aside my progressive views and delved back into Catholicism.

Was that enough? Did I earn my *H*?

What does it mean to be Latino, anyway? Is it the food you eat? The people you associate with? The music you listen to? Is it a matter of blood? Language? Loyalty? Back then, I thought suffering was the quintessential "Latino experience." You had to be hassled by the Migra or ignored by a cabdriver or denied an opportunity for which you distinctly qualified. As absurd as it sounds, I actually started wishing that my skin was darker, my accent thicker, so that I could endure the discrimination that befell real Mexicans—or, at the very least, lose some of the privilege I hadn't even earned and probably didn't deserve.

In short, I felt guilty. You've probably heard the term "white guilt" before. That's when white folks feel bad about descending from the people who, say, nearly obliterated this country's indigenous population. "Biracial guilt" is like that, only worse. If you're part white like me, it's the schizophrenic realization that half of your ancestry oppressed the other half. What do you do when a race war brews inside of you? Which side do you root for?

Most biracial people don't have a choice. Our physical appearance determines our role. We could be three-quarters white, but if our eyes slant or our hair kinks, we're people of color. That doesn't mean we're automatically accepted by our minority brothers and sisters, however. They have standards of their own. Our skin might be "too light" to be black, our hair "too wavy" to be Asian, our accents "too gringo" to be Latino. That's the hardest part of an internal race war: not belonging to either side.

That didn't stop me from trying, however. Throughout college, whenever anyone inquired about my ethnicity, I piped up: "Mexican! Chicana! Latina!"— never "Biracial! Half-breed! Mutt!" I delighted when minorities downgraded white people around me. They thought I was one of them! Acceptance!

Conversely, if a white person said something disparaging about Mexicans in my presence, I let them have it. "Who do you think you're talking to? *Soy Chicana!*" I would snap, then pray they wouldn't respond in Spanish.

I probably wouldn't understand.

That's right. Despite all my Mexifying in college, my Spanish never surpassed the level of Tarzan Lite. I had stockpiled language tapes and workbooks but rarely invested time in them—mainly because I couldn't fathom where it would get me besides, well, Mexico. And I had wanderlust. Bad. Grandma Griest's stories of my hobo uncle burned in my belly. I wanted to roam in his memory.

So I studied the language of the farthest nation on the map—Russian— and jetted off to Moscow with dreams of becoming a foreign correspondent. Russia had other plans in store, however, and I ended up falling in love with an ex-soldier who had escaped cleanup duty at Chernobyl by slitting his wrists (another bad idea). I set out for China next, hoping to stuff subversive messages into dumplings and slide them through the iron bars of prison cells of political dissidents. Instead, I rallied to print the Spice Girls on the entertainment page of the English mouthpiece of the Chinese Communist Party, where I worked as a "propaganda polisher."

Between 1996 and 2000, I visited a dozen (formerly) Communist lands, unrolling my sleeping bag in the mountains of Kyrgyzstan and riding ponies across the Mongolian steppe. Time and again, I was struck by how fervently Stalin and Mao Zedong had tried to exterminate centuries of religion, tradition, and ritual in their respective nations by forcing their citizens to conform to socialist culture. Yet, around the Bloc, millions of people defied their orders. Like the woman I met in Riga whose sister got shot while laying flowers at the feet of Milda, a statue symbolizing Latvian independence. Or the elderly Lithuanian I met in Vilnius who, at age 24, was imprisoned and then tortured because he refused to denounce Judaism. Or the Tibetan monk I met in Lhasa who smuggled copies of the Dalai Lama's works into his lamasery, shrugging off the deadly consequences of being caught.

All of these people had risked their lives to uphold their culture, while I had abandoned my own. Upon returning to the United States, I knew the time was ripe to delve inward, to travel to Mexico and search for what had been lost during my family's migration to Texas two generations ago.

There was just one problem: the very notion terrified me. I may have just circumnavigated the globe, but Mexico seemed like another planet. Ask any South Texan. To us, Mexico conjures kidnappings and carjackings, murderous narco-traffickers and explosive diarrhea. When I was in high school, a college student got snatched off the street while partying down in Matamoros during spring break. Bound and gagged, he was driven to a ranch run by a satanic cult. Next thing you know, he was menudo. One worshipper wore a belt made of his victims' spinal cords.

Equally worrisome was my lousy Spanish. What would Mexicans say when they heard it? "¿Tu mamá es mexicana? Híjale, what happened to you?"

And what if I finally did learn the language—and nothing changed? For years, this had been my pipe dream: *If only I spoke Spanish, I would be more Mexican.* But what if, after years of claiming (and even benefiting from) this heritage, I discovered I was not?

The stakes were high, and I couldn't rise to the challenge. Rather than venturing south of the border, I retreated north to New York, to try to make it as a writer. After publishing a memoir about my travel adventures, I found myself in a peculiar position. Latino media and organizations warmly embraced me as a "Latina author," but I had to decline their invitations to speak with Spanish-speaking audiences because I literally could not communicate with them. This resurrected sentiments I had been suppressing since college—of being a phony, a fake, a Chicana wanna-be.

And the guilt. Oh, the guilt. I was mired in it. Steeped.

Fast-forward to the spring of 2004. En route from Tucson to El Paso on a blisteringly hot day, I took what appeared to be a scenic farm road curving along the Mexican border and wound up in a desert choked with cactus and brush. Half an hour into the journey, it occurred to me that not one car—or anything else—had passed me on that road. Moreover, my gas gauge was nearly empty, my cell phone was roaming, and it was 100-plus degrees outside. My car, meanwhile, was thirteen years old and cranky. If it broke down, I would be toast. Better turn around and rejoin the main highway. My foot hovered above the brake as I grasped the stick shift.

Something appeared in the distance. Objects in the middle of the road. Moving sluggishly, then quickly. People! Most likely Mexicans, fleeing the border. I squeezed the brakes and blared the horn. Water! They must need water. I started slowing down, to offer a bottle. But . . . what if water wasn't all they needed? What if they asked me to take them somewhere? Of course I would say yes. How could I deny a ride to people in the middle of the desert? But . . . what if they didn't just want a lift? What if they wanted my car? Or what if they just took it? Tossed me into the cactus and roared away? That's what I would do, if the tables were turned: Throw out the gringa and go.

The irony was immediate. Nearly every accolade I had received in life was partly due to the genetic link I shared with these people charging through the snake-infested brush. What separated us was a twist of geographical fate that birthed me on one side of the border and them on the other. They were too Mexican; I was just enough.

And now they were gone. Water shimmered where they once stood. My heart thumping in my throat, I rolled back toward the highway. Rather than allow guilt to pool in my belly, as it always did, I made a vow instead. It was time to confront the nation, people, and bloodline that had haunted me all of my life. It was time to go to Mexico.

And so, on New Year's Eve that year, I quit my job, stuffed my possessions in storage, and hopped a plane to Mexico. In the eight months that followed, I traveled from the border town of Nuevo Laredo to the highlands of Chiapas. Adventures rapidly unfolded. I lived in a household of young gay artists and befriended a dominatrix. Sneaked into prisons to interview indigenous resistance fighters. Rallied with rebels on a plaza and camped with Zapatistas in a jungle. Fell heinously ill in San Cristobal and got hospitalized in Oaxaca. Found my ancestral village. Contemplated adopting a Zapotec girl. Wrote a memoir about what I saw and how it felt.

And yes. I learned the tongue of my mother. And of her mother. And of all the mothers that preceded them. Linguistic peace at last.

I know now that I will never be truly Mexican, not even if I moved there for the rest of my life and acquired all the requisite customs and traditions. Because what binds a people are their bedtime stories. The songs they sing on road trips. Political and historical events. Fads and crazes. Shared memories. Not skills that can be acquired, like language. Which isn't to suggest that my pursuit was a worthless endeavor. Cultural preservation is sacrosanct. But there is no point striving for an unobtainable state of being.

I did, however, realize that the schizophrenia of being biracial, of straddling two worlds but belonging to neither, probably gives me a deeper understanding of what it means to be Mexican than anything else. Mexico is, after all, biracial by definition. And the people I encountered there genuinely seemed to treasure their mestizo heritage, their blending of indigenous and colonial bloods. They believe that this makes them stronger, more complete. Una raza cósmica.

I've also decided that my history of existential identity crises makes me distinctly Latino. I've spent much of the past half-decade traveling around the United States talking with Latino groups, and am forever meeting caramel-skinned men and women who speak Spanish fluently, eat barbacoa, and salsa dance on weekends, yet who *still* don't feel Latino enough. This is especially ironic considering that white society created what it means to be Latino in the first place. Colonists diluted indigenous blood through conquest and rape; the US government drew up categories like "Hispanic," "White," "Black," and "Other" and made us choose. But poco a poco, we are coming into our own as a people, creating our own definitions of who we are and who we can aspire to be. Fulfilling the dreams of ancestors who struggled to root (or keep) us here.

I've learned a thing or two about guilt as well. For years, I've used it as a form of self-flagellation, as a way of paying penance for my privilege. But as far as emotions go, guilt is an empty one. Its sole concrete manifestation is a stomachache. There is only one proper way of dealing with privilege: seizing it like a baseball bat and knocking out injustice with all of your might.

3

Love, Prejudice, and Latinidad

Carla Trujillo

When I was thirteen, I had a crush on a guy I'd gone to grade school with—
Jimmy Alvarado. As a kid, he was skinny and knock-kneed, and he always ran
around the playground with a wide grin and a runny nose. But when I saw
him at thirteen, he had miraculously transformed into a really cute guy—an
impression influenced ever so possibly by my hormone-laden eyes. One day, I
was driving with my family through town when I saw him walking outside his
house. I remarked excitedly about seeing him, speaking in that impetuous, adolescent way of his good looks.

My mother glanced at my father, who scowled at me through the rearview
mirror, blurting out a gruff "I don't want you seeing him."

Startled by his reaction—more so since the town we lived in was small
and everyone knew one another—I asked him why. He replied that Jimmy was
"not like us." Confused, I persisted by asking him what he meant. After all, how
could he not approve? Jimmy wasn't a gangbanger, he went to church, and he
was shy and appeared kind, all in addition to his being Mexican. I couldn't figure
out what the problem was. And that's when my father muttered that "he's a different class of people."

Suddenly, I read through the lines. Jimmy was a Mexican. Maybe he was
born in the United States—I didn't know. And he was possibly a bit poorer than
we were, but it didn't matter because, in my parent's eyes, we were different,
since we'd been born in New Mexico which made us, in my father's words,
"New Mexican, not Mexican."

I found the whole basis of the argument irrelevant and idiotic. What
became far more disturbing was the realization that my parents, whom I had
previously envisioned as (only) opinionated and controlling, had instantly
morphed into people I didn't know. My father continued driving, acting like he'd
done nothing more than give me a well-intentioned directive. My mother clearly
agreed with him—so there was no hope in my asking her for support. I felt
angry and sick, like I'd been punched in the throat. And I vowed I'd never agree
with or abide by their point of view.

My father and mother kept the pressure on about who I dated all through
my junior and senior years in high school. Despite my fierce resistance, they for-
bade me from dating any boys who didn't meet their approval. During this time
I found out their racialized views about Mexicanos were similar to how they felt
about other people. (Now, given my propensity for girls, they probably regret
having been so strict. In fact, my father later questioned my mother whether my
being queer had anything to do with their boy-control efforts. I remarked that

it hadn't, though my parents still seem to struggle between love, prejudice, and homophobia.) Back then, I argued with my parents, who responded by threatening to kick me out of the house and disown me if I didn't obey them. Their ideas about people who were different made no sense to me. And like many young people, stuck between old-school parents and the multicultural world I inhabited, I did everything I could to sneak through the thin line negotiated between their desires and mine.

My parents received an ironic comeuppance when, about a year after the incident with Jimmy, my father went through a life-changing discrimination experience at work. He had been next in line for a long-awaited journeyman training program to become a welder. For some reason, he was bypassed for a white man. Furious, and certain his rights had been violated, my father took personal time off to go to the Equal Employment Opportunity Commission to file a complaint. He then contacted a lawyer (whom we couldn't afford), to begin processing a discrimination suit. Recognizing that the EEOC and the lawyer concurred with my father, the company said they had made an error and put him into the training program. The entire event became a profound learning experience for me, a deeply ingrained lesson on the importance of standing up for one's rights.

All of this, of course, gave me plenty to argue about with my parents on the illogic of their racism. I asked my dad how he could complain about his mistreatment for being Mexican, yet still have prejudice against other Mexicans. He said he didn't know, sounding genuinely befuddled. And I, for the life of me, couldn't understand it either.

My parents' prejudices confounded me all the more when they were placed alongside the teachings of the Catholic Church. Eight years of catechism taught me that I should love all beings equally, which really wasn't happening in our house. I know my parents weren't the only ones who did this sort of thing. I just had higher expectations for them. What was even more disturbing—which seems hard to imagine—were their feelings about Mexican immigrants.

When I told my dad we were the same people, all Mexicanos by origin, he said we weren't because we were "New Mexican. Born in the United States." Their point of view is not unique. My grandparents and great-grandparents were all born and raised in a state colonized so completely by the Spanish that the majority of its inhabitants still identify as Spanish (or now, more commonly, Hispanic). This makes them different (i.e., better) than those on the other side of the border, despite the fluidity of the border, or its having crossed them. Yet, in an interesting twist, my father, throughout my childhood, and contrary to many New Mexicans, didn't call himself Spanish. Instead, he proudly proclaimed his mixed heritage of being both Indian and Spanish. "Which," he said, with only slight hesitation, "does technically make us Mexican." My mother disagreed, leaving me thoroughly confused. Still, my parents felt they were higher on the food chain since they were American born. To add to the mix, they both knew New Mexico was once part of Mexico, which apparently didn't seem to matter because it hadn't been so since 1848.

It will come as no surprise (except perhaps to my mom and dad) that I received a fair share of differential treatment for being Chicana. It wasn't realistic, of course, that people would look at me and say, "Let's treat her differently because she looks New Mexican." Rather, they simply ascribed my appearance and origins to common stereotypes. And it didn't matter where I lived. Whether it was U.C. Davis for college, Wisconsin for graduate school, Texas for work, or California, where I now reside, I always have been and continue to be regarded as a Mexican.

As a product of the civil rights movement, I identified then, and still do now, as a Chicana. I recall even sewing a patch on my jean jacket at fourteen with the words "Chicano Power" emblazoned over a brown fist that I proudly wore 'til I outgrew it. Despite my parents pummeling me about being New Mexican, I considered it irrelevant to the far more important Chicano Movimiento, where I and others felt we had to work together to empower our people. This coexisted with the hegemonic consciousness of the American public, which possessed its own agenda, haranguing me throughout my life with a barrage of "What are you?" questions, from the irksome "What part of Mexico are you from?" to the equally clueless "Are you a barrio girl?" Now in an era when people want to be more careful about this sort of question, a middle-aged man recently asked me where my "face originated."

I finished graduate school, returned to California, and got a job at U.C. Berkeley. I quickly realized that, as a woman with an advanced degree and as a person able to interact with people from a variety of backgrounds, I still found myself pushed and pulled in and out of a privileged world depending on the circumstance. For example, for a number of years I did a great deal of solo travel. When I journeyed to Texas, I invariably got asked for directions to the hotel bathroom or lobby—no matter that I wore professional attire. Once while in Austin on business, I went to a nearby restaurant for dinner—crowded with non-Latinos waiting for a table. I don't know if it was because I was sitting alone, or if it was because I was Chicana (or perhaps a little of both, as one never really knows these things), but while I was waiting for my food, several waiting patrons leaned their butts against my table, drinking, laughing, and carrying on as if my presence didn't matter.

Somehow I found this more disconcerting than not being seen at all. Many people—particularly poor people and people of color—are cast into an ocean of invisibility every day of their lives. Privileging those with lighter skin or those who are wealthy goes on, as we all know, throughout the world. But the United States, through carefully constructed belief systems, prides itself as the land of equal opportunity, and I, like my parents, teachers, and classmates, had been thoroughly indoctrinated. As a child, I went to public schools with committed teachers who inspired me to go someplace further than the ordinary. Pumped with their enthusiasm, I felt I could do anything I put my mind to. Archeologist, doctor, and singer were just some of the things I wanted to be. One minor detail derailing several of my plans, however, was the lack of cash. (For instance, I used the school-owned drums in grade school since my parents couldn't afford to rent the flute I really wanted to play.) Despite this, I managed to conduct research, sing in a chorus, and land a job helping students into college. I don't know, maybe it's just me, but that heavily inculcated belief that "perseverance pays" gets a little shaken up when a bunch of people are sitting against your dinner table. Right then, it didn't matter who I was, where I'd come from, what I'd done that day, or even what I ordered. Those people chose not to see me. Unless you're officially blind, there's no excuse. I spoke to the manager, who moved me elsewhere.

Yet despite the aforementioned micro-aggressions, being a Chicana and a woman has its perks. As most writers are prone to do, I observe everything around me. When I'm rendered invisible or insignificant I am privy to information that wouldn't be uttered in other company. And due to these "opportunities," I see much more than the average American. Paradoxically, because of this invisibility (which I can't always control), I witness the often painful revelations of prejudice that many Americans insist is no longer present. This has informed the workshops I conduct on unlearning bias, as well as the work I do on increasing diversity on the Berkeley campus.

So back to the issue of being New Mexican. Although I realize there are differences in cultural and religious customs, languages, and appearances among US Chicanos, Mexicanos, and Latinos, I still feel a bond with anyone who identifies as such. Like others, this bond becomes a form of strength—strength to organize and work among ourselves and with our allies for the betterment of our people as well as others who are disenfranchised. Recently, I heard a group of young African American men talking to one another as they walked down Telegraph Avenue in Berkeley. One of the men loudly proclaimed with the confidence of insight and experience that "Mexicans are the new niggas," which catapulted me into acknowledging both the harshness and the truth of his words, as well as my own feelings about them. As everyone knows, many Mexicanos, particularly immigrants, keep our country going, doing some of the toughest work there is—often jobs no one else will do. But they are commonly rendered invisible, usually underpaid, undereducated, and exploited. In the past, the differences we possess as Chicanos, Mexicanos, and Latinos, as immigrants—legal or not—have kept us from working together to organize around key issues and collective empowerment. Thankfully, this is changing. More Chicanos and Latinos are graduating from high school and college. Many others are working interactively on collective goals, running for office, strategizing and fundraising for greater empowerment and visibility. Fear a brown nation? Watch what happens when we really get organized.

Though my parents demonstrated in a direct and odious manner their views about Mexicans versus New Mexicans, in my teenage mind I disagreed. Now I see the world as far more complex than I had originally envisioned. And despite the many changes and advances that have occurred in our country, it appears that Chicano/Latino people still represent a relatively monolithic Mexican community in the collective consciousness of the American public—especially if we're poor, non-English-speaking, or un(der)educated. I'd like to think this isn't so, and I know exceptions abound, yet I'm not naïve.

How then does all of this affect us as writers? As byproducts of a country founded on the principles of institutionalized racism, are we (in addition to others who are similarly racialized) able to surpass what mainstream Americans expect us to write? Of course we are, because we're already doing so. Will publishers print our work? I'd like to believe they will, since many already have, especially the smaller presses. Yet complications abound, involving agents, publishers, and reviewers, and whether they can push beyond formulaic visions of what a "Mexican" is and what they think Americans think a "Mexican" is. As we negotiate through this, how do we then retain our integrity as writers and communicate our own individualism and humanity?

These issues, on occasion, also follow us to the locales where we wish to hone our craft. I've attended several mainstream writers' conferences and taken many classes and workshops, all with the desire to improve my writing. Although most of my instructors were exceptional, the majority of my classmates commonly failed to understand my story's premise or the message I sought to convey. Comments regarding my work (as well as that of other writers of color who brought race or class issues into their writing) were typically minimal or bordered on the superficial, often focusing on whether they were able to understand the (limited) Spanish I used. This "feedback" left me frustrated and, more importantly, worried about the lack of knowledge many fellow writers had about the lives of people of color.

A wonderful exception was Macondo, where, over a number of years, I took a series of master's-level writing workshops in San Antonio, Texas. Macondo workshops were conceived and founded by Sandra Cisneros and attended by Mexicanos, Latinos, Chicanos, and non-Latinos during the dog days of summer. Much like the fictitious town Gabriel García Márquez speaks of (and where the Macondo writers' workshop got its name), Macondo is a special place. It retains a philosophy of selecting experienced writers who seek to refine their writing and who are also committed to serving their community. The workshops are challenging, as instructors have high expectations, but they're typically without the denigration often seen in other writing workshops or programs. Begun in 1998, Macondo has now become a self-sustaining program. As a participant in the first class, I was immediately struck by its difference. Finally I was in a place with other writers who thankfully knew enough about Latina/os that we could focus on the writing. It was a relief to find a socially conscious, dedicated group of writers cognizant of the complexities of our lives and offering constructive criticism that actually improved my work.

As I continue to write, I know I will compose stories unique to my own experience—lives I might have witnessed, heard of, or simply felt in my heart. Conversely, I may wish to write stories completely different than what others expect or think I should be writing. As writers of color, we need to get our stories out there, whatever they might be. And we should never feel we have to abide by preordained tropes, modes, or archetypes. How we actually accomplish this may not be easy since we have little to no work in the canon and a relatively small number of published works by Latina/o writers. Many of us, more than likely, have also received our literary training under the guidance of those who may have limited knowledge of Latina/o people, which can pinch back a story's depth and our professional development. Adding to all of this is the possibility that we might need to unlearn what we've been taught in order to accomplish something different.

Writing isn't easy, no matter who you are or what your writing background is. It takes courage to write from the heart, skill to do it well, thick skin to suffer its disappointments, and compassion to nurture others along the way. It also takes determination to wade through the extra challenges we face by being poor, overworked, overlooked, or "different." Yet despite it all, I still feel confident that we'll continue writing stories that mean something to us. And just like everything else we do, we'll manage to persevere.

4

Coyotes

ALEX ESPINOZA

I am at East Los Angeles City College standing in front of a group of students. This class is part of the Puente Project, an organization whose aim is to facilitate the transfer of Latino/as from a community college to a four-year institution. Through intensive writing and reading, group activities, and counseling and mentoring, Puente's goal is to instill in its students cultural awareness and pride, and a desire to continue studies beyond junior college. Nearly twenty years before, I had set foot in a similar classroom when I started my journey through academia; I was a Puentista from 1991 to 1992. Completely green, unsure and unprepared, I remember thinking that I needed to latch onto anything or anyone willing to provide me with answers to the questions swirling inside of me: *Do I belong here? Am I adequately prepared? What should I major in?* It was in a tiny classroom much like the one I stand in now—with broken desks, chipped plaster, and burned-out fluorescent lights—where I first developed my ability to write, where I first encountered Latino/a writers telling stories about experiences that mirrored my own. Here were people just like my brothers and sisters and their friends, breathing on the page, their lives and experiences being validated through literature, an artistic canon that I had thought, throughout much of high school, ignored us.

I tell this class that there was never an empty corner of the house where I grew up. Space was an issue in a three-bedroom house in suburban Los Angeles. There were people coming or going—relatives, friends of my brothers and sisters, an acquaintance escaping the physical and mental abuse of a mother who beat her with hangers and electrical cords and tried feeding her drain cleaner—at all hours. I was nothing at all like any other member in my family. My brothers caused trouble, picked fights, and sniffed glue in empty lots. My sisters were rude and opinionated; they learned to fight with fists better than my brothers. My siblings were independent, strong-willed, brash. They regularly ignored my mother and loved challenging her authority, something I never dared to do. My mother watched me, held me, let no harm come to her baby. Hold him tight, my grandmother would tell her, don't let that boy out of your sight, because the minute you do, the world will eat him up, crush him. I was taught never to question. Letting others—aunts, uncles, siblings, even cousins younger than I—do for me was the way my life was to be. Growing up Mexican and poor is one thing, but growing up Mexican, poor, and disabled was something else entirely.

The statistics will tell you a sad story about a kid like me, a kid who, by all accounts, should be either dead or strung out or in jail, or, if I was lucky, holding down a dead-end job, a red shirt, part of the silent workforce that cleans and washes and mows and asks no questions. Home wasn't a sanctuary, wasn't a safe haven from the crime and poverty, the daily assaults and dramas. My father drank heavily. My brother was a heroin addict who would shoot up in the bathroom, twigs of burnt matches and bent spoons shoved behind bottles of conditioner and bars of soap.

I almost dropped out of high school, and I would have been lost were it not for my passion for books and stories, for works of literature and writing that opened windows into realms of other possibilities. This was how I gained the ability to resist the prescribed notions of what an infirm and weak and crippled brown boy should do: sit down, shut up, keep your head down, be vulnerable, helpless, never ask questions, never ask anything.

Today's talk is one I've given variants of many times as I've crisscrossed the state in my car, from one end of California to the other, visiting classes, talking to students, trying in my own way to motivate them, to keep them focused. It is hard work, exhausting, and I wonder how these community college teachers do it day in and day out for years. The teacher had assigned my novel, and the students are now firing questions at me from all sides. I'm having trouble keeping up. Then a girl with dark lipstick and flat hair asks, "So, how do you do this?" She waves my book in front of her face. By *this*, I know she means more than just my book. It seems that, wherever I go, whatever campus I visit, in each Puente class I talk to, I always encounter the same question, the same group of students seeking the path to academic enlightenment. The ELACC Puentistas are no different. Their gazes are deep, unflinching, penetrating; they remind me so much of the person I once was.

"Home wasn't a sanctuary," I tell the class and am met with several approving nods when I admit this. "With no walls to shield me, with nothing motivating me, no thoughts of anything beyond the streets of my hometown in suburban Los Angeles, things were bleak, hopeless," I say. I talk about how I almost dropped out, how I would have been lost had it not been for my passion for books and stories. After graduating from high school, it was community college or nothing. Vocational training was out of the question, because a physical disability limited the kind of work I could do. The trade schools advertised on television showed men in overalls using both hands to weld, or people dressed in scrubs taking a patient's blood pressure.

Luckily, I say, with relief, my own voice quivering, there were programs like Puente, programs that saw enough to take a chance on a poor kid like me, programs that told me what it was I was good at rather than what it was I was bad at, programs that created a space for me to fully explore my creativity, programs that now, as California struggles with economic woes, are in danger of being eliminated altogether. It was Puente that allowed for the creation of a classroom space that acted as a buffer from the noise and daily assaults bombarding me. That classroom so long ago, I tell the students, became a sacred space, a space in which to freely pursue my writing, an ability I had but never knew and was never encouraged to pursue. The life dramas, I go on, continued and intensified, well past my community college years, into my time at UC

Riverside, where I received my BA in Creative Writing, and into my graduate studies at UC Irvine. I discovered, created, or reclaimed sacred spaces at each school, finding solace in the Tomas Rivera library, named for a Chicano writer who became the first Mexican American chancellor in the UC system; or in the workshop at UCI, where I sat at the same table where writers like Gary Soto and Helena Viramontes had once sat.

"I shouldn't be here," I tell this class, just as I tell the countless community college classes I visit. I'm a statistical anomaly, someone who beat the odds, who found a way out, who fought against the prescribed notions of what a poor brown kid from Tijuana, the youngest of eleven, the runt of the litter, is supposed to do. "I shouldn't be here," I say again.

How is it that I am here? That seems to be what they want answered, the source of their befuddlement. I tell them again and again what worked for me, that the way, the truth, the light was in literature and writing, that programs like Puente made that line of escape possible. I tell them about the need to create sacred spaces, sites where they can liberate themselves from the shackles weighing them down. They nod, but sometimes I fear there's just too much noise around them for them to hear me.

It's early May now, a few weeks after my lecture at East Los Angeles City College. The talks about the dwindling California economy, the rumors about drastic budget cuts and mandatory furlough days threatening both the UC and Cal State systems, have everyone around campus on edge. Senior faculty members tell me, panic in their eyes and a somber pitch in their voices, about previous budget cuts, about whole departments vanishing, about tenured faculty being fired.

"I'm so thankful I have tenure," one admits to me in the hallway, her arms full of student essays marked up in green ink.

"Lucky you," I say.

"Well, you'll be fine," she adds, smiling uncomfortably, tucking a strand of blond hair behind her ear with her free hand.

In a city where nearly half the residents are from Mexico and Central America, at an institution where over 30 percent of the student body is Latino/a, only 7 percent of our university's faculty is Chicano/a or Latino/a. With no regular offerings of Chicano/a literature courses in the department where I teach, I worry many of our students here have fallen prey to the same institutional amnesia that plagued me in high school. I worry that they aren't seeing themselves in literature, that they aren't being exposed to the complex body of our literary canon. I make attempts to rectify this, to fill the gap, by intervening on their behalf, but the process is a slow one, the politics surrounding such moves tricky and dangerous.

I think of the word "coyote" and all the negative connotations associated with such a term. There are the ferocious hunters wandering throughout Central and North America, as far south as Panama, as far north as Alaska. There are the coyotes along the border who, more often than not, rob and even kill the undocumented paisanos they are smuggling across the vast and dark deserts of the American Southwest. But then I think of Huehuecoyotl, the Aztec god of music and song, a trickster, a shape shifter, whose name in Nahuatl means "very old coyote," a singer, a storyteller. And this is who I become, the negative, the positive, even the ambivalent characteristics of this figure, this trickster, this shape-shifter. I smuggle in essays, stories, poems by my favorite Chicano/a writers, the same stories I read years ago as a Puente student in community college, the same stories that made me realize that writing was my passion, my salvation, my escape. I give these to my students, both brown and otherwise, and almost always a Chicano/a comes up to me after class, once the room is empty and I'm gathering my things. I hear something in their voices and see a glimmer in their eyes that tells me they've recognized themselves on the page, in that story or poem or essay.

I'm a coyote, gathering together my Latino/a graduate students at my home. I offer them amnesty and nourish them with the manna of the Chicano/a word. I beam with pride when I look at them, when I repeat their last names to myself—Jimenez, Rosado, Muñoz, Sanchez, Guzman. We gather around my dining table, share work, and talk. They reveal aspects of themselves and our culture that they'd never address outside of our circle. I again hear the same anxiety in their voices, and I feel the same apprehension and confusion I once held and bottled up.

We talk about bettering our writing, about being better critics of our work, about holding one another more accountable. We talk about our position as writers and artists within our respective communities, about viewing ourselves not just as Chicano/a writers but as American writers. We need, I say to them, to nurture a mind that speaks from honesty, for it is through brute honesty, through careful analysis and examination, that great thinkers are cultivated. This, in turn, gives rise to great works of art, great novels and stories that stand up to the winds of criticism and remain long after we have passed. We talk about how, far too often, the very idea of criticism is discouraged, is seen as hostile, a betrayal of our community, a betrayal of the voices coming out of our immigrant experiences. It is not a betrayal of culture to analyze such works this way, I say to them. Rather, it is respect for art, respect for creative endeavors, respect for our immigrant voices that are the true intentions and motivations for such criticism.

I think about Virginia Woolf, about how, in her essay "A Room of One's Own," she imagines a woman named Judith, sister to William Shakespeare, a woman just as talented as her brother, a woman not allowed to pursue her abilities because of the social constraints of the time. A woman, Woolf explains, needs a space and financial stability to create art. I think how the Latino/a artists, students, and scholars too need a room, space to allow for the formation of individual and original thought, if they are to become the thinkers and critics our communities need them to be.

But the rooms are overcrowded, bursting at the seams; my class caps, I learn just as the semester ends, will be increased to a pedagogically unsound number the following year. Doors are slammed in the faces of my potential students; thousands are denied enrollment or are simply turned away. These are the children of the field hands, the cooks, the janitors, and the factory workers. These are brown children seeking solace, a voice, a promise made to them long before their names were ever whispered.

I am constantly confronting the specter of my former self these days. I see him in the faces of those community college students struggling to balance their crammed class loads with full-time jobs, dwindling funds, vanishing resources— no rooms of their own. I see him in my undergraduates, the ones who remain; these are the first-generation college students who come from Michoacán or Jalisco or Guerrero, whose parents harvest and mow and wash. I see him in the faces of my Latino/a graduate students pursuing their MFAs. *Where will my literature fit?* they ask. *Why does our culture often work against us, against our own best interests?*

I worry a lot, though, because I am one person, because there are so few of us, because the world outside still rages on, because every day the chances of success for the Latino/a, the Chicano/a—of rising above the oppression many of us wade in—goes away little by little. When I'm alone in my office—pecking out words in the heat of a Central California night as mosquitoes bat their thin wings against the windows—I think what a privilege it is that I can call myself a writer, a scholar, an educator, during such fiscally precarious times, when the institutions of higher education meant to serve the children of the disenfran- chised, the less fortunate, los de abajo, ignore one of the largest, most under- served segments of the population. Friends—from New York to Texas, Illinois to Arizona—tell me it's bad everywhere for us, and it is, but it's especially bad here. The most populated state in the country is imploding. Public institutions like the UC and Cal State systems, meant to be accessible to those who need it the most, have become too expensive. It seems the only choice a poor brown kid has for getting out is the service, either that or the prison industrial complex, also facing overcrowding and diminishing resources. We are a dying breed, I fear, those of us who managed, through literature or art or science, to slip through the cracks, to break free, to rise above the expectations, to claim the halls of academia as our own. Those at our heels, those that we need to take our place when we depart, are facing a present and future that is anything but optimistic, that doesn't even hint at an illusion for success and stability.

My father was several years younger than I am now when he boarded a train steaming north from his native Michoacán. Leaving my mother and a hand- ful of my brothers and sisters behind, he snuck across the border and made his way to Chicago. He found a job in a factory and, later, sent for the rest of his family. He worked as a machinist for many years, up until his death when I was a teenager. He came here for the same reasons many of us have and will con- tinue to come: his family was starving and poor and his children deserved some- thing better, a quality education. I was educated in the California public school system, from elementary school all the way up to graduate school. California State University, the largest public institution of higher education in our country, now employs me. Pell grants and student loans, low fees, and programs like Puente helped me along the way, but those resources are fading fast.

This is what I do when I sit here, alone, in my office, in the house I purchased with the money I earned from my two novels. I stare at the pictures of my deceased grandparents and parents crowding my bookcases and think about the past, the legacy of broken dreams and failed attempts, of struggle and sacrifice, the things I managed to avoid. I wonder what it's like to have no place to escape to, no place to be alone with just my thoughts, without the screaming and yelling. I wonder what it's like to have no say, to have no choice. Even though it's hot outside, I shiver.

I am at the edge of the continent. To my right is the sea, to my left are the mountains. I am facing south, precariously dangling on a sliver of land that is always moving and shifting. I think of them out there, all those boys and girls so like I once was, hunkered down in the dead of night, in the dark night, hoping for salvation, for someone to lead them through the thick brush toward a scattering of dim lights in the distance.

5

A Latinidad Litmus Test

TERESA DOVALPAGE

Normally I don't think of myself in terms of origin or ethnicity. I am just . . .
Teresita. La Te. But when asked about my Latina condition, this gives me food
for thought. One thing I know for sure: I am Cuban. I was born in Havana in
1966, so there is no doubt about that. But the Cuban American label is debat-
able. According to scholars like Gustavo Perez Firmat, it is reserved for those
born in the United States to Cuban parents, or for Cuban-born persons who
were raised and educated in United States. I wouldn't place myself in either category since I came to the United States when I was twenty-nine years old.

And what about my being Latina? Does being from Latin America make
me a Latina by default? How does one measure one's Latinidad? The literary
critic William Luis states that Latinidad in writers is threefold: (1) The writer is
from a Spanish-speaking background or heritage with some connection to Latin
America; (2) The writer is inculcated in the US experience and writes in English;
and (3) The writer self-identifies as Latino or Latina. I fulfill the first and last conditions. As for the second one, I confess that I have doubts. I am not sure how
"inculcated" I am in the US experience, though I write in English as often as in
Spanish and I now have American citizenship. Yet I still think in Spanish, dream
in Spanish, sing in Spanish when I shower, and if I cut my finger with a knife, I
yell "¡Ay!" not "Ouch!"

Are we what we speak? If the answer to the Latinidad question lies in the
language spoken every day, I may not be a one hundred percent Latina right
now. At home I speak mostly English, with the possible exception of curse
words. My husband doesn't understand Spanish so, in order to achieve effective
communication, English has become the lingua franca en casa. At the University
of New Mexico–Taos, where I am a Spanish instructor, the language used in my
classes is half and half.

I do not use Spanglish, though. Merriam-Webster's dictionary defines this
term as "Spanish marked by numerous borrowings from English; broadly: any of
various combinations of Spanish and English." I prefer to communicate clearly
in one language, rather than risk being misunderstood in two. However, I sometimes spice my English sentences with one or two Spanish words, making sure
that they are understood in the context. ¿Comprenden? Because I teach basic
and intermediate Spanish, most explanations are conveyed in English, so I have
to repeat over and over, in Spanish 101, that un torito is *not* a little dog.

And yet I must confess that I am guilty of deletear or forwardear un men-
saje, as well as of yelling to my husband to get his troca out of the way so I
can parquear el carro. In the first case, my use of the English terms in a Spanish

context is somewhat justifiable. They are pertaining to the realm of computers and Internet, and I learned them in English, so the Spanish word doesn't come naturally to me. Secondly, my use of Spanglish is purely influenced from my taoseño friends, who seldom use "truck." It is always la troca as lunch is el lonche. But when writing, I shy away from Spanglish. Its use often results in inelegant and ungrammatical sentences, though it can be muy comical. Spanish editors are particularly sensitive to the use of Spanglish. They don't even like terms like the aforementioned parquear though my Spanish spellchecker recognizes the word. In formal conversations with people who don't speak Spanish I prefer not to use Spanglish because I assume that they already have enough trouble deciphering my Cuban accent. But in conversations with local friends and in informal emails I use more Spanglish than what I thought at first or even wanted to admit, que no?

Are we what we write . . . or what we read? My first novel, *A Girl Like Che Guevara*, is in English. I didn't know there was a market for Spanish language books in the United States when I wrote it. Still unfamiliar with the powerful Latino movement in this country (particularly in California, where I lived at the time) I thought that publishing and selling a book written in Spanish would be almost impossible. And when I discovered that there was indeed a market for Spanish-language authors, I was halfway through the novel, so I went on. I also write articles, book reviews, and now I am working on a novella in English. As for reading, I read more in English than in Spanish, just because of the availability of materials. I live in Taos, New Mexico, and though the majority of the population is of Spanish ancestry, or so they say, we don't have even one bookstore that carries Spanish-language books or magazines. Una vergüenza, a total shame! Hijole, did I fail the Latinidad language test? No sé, José.

Are we what we eat? I consulted (in Spanish, by the way) with my friend Merceditas on this issue. She said that cooking style was an accurate way to define one's identity. "What kind of food do you cook?" she asked me. "Flavorless gringo stuff? Spicy Cuban meals?" Hmm . . . Inadvertently, we stumbled into prejudice. Neither are all American foods flavorless (think apple pie!) nor are all Cuban meals spicy. Cuban cuisine relies on a few basic spices like cumin, garlic, and pepper, which make our dishes rather bland. Where the hot chile habanero came from I would like to find out, but definitely it wasn't from Havana. Most Habaneros don't even know what chiles are. And then, I seldom cook. That is my husband's task. And he does it so well that I see no reason to update my culinary skills. But that means we eat mostly American food. Well, sometimes, when inspired, I make black beans (from a Goya can, of course), rice, and picadillo (hash meat), but that happens de Pascuas a San Juan, once in a blue moon.

Are we what we look like? I am petite and fair skinned, with light-brown hair. Una güerita, my Mexican friends call me. Unfortunately, I don't look like the curvaceous mulattas who have become the symbol of Cuba in promotional ads. On the island they used to call me "bola," a pejorative term reserved for Russian women. Bola, which literally means "beach ball," describes the supposedly pale and shapeless body of Russian women, as opposed to the Cuban women who (supposedly, too) have a well-defined waist, big hips, and a prominent rear end. I lacked these three elements and didn't tan easily so, even though I wasn't fat, I was considered a bolita.

Here, until I open my mouth, I blend quite well with the Anglo crowd, which sometimes causes embarrassing situations. At the Miami Book Fair where I went to present *A Girl Like Che Guevara*, there were some older Cuban exiles. They took me for an American writing about Cuba, and one white-haired señor told me: "Mira, mijita (look, my dear), I'm going to tell you how things really are in Cuba because you don't have a clue." Offended, I explained to him that I certainly knew since I was born and raised there. And then he said, "But, mijita, the problem is that you look just like an American with your blond hair and white skin." And this was a Cuban-born guy who should have known better!

Does all that mean that I am not Latina enough? But what, exactly, is a Latina? Going back to the language, I speak only Spanish with my girlfriends. My best friends here in New Mexico are Spanish speakers (one Mexican, one Puerto Rican, and another Cuban), and when we get together, we chatter sólo en español. Even at home, as I mentioned before, I spice my English sentences with Spanish, sometimes purely Cuban, terms. This can create some confusion, as when I said to a friend's child that a word he had just said was una grosería, a rude term. Gary, my husband, overheard the word grosería and associated it with groceries so the next time he went to the supermarket he offered to bring me a few groserías. I told him I had all the groserías I needed, thank you very much. The chapter of linguistic misunderstandings is long and storied. Shortly after my arrival from Cuba, I said I had to buy new bloomers, and my husband couldn't understand why I wanted to wear such an old-fashioned item. In Cuba we called panties "bloomers," so I assumed that it would be the proper word in English too.

As for my writing, I have three novels and two theater plays in Spanish. In Spain, I was a runner-up for the Herralde Award with my novel *Muerte de un murciano en la Habana* (*Death of a Murcian in Havana*), and my novella *El difunto Fidel* (*The Late Fidel*) won the Rincon de la Victoria Award in Málaga in May 2009. I still read in Spanish, the old books I brought with me from Cuba and new books I have bought in Miami, Mexico City, and Barcelona. I am a follower of several Cuban blogs, and I write regularly for a couple of them. And then most of what I write about (in English or in Spanish) has to do with Cuba or is connected to the island in some way. So maybe I passed the language test, after all.

Let's move back into the kitchen. I may not cook Cuban food but I certainly love to eat it. I have taught my husband how to make picadillo a la criolla, Cuban-style hash meat that he prepares like a chef from Havana. Last November, during the Miami Book Fair, I gained two pounds in five days because I practically lived at the little Cuban restaurants in Calle Ocho. And Cuban food—with its fried yucca, fried pork chops, fried chicken . . . fried everything—is muy fattening. Ay, the sinful crunch of chicharrones! Eating cracklings goes against the South Beach diet that I have tried to follow for years. Yet is there anything better than the sweet smells of fried mashed plantains? Or the saucy tanginess of ropa vieja, which literally translates as "old clothes," but is meat cooked so tenderly that it melts in your mouth? When I eat out, I always order dishes that resemble Cuban stuff like chicken-fried steak and caramel custard. And I just found a simple recipe for Cuban flan, which I will try making someday.

There is still the güerita issue. I can't change the way I look, but I must remember (and remind other people of it) that Latinas come in all shapes, colors, and sizes. We Hispanics came to Latin America from all parts of the globe, just as immigrants have come to the United States from everywhere else. So being Hispanic shouldn't be associated with a particular race. We are held together by our culture and our language, not by the color of our skin. There are freckled Colombians, red-haired Cubans, and platinum blond Mexicans. Race is not, and shouldn't be, an ethnicity mark. Don't judge a book by its cover or a Latina by her looks. So I am a Latina indeed, though I still prefer to be called a Cuban. Cubanita.

And what does a Latina writer write about? Ay, por favor, don't bring up chica lit. I have the utmost respect for all literary genres and I can devour a chica lit story as happily as anybody else. I enjoyed *The Dirty Girls Social Club* by Alissa Valdes Rodriguez and everything by Mary Castillo, a Mexican American writer, the author of *In Between Men* and *Hot Tamara*. But it would be nice if publishers didn't expect all of us to write about shopping and getting manicures, boyfriends or massages. Now I am working on a Spanish-language novel about an Andalusian priest who goes to Cuba, and the first question I was asked by someone in the literary industry was, "What do you know about Spanish priests?"

Publishers, and also readers in general, have expectations about what Latina writers should deal with. And these expectations even run among family and friends. My mother, in Cuba, often asks me when I am going to write something bonito (pretty and sweet) instead of the somber reality I reflect in my books. "Mija, if I want to see ugliness, blackouts, and fights, I just need to look all around me and it's everywhere," she says. "Why would I read a book about it?" My answer is: "I like to reflect the world as I see it. If I wanted to create 'pink and fluffy' literature, I would write romance novels, Harlequin-style . . . and make more money at it."

Around a year ago I was asked to write a play based on the theme of *Death of a Salesman*. We had to adapt it to the circumstances of a Latino immigrant living in the United States. At first I started the play based on a female character, a Willy Loman in a skirt (or rather, in a power suit, with Bobby Brown makeup). She had a husband and two kids. She was a real estate agent who, due to the mortgage crisis, had lost her job and was in financial straits. Quite a common situation, these days, I thought, and perfect for a modern version of the play.

But none of those who read the first draft found that plot believable. There was no conflict, they told me. The protagonist wasn't really in trouble. They all repeated the same song: "She still has a husband. She has her kids. What's her problem?" Even when they agreed that this was a real-life, typical situation, they still couldn't see it as the material for a compelling play. One person (a Latina woman, no less) said to me: "If she were a gringa, it would make more sense. But a *señora* Latina . . . forget it. Her husband will take care of the money issue." Indeed, there is still a double standard. The measurement of success for a Latina is not the same as for a Latino. Much less is still expected from women, it seems, in terms of career advancement and workplace success. I finally wrote a play based on the male character, *Hasta que el mortgage nos separe* (Until Mortgage Do Us Part). Yes, I censored myself. Sometimes one has to make compromises, I thought then—though that should be no excuse. Fortunately, I am working on another play, a counterpart to the first one, from the female point of view and with a very loudmouthed heroine. A Latina heroine, if you will.

Now, does our name define our ethnicity or origin? My maiden name is Doval. Doval has Celtic roots; my paternal grandparents were from Galicia, Spain. When I came to the United States, not wanting to lose my maiden name, I kept it and added my first husband's surname, Page, to it. I became Teresa Dovalpage. But the editor of my first book suggested that I publish it as Teresa Doval and add my middle name (de la Caridad) so readers would know that, even though I was writing in English, I was a "Latina" writer.

Again, I made a compromise. Not too smart, I discovered later, because now it seems as if my English and my Spanish novels were written by two different people. A case of split personality! I realize now that I agreed to use Doval because, at that particular moment, in 2003, I wasn't too sure of who I really was. Teresita Doval? Teresa Dovalpage? Cuban? Cuban American? After only seven years in my new country, my identity-in-progress wasn't yet clearly defined. If I could do it again, I would insist on signing the book with my real name. I am Teresita la Cubana, but my half-American surname represents my new life.

Spanish publishers did not fret over the sound of my last name. None of them ever cared about that. It makes me wonder, is this concern about names an American issue? When I was part of a panel at the 2006 Family Book Festival in Houston, we were asked if publishers preferred authors with English, rather than Spanish, surnames. I answered that my editor wanted to telegraph or somehow hint at my ethnicity by urging me to use only my middle and maiden names, but not out of bias for Spanish surnames. In fact, she thought that using "de la Caridad Doval" would make readers curious. They might have wondered something like this: "She is Cuban, but she wrote this novel in English? How quaint."

After reading many articles on the subject, I kept pondering my Latinidad. Vaya, I was on an identity quest. Was I Hispanic, Latina, or Cuban? Would I behave differently if I knew the answer? And is there an answer? A "right" one?

In my quest to find it, I met with my friends Lisette Rosenberg, a Jewish Cuban, and Raquel Troyce, a Jewish Mexican. We were at a Taos teahouse discussing the matter over scones and herbal teas when Raquel pointed out that most people confused the terms Latino and Hispanic. She informed me that Latinos are those whose native language has roots in ancient Latin, so Romanians, Italians, and French can safely be placed under the Latino category, but nobody would call them Hispanic. This term, she emphasized, is reserved for those whose native language is Spanish. Consequently Mexicans, Cubans, even Spaniards . . . we are all Hispanic and Latino at the same time.

Lisette, a retired teacher, didn't consider this distinction relevant. She brought up the difficulties that her students had understanding that being Hispanic (or Latina) did not mean having an accent. Her students were all American-born but had a distinctive New Mexican accent. They were not second-generation immigrants; their families had been in Taos for over three hundred years. And they consider anyone who does not speak like they do to be an outsider. So Lisette, who has, after forty-nine years in the United States, lost her Cuban accent, was not accepted as a local until she started spouting out her Spanish.

That problem I don't have. My accent is still fairly noticeable and my taoseño friends know I am not "from the mainstream." Or, as one of them told me, "I know you aren't white bread and mayonnaise." "Pos no, I am whole-wheat bread, in any case," I replied, "with butter and a slice of ham." That is, a Cuban sandwich.

After the conversation with Lisette and Raquel, still lost in my quest, I resorted to Gustavo Pérez Firmat and his delightful book, *Next Year in Cuba,* wherein Pérez Firmat declares: "To tell the truth, the Latino is a statistical fiction. Part hype and part hypothesis, the term Latino exists principally for the purposes of politicians, ideologues, salsa singers and Americans of non-Hispanic descent. The Latino's brown face has greenbacks plastered all over it, and in fact, most people to whom the label is applied reject it, opting instead for a national designation: Mexican, Puerto Rican, Cuban."[1] Later on, the author refers to a Cuban sandwich he and his friend Roberto Fernandez ordered at what used to be a Cuban restaurant on Calle Ocho: "It tasted nothing like the way it was supposed to. Roberto said it was because my Cuban sandwich had become a Latino sandwich."

Bingo! I sided with Pérez Firmat. For a while I was afraid of losing my "Cuban flavor" just like the sandwich did. Losing my cultural identity as a Cuban was the same as losing my distinctive flavor. Becoming Latina, in this case, would have meant becoming bland, or maybe tasteless. But that will never happen; I finally found out. This search for identity helped me understand that my Cubanidad is an integral part of my Latinidad, as the ham is an integral part of the Cuban sandwich. (You can't have a Cuban sandwich made with salami or pastrami.) So if someone calls me a Latina or a Hispanic woman, I will accept the label, ni modo, and won't be offended by it. But I fervently hope never to lose my Cuban flavor, eh!

Note

1. Gustavo Pérez Firmat, *Next Year in Cuba: A Cubano's Coming of Age in America* (Houston: Arte Público Press, 2005).

6

When We Were Spanish

LORRAINE M. LÓPEZ

"We are Spanish," my mother told me, my sisters, and my brother over and over again. She was a woman of prodigious bluntness and honesty, nearly a menace with the truth, but on the rare occasions when she told lies, they were whoppers, and this was one of those. "We are not Mexican," she would say, though she had nothing against Mexicans. Wasn't her best friend for life, Mary Acosta, a Mexican American, after all? Instead, my mother would point out that our family had never been to Mexico, and until my cousins ventured across the border to purchase recreational drugs in the late 1960s, this was largely true. Her family could trace its presence in central New Mexico from the 1600s. She was descended from Sephardic Jews who immigrated during the Inquisition and then promptly and bizarrely converted to Roman Catholicism. My father's forebearers migrated from Mexico in the early 1800s. Both families, though, resided in territory that belonged to Mexico until 1848, when the Treaty of Guadalupe Hidalgo was signed. To my knowledge, our ancestors never crossed the border illegally; instead, in the words of the actor portraying a Latino busboy in the film *Bobby*, "the border crossed us."

To complicate matters, my parents relocated from central New Mexico, where most people shared similar cultural heritage, to Los Angeles after my ex-serviceman father had trouble finding work in postwar New Mexico. In Los Angeles, he was snapped up by the Department of Water and Power, where he was employed for over forty years. There, we grew up among Mexicanos and Chicanos; Cubanos; Puertoriqueños; Dominicanos; Central and South Americans; Filipinos; Japanese, Chinese, Korean, and African Americans; even Middle Easterners; and of course, a smattering of white people of unspecific European heritage. But really the majority of white people we encountered resided in our television set and on movie screens—characters larger than life yet, at the same time, few in number when it came to daily encounters. In Southern California, we met even fewer people who were like us, Españos de Nuevo Mexico, or as my mother would insist, "Spanish."

To be fair, my mother herself was nothing like the demographic profile of the Mexican mother that I studied in teacher training. Instead of being that small, self-effacing, nearly invisible but deeply revered figure in the background, she was large, outspoken, opinionated, and annoyingly omnipresent. Her favorite activity had to be public speaking. In elementary school, I could not attend an assembly without facing my mother onstage, though she was not even a teacher at the time, but an officer in the PTA, addressing students and faculty with her big booming voice. By the time I was middle-school age, she was teaching at the same parochial school I attended. Only in high school did I escape her public presence, though she appeared on campus any time a meeting concerning parents transpired. She spoke Spanish and English, both at top volume, and despite her views on our heritage, she was diplomatic enough not to offend Mexicans and Mexican Americans, who comprised the majority of people she addressed.

My father, though wisely silent in my mother's presence, is at least as verbose but a lot less opinionated than my mother. He is a man with an infinite capacity to be laid back. To this day, very little fazes him. But when we were growing up, he occasionally reminded us of one line we should never cross. "If you ever dye your hair blond, then that's it," he would say, "you can't live in this house anymore." In the context of his laissez-faire parenting style, the subtext issued with crystalline clarity: He didn't care what we did so long as we did not mask our ethnicity. I suppose I could extrapolate from this a more global prohibition related to denying the self, but given his reluctance to set too many parameters, that might be going a bit far.

My father's message stayed with me, formulating, when I was very young, into an idea on constructs of reality and being. There were real people, people like us whose parents and relatives spoke Spanish; who ate enchiladas, sopaipillas, and caldos; warm and comfortable people with lilting voices; people who, when sniffed, emitted the fragrance of masa, roasted chili, and crushed cilantro. And then there were not-so-real people who sometimes had blond hair and usually had fair skin; who spoke flat, unaccented English; people who, though they consumed tasty things like hamburgers, hotdogs, and apple pies, nevertheless smelled slightly soapy to me.

This simple construction of self and other morphed for me into a confluence of revulsion and pity toward my playmates who were not fortunate enough to have been born with dark hair and to families who spoke at least some Spanish. I remember one friend, Arlene, a sturdy blonde, who visited my house one afternoon and asked if she could use my hairbrush. I hesitated, but eventually relented, permitting her to stroke those amber waves with my battered brush. After she went home, I stared long and hard at the bristles, the disgusting yellow strands, like metallic filaments, trapped in them. I quailed at the prospect of removing them by hand or even with the teeth of my untouched-by-blond-hair comb, so I ended up throwing the thing away.

Growing up in the age of television, I rarely encountered representations that informed my quest for cultural identity in a helpful way. I am old enough to remember the Frito Bandito, Speedy Gonzales and a host of slumbering, sombrero-wearing Mexicans in westerns who were about as significant as cacti to the gun-slinging white hero. In *The Good, the Bad, and the Ugly*, the Mexican, while not bad, was ugly, which—to me—was much worse than being bad, and played by Eli Wallach, a Jew. On television and in films, the white people, those I construed to be the not-so-real people, made choices and took action, though they were not like me or anyone in my family. They had surnames like Anderson, Reed, and Cleaver, and though they had few family members, they owned large houses with well-manicured lawns on streets unlike any in our neighborhood. As a child, I found it difficult to witness them onscreen living their amusing and exciting lives without wanting to be at least a little less real.

This contributed to a confusing state of affairs for me, especially in adolescence when I embarked on the ontological journey to define the self. Who was I? I wondered. And *what* was I? Satisfying answers to these questions came more easily for my older sister, who identified and aligned with our Mexican American and Chicano schoolmates and neighbors in the pre-gentrified Echo Park District where we grew up. "Somos Chicanos!" She took to the language— its inflections and idioms, customs, and especially the politics—with ease, completely eliding our more complicated New Mexican roots. By the definition I now apply in determining Chicano identity (some mestizo heritage, inculcation in the US experience, or self-identification as Chicano), she was perfectly right to do this, to self-declare as a Chicana. Her assessment, in truth, was more accurate than my mother's insistence that we were Spanish. The early Spaniards, the conquistadores and even those fleeing the Inquisition, were usually men. Survival entailed reproduction; reproduction meant miscegenation somewhere along the line, and in fact, we now know our paternal grandfather was born of a union between an Hispano and a Pueblo woman. Though unaffiliated with present-day Mexico, we certainly were of "mixed blood," or mestizos, from which the word Mexican derives.

Nevertheless, the fundamental logic that created for my sister an easy assimilation into this cultural context was a bit more difficult for me. Everywhere I looked, it seemed, the not-so-real people were in charge and telling the real people what to do, from my father's big bosses at the DWP to the principal, a French Canadian nun, at the school where my mother taught. As I grew into adolescence, my simple categories began to tumble and rearrange themselves: those whom I had believed to be real seemed more and more compromised in authority, while those I once deemed to be not-so-real had it all. Traits like accented speech and appearance, racial markers like height, skin and hair color, and even last names unfurled certain delimiting and abbreviated narratives that sometimes cut off opportunities to forge identity and create the self as a unique individual, even as a sentient being. Instead, one became "that Mexican," which was especially frustrating to my mother, and to me, because we had never even seen Mexico.

Early on, I decided I did not want to be defined in a limited way, and I had no desire to lose opportunities because of this; but moreover, with my height, fair skin, and European features, I found that I could pass. And so I tried to do this, to be real and not-so-real, whichever was which and whenever it suited me. One can likely guess how well that worked. In my Chicana life, I partook of social events with my more outgoing sister, working hard at not being called out for my lamentable Spanish and lack of nostalgia for Mexico. This was fine, but as I grew into adulthood, I found the male-female dynamic in these contexts appalling; machismo really pissed me off. After graduating from high school, I converted from being a *Cosmo* girl into a regular subscriber to *Ms.* magazine and launched myself via consciousness-raising toward feminism, discovering Steinem, Rich, and Friedan as my trusty, wise guides along the way.

Nothing in my experience of the world convinced me that one sex was entitled to dominate another. No male I encountered exhibited judgment I deemed worthy of preempting my own (that unfortunate illusion would come later) and I had limited skill and patience for flirtation or feigning admiration for the opposite sex. So, while it suited my girlfriends to sit ardently listening to their Chicano musician boyfriends play guitar with their bandmates, practicing the same mind-numbing chords for hours on end, this drove me to contemplate mass murder. When we both attended California State University, Northridge, my sister prevailed on me to join MECHA, a student-activist Chicano group on campus, eventually convincing me to attend a meeting with her. At this meeting, one male leader after another addressed the group, and I remember thinking that if I wanted to hear some man or another go on and on, uninterrupted and unquestioned, why, I could just go back to attending Mass. At the conclusion of the meeting, the final speaker issued this unforgettable announcement: "Now, if the girls will go to the kitchen in back, we've got stuff for you to make tostadas!" Here, I rose from my seat and, pushing past the tide of willing young women marching toward the kitchen, I walked out, never to return again.

To be fair, my sister also persuaded me to take a Chicano Studies class at CSUN. This course was taught by the brilliant Rodolfo Acuña, a man I soon came to admire honestly and even emulate in the university classes I now teach. Professor Rudy Acuña presented me with the full gallery of heroes—men and women—on whose backs the Chicano Movement was built. He introduced me to Chicana feminists including Dolores Huerta, Mirta Vidal, Anna NietoGomez, Martha Cortera, and Gloria Anzaldúa, and he did not shy away from the shameful truth about the Denver Youth Conference of 1969, wherein the male leadership determined that "[i]t was the consensus of the group that the Chicana woman does not want to be liberated," sparking fierce outrage among the women present and leading to the inception of the Chicana Feminist Movement.

Although I was too young to participate in the Chicano Movement, I was vindicated to learn about these pioneering women leaders and their struggle to be recognized beyond the few obligatory lines in Corky Gonzales's long, seminal poem about Chicano identity, wherein women, when they appear, are portrayed weeping over their slain men. Despite Rudy Acuña's respect for Chicana feminists and recognition of their contributions to the movement, by the time I came along, in the late 1970s, Chicano student activists, at least at CSUN, had resumed business as usual: men in charge and ordering women into the kitchen to whip up tostadas. Had she known about this, my mother would not have been able to resist pointing out that this particular dish, the tostada—also known as the chalupa and composed of a crisp corn tortilla layered with refried beans, cheese, lettuce, and chopped tomatoes—is not something we eat, much less prepare. It is Mexican food, and she would have said, "We are Spanish."

My first husband, a bona fide Mexican American, a Chicano, even, with immigrant parents, blessedly had little in common with his brethren in MECHA. Luis was a relatively liberated male who grew up in a suburban Van Nuys neighborhood. His parents owned a dry-cleaning business that required them to spend long hours away from home, so Luis, their firstborn, was expected to watch over his younger siblings, keep house, and prepare the family's evening meal. He became so adept at these tasks that he opened my mind to the concept that food can actually have taste and even be flavorful, something I was not aware of due to my mother's ineptitude in the kitchen, which was not masked by the New Mexican custom of smothering most dishes in mouth-excoriating chili. Luis prepared a broad range of edible Mexican foods, even disgusting-sounding things like tripas (tripe) and trickier dishes like chiles rellenos—all of his concoctions sublime. And he kept our small house immaculate, often chastising me for leaving clothing scattered about. When I think of him these days, the image that flashes before me derives from a time I arrived home from school to find him suctioning the dust out of our fishbowl-sized terrarium with a teensy, battery-operated vacuum. He did not seem to mind that I would not take his last name (Bermudez) when we wed, but he certainly looked baffled when I gave my reason for this: "It would be redundant."

Indeed, his last name told the same story that my last name told. No matter that the narratives behind these similar sounding names—López and Bermudez—were and still are distinctly different. Going by his last name was the same for me as using my maiden name; this gave away too much and at the same time it told nothing at all about me. I was still trying to pass and not pass. In the words of Lawrence Durrell, I wanted to belong and to be free, and I imagined with all my might that this could be possible. And though the men I subsequently married had ordinary Anglicized names, I was never fully able to hide my otherness behind these. In fact, the names and the in-laws that came with them seemed to exacerbate my outsider status, to inflect my exoticism. I stood out in holiday photos—the dark-haired one, angled away from the group, smiling that tight smile and holding herself stiffly.

As a writer, I have found that the limitations imposed by my ethnic identity complicate artistic production. In a graduate creative writing workshop, I was taken aside by my professor, who informed me that my characters, though they had Spanish-sounding surnames, struck him as "just people, and not really ethnic types." He kindly lent me a book by a Chicano author to help me understand how to write in a more culturally appropriate way. Respect for this poet and his writing prevented me from mentioning that his poetry did not strike me as particularly Jewish, and as a Jewish writer did it not behoove him to write in a more culturally appropriate way. I could have recommended Saul Bellow, Isaac Bashevis Singer, or Phillip Roth to him. And here again, I want it both ways. I cry racism when readers complain about my use of Spanish in my novels and point out that no one thinks less of T. S. Eliot for the Sanskrit that pops up in *The Wasteland*, as if old T. S. and I are colleagues from the same peer-writing group.

Though it usually compounds my troubles, at times my cultural ambivalence has worked to my advantage, probably oftener than I know. When I relocated to the South, I was hired by a covertly racist community organizer who was required to staff the federally funded agency she directed with diverse employees. In her eyes, someone who could pass and not pass, a woman of color who looked and sounded white, provided a workable compromise to this mandate. So my genetic luck and hard work to eradicate markers of ethnicity, such as accented speech, paid off when I first moved to Georgia and was desperate to escape the particularly perverse hell that is substitute teaching. Unlike my family members, including siblings, my spoken English is accent-free, and I will never forget being initially mystified when a coworker told me "some Spanish guy" phoned the agency, asking for me. I found out later that this was my brother, a native English-speaker like me, but culturally identified by his accented speech. While I no doubt benefited from masking cultural signifiers, usually this ambivalence created internal conflict, feelings of guilt, betrayal, and undeserved privilege when I took advantage of opportunities such as the aforementioned job.

And once, my chameleon act lost me a position. Just before I finished my dissertation, I applied for a creative writing fellowship at a two-year college in Phoenix, Arizona. I had already lined up an assistantship to the editors at the *Georgia Review*, but this one-year teaching position that came with a real salary enticed me. When invited to fly out for an interview, I accepted, thinking at the very least I would have an opportunity to visit with a friend who was at the Arizona State University in nearby Tempe. The interview, I thought, went well. I remember slogging across molten asphalt in the parking lot, thinking I would likely reject the offer because of the relentless heat. I was confident an offer would be made. I should have been suspicious when escorted to meet ESOL faculty, but I was only naively curious about their pedagogical questions related to teaching English to nonnative speakers.

Within a week, I had a call from the college in Phoenix. To my chagrin, I did not get the fellowship. The chair of the selection committee told me they had hired another candidate who they believed would relate better to their students, someone "a bit more Latina," she blithely told me; she then offered me another position with the same college. "Tenure-track," she said, as if tempting me with something more desirable than the twelve-month fellowship and not merely tossing me a consolation prize for my coming up short in the Latinidad department. The dean, she explained, wanted me to teach ESOL in the fall. "Oh?" I said, immediately realizing that I was to be part of a twofer for this college, in which they would acquire a pair of Latinas in one hiring swoop. I asked her to let me think about this, but really I wanted time to figure out how to say no and not sound angry about it. When I called to reject the offer, the chair asked why I turned them down. I said I had another offer, but the woman persisted, wanting to know what this was, perhaps suspecting the boondoggle aspect to my visit on their dime. I told her about the *Georgia Review* and stressed that I did not want to teach ESOL

Yet I must look like an ESOL instructor in some indefinable way, for that is the assumption I encounter these days when people who know my last name learn that I now teach at Vanderbilt University. No matter that we have no department specializing in English language acquisition and do not even offer linguistics courses through the English department. Or else I am asked if I teach

Spanish. Here in the South, "Spanish" is the polite word to use when talking about Hispanics or Latinos. With the influx of immigrant labor stirring nationalist foment and a persistent "English-only" movement, the word "Mexican" has devolved into a slur here in my adopted home state of Tennessee, and "Chicano" has not yet worked itself into the vernacular. When I stroll into my local supermarket to find salsa, I head for the aisle labeled "Spanish Foods," so strong is reluctance to use the "M" word. I often wonder what Spaniards would think perusing such an aisle. A tortilla in Spain, for instance, is an omelet and nothing like the flat wheat or corn flour wrapping for beans and meat. What would a Galician make of pickled yucca and bottled tomatillos?

In the South, where people are friendly but inquisitive, I am often questioned about my church affiliation, and when people find out my last name or are puzzled by my dark hair and eyes, I am asked if I am Spanish. At times like this, I flash on an image of my mother, her immense arms crossed, a what-did-I-tell-you-look on her broad face. She's raising one eyebrow, pursing her lips, and she's nodding at me.

7

My Word Hunger

Judith Ortiz Cofer

According to legend, the first machine translation program was given the sentence "The flesh is weak, but the spirit willing." The translation (into Russian) was then translated back to English, yielding, "The meat is spoiled, but the vodka is good."

—Gary Marcus, *Kluge: The Haphazard Evolution of the Human Mind*

It can strike me anytime, but it usually happens summers when I'm reunited with my mother in Puerto Rico. Not when we embrace, and she tells me I'm too thin and gives me her blessing, "Dios te bendiga, Hija," and I respond automatically, "Gracias, Mami." Nor when I tell her she looks younger than ever, and she answers, "Gracias, Hija." And it doesn't happen over the much-anticipated traditional dinner she has prepared for my husband and me—arroz, habichuelas, pollo, platanos dulces, followed by ultra-sweet café con leche and a budín, a small high-density square of such deeply satisfying sweetness that I suspect (but never want to confirm) it contains an entire day's worth of calories for most moderately active adults. It may not even happen while we are discussing the family gossip and health problems: my uncle with diabetes, aunts getting on in age, and the family curse of arthritis—the ailment that is slowly but certainly descending over most of us in the immediate and extended maternal side of my family. Diabetes, arthritis—di-ah-beh-tis, ar-tree-tis—both have cognates in Spanish.

It usually accosts me when the conversation takes a turn, entering any subject in Spanish that I live with only in English: politics; medical conditions that I have not encountered during my previous visits; the intricacies of topics such as cooking, house building, and sex (this subject hardly ever a problem unless my mother is reading about a sex-change operation or the sexual preferences of a celebrity in her *Vanidades* magazine); and many other areas of interest to her and my Spanish-only relatives. It is in those awkward pauses in conversation that I can now identify the beginning of my episodes; for example, if I am asked a question, or if it is my turn to comment on the high price of renovating a part of a house that I have never spoken of in Spanish. This is an area that, as a homeowner in Georgia, I have learned to communicate well in Southern English, my daily dialect: "And, Sir," I will say to the handyman assiduously avoiding my interference as he climbs up on the roof of our house, "Sir, will you be able to put in that new gutter lickety-split? It looks like this rain's going to be a gulley-washer."

In my mother's conversation groups, however, I am always the contestant, on the spot, playing Double Jeopardy, and the question is "¿Come se dice———"¿

"¿Qué crees?" someone will invite me to offer my opinion, and I am muted by an invisible remote control aimed at me from above. I am suffering the first symptoms of *word hunger*. I search frantically through my brain files for an equivalent. Awkward moment of silence. Exchange of dubious looks, not subtle; Puerto Rican–style irony can become visual aggression. La Profesora cannot cough up a simple answer to a simple question? Usually my mother, a great improvisational dancer, both on the dance floor and off, makes her move to rescue me, translating the unknown into a synonymous concept.

"Prices here for una instalación de unos altos (an addition to the house) are twice as much as in the United States ¿No creen?"

Even with my desperate segues and my mother's conversational diversions, La Profesora loses face. I have an academic title (my area is creative writing and American literature) and teach at the University of Georgia, where I am only now encountering the occasional Latina/o student in my classrooms—and they usually want to speak in English. I rarely get to speak Spanish, even when I am asked to give readings to Latinos in the United States. My North American, Bolivia-raised son-in-law, who is teaching my two-year-old grandson Spanish, knows more words than I because he speaks it every day; currently his most extensive vocabulary entails baby concerns, not complex scientific terminology, in which I am sure he is also fluent. My excuse for ignorance in infant-care terminology is that I never had a reason to learn those words in Spanish: pañales, pediatra, andadora, mecedora—not a difficult vocabulary, but these words are simply not on the tip of my brain. I keep a Spanish-English dictionary handy when my nieto and his papi are around. With language, it is a natural but frustrating process of use it or lose it, as it is with any human function: for most of my life since our move to the United States, I have been undergoing the change from being a primary Spanish speaker toward English becoming my first language—this is not a choice, any more than is having one arm stronger than the other because I use it more often. I have kept the Spanish vocabulary I use and have been losing the words I don't need. In the meantime my English has grown and evolved as the language of my everyday concerns and of my professional life.

Occasionally, my mother lets me suffer through a word vacuum, at least for a minute or two, long enough to allow me to dig up la palabra—if it happens to still exist somewhere in the deep recesses of my brain area—for my own good, she claims; I can regain my Spanish, she insists. She lends me her *Buenhogar* and *People en español* magazines, so I can continue to acquire a conversational vocabulary. And it works. I can discuss the lives of celebrities with some competence, and if the topic of setting up a buffet meal for twenty comes up, I can probably get a few words into the conversation. I usually spend the time at her house reading books by contemporary Puerto Rican writers such as Rosario

Ferré, Ana Lydia Vega, Carmen Lugo Filippi, and many others, and marveling at the beauty of my native tongue, especially when it sings at the hands of a talented wordsmith. I fall in love again with its cadences, its music. Spanish is a delicious language, miel en la boca, and I often feel like an onlooker at a banquet, kept out of the festivities mainly because of a speech impediment. Pero en mi vida, I had to choose a tongue to serve me, and it had to be English. But I can dream in Spanish. ¿No creen?

Yet there are times when the word hunger defeats me. It happens when I am trying to share with my mother or a relative or friend on the Island something that is both complicated and serious, and all the words I can come up with date back to the last stages in my life when I was more Spanish than English speaking, my adolescence. I stopped acquiring working vocabularies in what became my second language then; it is as if I became frozen within the boundaries of my native language at the point I had reached at age fifteen. During my formative years we lived mainly in Paterson, New Jersey, and it was a hard city for Puerto Rican kids who did not have a grasp of survival English—preferably in tough, street-wise, Italian-mafia affected cadences. I was also required to speak polite English at St. Joseph's Catholic School. Spanish became intrinsically related to our family's apartment interactions, and to visits to the homes of my relatives, where the children talked in English among themselves, while our parents discussed their luchas and travails in passionate Spanish. Mainly, in those years of rebellion, I used my Spanish with and against my mother. I had a good fighting vocabulary.

"No soy tu prisionera. Todos mis amigos salen en dates con muchachos. No vivimos en tu isla. Es el twentieth century, Mami. Estamos en America. Sí, voy a usar makeup. Esta bien, no voy a usar makeup, for now. Mami, necesito dinero."

I never had a reason to discuss paradigms, dichotomies or dialectics, pedagogy or gender issues with my mother, unless it was the constant argument about what a good mujer should be, and when it was appropriate to wear makeup (never), date boys (never), or increase my allowance (that is for your father to decide). I could probably still defend myself well in these areas, but no longer have to.

But I exaggerate a bit, as is my cultural privilege. Mother taught us how to write in basic familial Spanish so we could correspond with our grandparents, and because I was her interpreter, I learned how to deal with doctors, clerks, the US Navy, the Red Cross, and the occasional lawyer. But I was her recording device and her trained parrot; none of these matters were my causes; therefore, I forgot many words that did not interest me as I distanced myself from my childhood roles.

Recently I was in line at a gate in Hartsfield Airport in Atlanta. An irate airline employee was dealing with angry passengers experiencing many delays and missed connections. In front of me, a woman was desperately trying to find out why her flight to San Juan had been canceled. The attendant kept motioning her to move aside, telling her that he had requested a Spanish speaker to come talk to her. I normally do not get involved in airline disputes, as I have learned that next to the famously impassive New York City waiters, airline agents are the most adept public service personnel at avoiding your gaze and ignoring your presence at their counters (or supplicants' altars, as I think of these barriers to communication). You are made to wait until you have to declare temporary residency at the gate, or for the next shift to take over, then grovel and ingratiate yourself to them as best you can under the weight of travel fatigue and carry-on luggage. Travel is a humbling experience. Yet something in this woman's voice told me I needed to offer her my emergency Spanish. I asked her what the problem was. She told me she had to get home for her mother's funeral; she had been visiting her son at Fort Benning. He was soon to be deployed to Iraq, and as a result, she had missed being at her mamá's deathbed. *Madre, morir*—two of the most dramatic and connotative words in Spanish brought me to full attention. I could not understand any more of what she said as she broke down crying, but I knew I had to use my survival language to help her. I explained the situation to the attendant, who actually showed a small, measured sympathetic response. I also made sure that the fidgety people behind us heard me explaining the dire circumstances, which I described in my best lecturing mode. *Please understand, death in the family, a son, fighting for OUR country*. There was a palpable shift in attitudes, an almost imperceptible making of a bit of space for this suffering woman. Soon enough she was put on another airline's flight to the Island. My survival English had met the challenge and my emergency Spanish had sufficed. This time.

Not long after that, I faced a different, more frustrating situation. I was asked to give a talk at a Spanish-language academic conference. After all, I have various books about my experiences in two cultures, I was perfectly suited for the task; here was an opportunity to feature the Puerto Rican in my Puerto Rican American identity: could I deliver a paper? The time had come for me to admit that although I speak Spanish, I am not bilingual beyond a certain conversational level. I would have had to ask my friend and translator of my books, Dr. Elena Olazagasti-Segovia, Vanderbilt University professor, PhD in Spanish, University of Puerto Rico, to translate my paper, and then learn to pronounce academese in Spanish (hard enough in English). I found the task not within my zone of Spanish-language comfort. It was hard to explain to my dominant-Spanish colegas in academia, many of whom seem to feel little or no embarrassment in speaking in heavily accented English and using translators for their work, that I am a Spanish-fluent, non-bilingual, English-dominant Latina, not out of choice, but due to circumstances I could not control when, as a pre-literate child, I was brought to the United States by my parents. Yet, it is as if it is my responsibility as the speaker of the language not of the minority group, which is English, to make the effort. But that is not how I see the situation. It was not my personal decision to become English-dominant. My formal education has been in English; my cultural education has been split between heart and mind, with Spanish remaining at the core of my identity, while English increasingly became the language of both my survival and my art. I use Spanish in my work to distinguish the English as that of a Latina, to dramatize and to emphasize my words. I use it to add humor and spice, as well as to indicate nuances of joy and pain. My Spanish flavors my writing as it does the most memorable meals of my life. Spanish is still the language de mi corazón. But I have to declare this in my best words, so I say it using my best English, with a little Spanish added, which is, I believe, the best language for expressing amor. English is my first language now. This is simply how it is, not how I decided it should be.

But on the surface, it must appear to the individuals who bind identity so strictly to the choice of a primary language that mine is betrayal of the mother tongue—a puertorriqueña who will not write or give a talk in her native language. Shame! ¡Que verguenza! I also did not mention this to distinguished colleagues—that, until recently, I too suffered from bilingualism-paradigm confusion; either you *is* bilingual *honey*, or you *ain't*. ¿Como se dice paradigm en español? I once heard two Latino academics practicing their paradigm insider joke at a conference. One asks, "What is a paradigm?" The other answers "Four nickels?" The conclusion I have come to is that the level of my bilingualism depends on my particular circumstances and needs—how much Spanish I will speak is a personal decision for me, one I will not make based on someone else's dogmatic views on ethnic identity.

There was a situation recently that left me feeling truly word-starved because it was a family matter of great importance to me, and yet I failed to find the words to meet the challenge. It had to do with my mother's decision to let me ask her many difficult questions about my father's long battle with depression and about the psychological traumas I suspected he had experienced during his lifetime career in the military, which I had only heard about in snatches and rumors, and which I suspected were at the root of his malady. But more significant to my understanding of the loss my family suffered, I needed to know more facts about his early death in a car accident during one of his worst bouts with what my mother has always referred to as la tristeza, the chronic sadness he wore daily like a heavy coat he could not or would not take off. I had always respected her reticence on this subject and had tried to piece together my father's story through other channels, such as questions I occasionally asked of his brothers and sisters, who, like me, only knew what he and my mother chose to reveal.

But one day, alone with her in her house on the Island, not long after she lost her beloved father to old age, after a prolonged bout with dementia and other agonies of the mind and body in his final years, we sat together in camaraderie. We sat and talked of many things, like friends, like what we are, two women in late middle age reminiscing about family times of joy, the birth of my grandson, her great-grandson, and the tristeza we will all experience in the end: birth and death, the bookends of all our lives. Here was my chance to ask the source, the keeper of our shared memories and the witness to my father's life story, to tell me what I needed to know about him. And I knew what questions I needed to ask, but they had to be phrased exactly right. We were both feeling emotional, and I could not very well run out of the room to find a dictionary, or power up my laptop to google translations when I could not come up with las palabras. In my desperate need to phrase it just right, the moment passed, the window closed. I had felt the pangs, the spiritual hunger, but I had been unable to make the right sentences out of the wordless pain. Now it would have to wait until another time, when all the elements were aligned again. When I came home to my English-language life, I wrote everything out and laboriously translated it, committing the right words to memory, preparing my *passionate* Spanish, the dream tongue I will always need, for when the time comes. I will be ready.

Do I speak Spanish? Yes, I speak Spanish. I speak survival Spanish. I speak yearning Spanish, I speak nostalgic Spanish. I dream in Spanish. The dream-Spanish trickles down into my poems, stories, and essays. And en mi vida, el español de mis sueños y mi corazón suffices.

8

Jotonovela

ERASMO GUERRA

The night hours pitched toward morning—and still no call from my boyfriend Josh. I fired up my computer and, feeling as melodramatic as my mother when she used to sniff my father's work clothes for another woman's perfume, I cracked one of Josh's email accounts by guessing the password as his phone number.

This was the summer of 2001 and in the seven months that Josh and I had been seeing each other, I had my suspicions that he was seeing other men. For one thing, he insisted unsentimentally that "everybody cheated." So I had doubts about his "friend" Dave, with whom he was having dinner earlier that night. Like a lot of gay men, they'd hooked up years ago when they first met and had since settled into a friendship. Thinking there was more going on, I scanned Josh's inbox, clicked an already opened message from Dave, and found a link to a gay personals ad site. When the link refused to connect, I broke into Josh's other account—he used the same password—and this time the link worked.

As I scrolled through Josh's profile, headlined "Open to Anything (29 years old)," whatever guilt I felt collapsed into grief. He described himself in one swoop as good-looking and smart and nonjudgmental; he sought the same in others and looked for a down-to-earth, no-attitude guy in touch with his sexuality, with uncut a plus. Not that he would say no to "circumsized" men.

Height: Five Eleven (an inch more than the truth). Body Type: Defined (from playing tennis twice a week). Ethnic Origin: Asian (though he insisted that Filipinos were not so much Asians as Pacific Islanders with a long history of Spanish colonialism). Hair Color: Black. Eyes: Brown.

He checked off that he was a "Single Gay Man" interested in meeting "A Single Man," "A Gay Male Couple," "A Group for Friendship" or "Email/Chat," or for "1-on-1 Sex" or "Group Sex" or "Other Activities." Under "Practice Safe Sex" he indicated "Rather Not Say."

I sat in front of my computer, stunned, as if a flock of doves had been rattled out of my heart. At least Josh hadn't included a photo like Dave, whose profile I found later. In one frame he was dressed in his police officer's uniform. In another, he was naked, offering a close-up of his pale ass. Until then, I'd only heard stories of Dave through Josh, so this was the first time I'd ever seen what he looked like.

A moment later, digging through more of Josh's emails, I got an instant message from Dave, who must have thought Josh was online. The note thanked Josh for their night out.

"You're still the best kisser," he wrote at the bottom, where a smiley-face emoticon punctuated the end.

I closed out of my computer and called Josh's apartment. He answered with a drowsy hello.

"It's over," I said. "And you know why."

He told me he didn't know what I was talking about, but in the ensuing quiet he must have thought better of his denial. He asked if all this "drama" was about the kiss with Dave.

"It was nothing," he defended. "We were drunk. If I wanted to cheat I would've gone somewhere else and not given him that nothing kiss in front of my building."

Josh rented a one-room studio in the landmark Times Square Hotel, which had been renovated into subsidized housing for struggling artists, actors, and the aged. I lived in a Hell's Kitchen share that was ten streets and one avenue away. Josh must've thought I'd been nearby and seen them together. I told him I'd found his personals ad.

"I only registered to get free naked pictures from other guys," he explained, as if that made everything okay—which it didn't. "Dave signed me up that night as a joke."

Maybe I was taking this too seriously and being over-dramatic. Growing up in South Texas, my own family had labeled me early on as an "exagerado," an exaggerator, someone who added more to the story and rendered it unrecognizable from the truth. Shamed, I kept my mouth shut and rode the four miles from our house to my grandmother's when my fingers got caught in the door of the El Camino; I huddled behind a couch while at a barbecue at a family friend's house when their dog bit my arm; and I locked myself in my bedroom when I fell and broke my nose. In each case I didn't want to cause trouble or make a scene.

That changed when a high school teacher forced us to keep a journal as part of her senior English class. For the first time, I told without judgment and continued the practice after graduation. And while I never consciously sought out conflict, I never shied away from writing about it in my spiral-bound notebooks. By the time I outgrew my boyhood, most of my story material was drawn exclusively from boyfriends.

I just never considered myself a drama queen, looking for messes or manufacturing them, the way Josh accused me of doing. Never mind that he was the one who behaved over-the-top. He'd trained in musical theater in Manila, and though he gave up on making a career of it after a few discouraging years in New York, he still seemed to live on a stage of his imagination, like when he made huge productions of "catching" me looking at other guys in public—but only to draw the other guy's attention to himself, leading me to think that he was guiltily projecting his own possible infidelities.

The nights I went over to his place, I shut myself in his bathroom and dug through the hamper, pulling out the pockets of his pants in search of scraps on which other guys may have written their names and numbers and email addresses. I'd seen this done by my mother, a child of Mexican immigrants, who was born along the Texas-Mexico border and raised on songs of romantic doom like "Paloma Negra," an anguished cucurrucucú of breakup. The refrain was an operatic wail to a mythic black dove, or maybe it was just the lover transformed.

¡Paloma Negra! ¡Paloma Negra!
¿Donde? ¿Donde estaras?

Not that you hoped for peace. You rode the bird's wings into the winds of emotional upset, the heavens going dark, and you cried as if misery was a country beautiful and adored.

My mother had "known" only one man in her life, my father, whose beer-fueled rages she endured to spare us kids the disgrace of divorce and the further humiliation of other people's talk. Not that she was doing us any favors, since the nights we went out looking for him, my mother and older sister remained in the car while my little brother and I were forced to enter the south-side cantinas, our eyes barely clearing the raw-wood tabletops.

In New York, where I'd been living for the past eight years, there were no romantic black doves, only gritty pigeons that wheeled over grimy rooftops and shit on everything. As a thirty-one-year-old gay man, who'd come of age roller skating to Pat Benatar and whose favorite song that summer of 2001 was the hip-hop hit "No More Drama" by Mary J. Blige, I'd come to believe that if one guy wasn't working out, I was free to find another without worrying what anyone else was going to think or say. I didn't have any responsibilities holding me back either. So while my mother had been trapped, I was always prepared to escape through any trapdoor I could find. I swore I'd never allow myself to become like my mother. There was no need for that.

Still, hours after I called it off with Josh, I wanted him to come pounding on the front door of my apartment. But he never came to defend himself. Even at the midtown office where I worked the front desk, each knock, each ring on the phone, was Josh for one deluded moment, and then it was whoever it was.

I called my best friend, an Argentine writer prone to self-described Evita impersonations, who lived in Williamsburg with his Filipino slam-poet boyfriend. When I told him the news, his support came in a half-apologetic tone; he was busy that weekend, dealing with his own crumbling relationship and carrying hopes for a new guy he'd just met. I told him not to worry. I'll be fine, I said, though by the time we hung up I wanted to break up with him, too.

I had other friends. Or so I thought.

The older French guy, with whom I'd had a thing when I first moved to New York, took me to dinner and advised me to have a fling. He suggested I go to the steam room at my gym. I had told him stories. (Sharing accounts of your sex life with others when you were no longer interested in one another seemed to be the polite thing to do. And, as a writer, it was good narrative practice.) "Don't even bother with the pretense of working out," he said, before heading out to a male strip show.

Later that night, I met up with a female coworker who lived in the neighborhood. We headed to Barrage, the local bar where I'd met Josh. Afraid and hopeful about seeing him, I was relieved that the line outside was long and we refused to wait. We went to Posh instead, the bar where Josh and I had our first date; I pointed out the leather couches in the back where Josh and I had made out.

The night I first met him, Josh stood in the middle of Barrage, chopped bangs covering his bug eyes. His face was pocked and his forehead shone with a few pimples. His teeth were bonded or capped or otherwise held together by cheap dental cosmetology. A scar collapsed the bridge of his nose.

He wasn't handsome, but something about the way he ignored me compelled me to go over to say hello. I lied about having seen him in the neighborhood. I had so convinced myself of my line that I felt indignant when he sneered, no, I hadn't seen him. I didn't know how he could've been so certain even as I made up details about watching him walk down Ninth Avenue.

Months later he was still calling me a liar. I didn't take it personally because I knew I wasn't a terrific fiction writer. I was better at nonfiction and reportage, dramatizing real incidents. Maybe I took some literary license when I used more figurative language, but otherwise I stuck to the truth. Which was why I was so taken by Josh that first night when he bluntly called me out on my wishful thinking.

I soon fell for the fact that he was tri-lingual—English, Tagalog, and a bit of Spanish—and for the way he played with words. What attracted me most, however, was that he liked to read. Sure, he checked out young adult romances from the Jefferson Market Library—he loved the *Sweet Valley High* series—but he also read E. M. Forster and a number of *New York Times* best sellers. He turned to literature for its entertainment value and left all the obscure, plotless, hard-to-read material to me.

What more could a writer ask for in a boyfriend? Though Josh was adamant that he didn't want me to write about him. Or, if I did, he wanted to be made beautiful and given the name "Josh." He wanted me to turn him into one of those white-boy characters he loved to read about so much.

As for making him "beautiful," I only had to take inventory of my own physical defects—like my crooked nose, smashed from that childhood fall on my face—and by comparison Josh wasn't too bad. He insisted I was the most gorgeous guy he'd ever dated. I felt he was just telling me a well-intentioned lie similar to the one I told when I approached him at the bar.

The Saturday after our breakup, I sat at one of the outdoor tables at Good & Plenty, a take-out spot Josh and I went to regularly for weekend breakfast, and I waited for him to pass on his mid-morning trip to the gym. As afraid as I was of seeing him, I was more afraid of not seeing him.

I turned to every flash of khaki shorts, looked up when I heard the scrape of sandals dragging the sidewalk, but it was always someone else, and I returned to my spiral notebook to write about what had happened between us. Most of my published work is based on the men who've moved in and out of my life.

My mother, who has read some of it, considers my work nothing more than pornography, either for the gay sexual situations I depict, or because of my total disregard for suffering silently.

Later that afternoon, I hit the basement steam room at my eastside gym. It depressed me to think that Josh was on the other side of town, slumped against the tiles of the steam room at his own gym. Without any desire to participate, I watched the older men, shapeless and sad in the hot clouds, circle the younger guys, who ignored them as they chased the ones who were better looking. The men gathered in the steam and then spooled out to the showers or the sauna before flocking back to the sweaty tiles for another round.

Barrage wasn't much better later that night. The walls were strung with laminated tear sheets of all the homoerotic ad campaigns from Abercrombie to Versace, making the bar look like a photographer's darkroom. Working my way through the Saturday night crowd I ordered a Jack on the rocks and told myself I was not here to find a one-night stand. I was out to make a friend.

Josh was of the mind that gay bars were nothing but hook-up joints and said I was lying to myself if I thought otherwise. And, sure enough, after meeting a guy I'll call Tristan—that was the other name Josh wanted me to use if I ever wrote about him—we hurried to Tristan's high-rise apartment on West 57th Street.

On the walk, Tristan told me that he was an actor, and that he had just finished a Woody Allen movie. "Woody cast me as the Voice of Doom," he squeaked, his voice far from threatening, which must've been the point.

Up at his place, the bedroom windows looked over the red river of tail-lights of Ninth Avenue traffic. The computer in the corner was tuned to a chat room where the dialogue scrolled up the monitor, making me wonder, as Tristan lit votives, whether Josh was online at that hour.

The best part of the encounter was settling the score with Josh and being able to return home by midnight to get a good night's sleep.

The next night at Barrage, I repeated to myself that I was here to make a friend instead of settling for sex. Wasn't that what my father had gone searching for at those cantinas? A drinking buddy who understood his burdens as a middle-aged, working-class, married man?

Or was I just repeating my mother's routine, hitting up all the watering holes she knew my father went to? Because as much as I hated those late-night trips to fetch my father, I realize now that I was still making the rounds as an adult, searching the New York gay bars for someone to bring home.

Disoriented about who I was, deluded about what exactly I was doing there, I sat under the laundry line of photos and sipped my Jack as the bar filled up with a delinquent Sunday night crowd. As everyone else admired the photos, giving these commercial ideals more attention than the real guys at the bar, I imagined these slick fantasies of gay life stacked one on top of the other and stapled and sold as a gay fotonovela—call it a jotonovela—a story told in pictures. Never mind the happy ending. Give it no ending at all. Let it be one night after another of faces and bodies that never grow tired or old or die.

Josh called me at work the following Monday and asked, "Why aren't you talking to me, Amores Guerra?"

He liked to play with my name, mixing up the letters to form other words, and I loved the way he exaggerated the Spanish. Then again, "Amores Guerra" also sounded like he was saying "Love Is War."

"I didn't cheat on you," he groaned. "There are a thousand other reasons for you to break up with me. I know I can be mean sometimes. I have double standards. I should have spent more time with you and your friends. And I should've introduced you to mine. But you can't break up with me for cheating, because nothing happened."

Josh cleared his throat. "Did you miss me?"

"I cried all weekend," I said, embellishing.

A more terrible grief hit weeks later in early September. Josh and I broke up for a second time. And, the next day, the morning of September 11, as I was walking to work from Josh's apartment, his friend Dave was rushing into the burning towers of the World Trade Center. Other than the stories Josh had told me about Dave, the profile and pictures of him I'd found online, the instant message he'd unknowingly sent me, I never got the chance to meet him. For years he's been a name, a name that has haunted me with so much speculation and sorrow that I had doubts about sharing his real name—just as Josh must've had doubts about introducing me to him at all—and therefore have decided to call him "Dave" in this story. The night he and Josh had dinner and shared that kiss turned out to be the last time they saw each other. And years later I still tear up about how ridiculous I'd been for begrudging them that kiss.

That night Josh wanted to talk things out; he arrived at my apartment after work and I ran downstairs to meet him on the worn stoop. After a weekend of strangers in bars, he seemed a little more human, a little more handsome, his skin darkened, pocks faded by a tennis-playing tan.

He wore a new red-check shirt, three-quarter-length khakis, sandals. He surprised me with a bouquet of bodega flowers, wrapped in cellophane, jammed in a vase. He thrust them toward me and announced, a little too sure of himself, "You're not mad anymore."

Running the five flights back up to my apartment to drop off the flowers, I told myself, okay, even though I wasn't mad, it didn't mean we were back together. I told him as much as we headed to the restaurants on Ninth Avenue. His eyes reddened.

"So? This is it?" he said.

It wasn't much of an emotional display. Passersby would've noticed nothing more than two guys trying to make up their minds about where to eat. But those red eyes meant a lot. This was the first time in the months we'd been together that I ever saw Josh express an authentic emotion. Until then, everything had always seemed like a caricature, a musical-theater adaptation of our relationship—his comedy to my tragedy—but for a single moment on that Hell's Kitchen sidewalk it was as if he was trying to get no one else's attention except mine.

"Baby, you don't know how much I love you and how important you are to me. You're the only one who puts up with me."

And there it was. I'd become my mother after all. Or, rather, I'd been my mother's son all along, someone "que aguanta," as we called it, someone who "endures" and "puts up with."

Josh, who recognized that, who pointed out yet again how I continued to lie to myself about who I was and what I'd come from, took my hands and studied them for a long moment. He looked up at me with an exaggerated sigh. "Baby, tell me now. Are you open to negotiation? Or have you made up your mind?"

I suspected we were taking our dinner to go because the cruisy guys at our usual Thai joint would have distracted Josh. Or me, which was what I expected him to say, accusing me rather than admit any temptation on his part. At the counter, placing our order, Josh hissed when I called him baby because he said it wasn't as if we were back together yet.

Like I said, Josh was great at switching and mixing things around—letters, words, blame—sometimes delighting me with what he came up with, and other times confusing me with his blatant contradictions.

Back at my apartment, we ate our roast duck salad and spoke about our weekends. Now he insisted that we hadn't really broken up. He'd let me have my two days alone, he said, to make me realize how dumb I was to break up with him.

He asked me, "You sure you didn't meet anyone this weekend?"

I said no, but he was certain that I had, and he put aside his chopsticks and insisted that I admit it. When I tried to switch it around and asked Josh if he'd met anyone, he hammered me with a speech about how he didn't need to sleep with some guy in order to forget me and feel better about himself. It sounded like something lifted out of *Sweet Valley High*. (If only I'd written it down!)

He asked, "Did you go to Barrage?"

I said I had.

"*¡You met someone!*" He said it in American English, but the emotion was all Mexican telenovela. The bedside lamp served as a spotlight.

"I don't want to know any more," Josh said. But it was obvious he knew, or at least sensed, all there was to know.

We had our make-up sex, and when we were done, we headed to Josh's apartment for the night. As we walked, I looked down the avenue, glancing over at destiny's side streets, guarding against an accidental run-in with the actor and carefully sidestepping the pigeons.

9

Island of Bones

Joy Castro

Home

The anthologies don't mention us. When I teach Latino Studies, I have to take supplemental materials into class so that students know Cubans existed here in the United States before 1959.

In the public narrative of Cuban immigration—the narrative we most often hear and read—we're told that, fleeing Castro's revolution, the very "*first* wave of Cubans, approximately 250,000, arrived from 1959 to 1964," as Guillermo Grenier writes in his study of Cuban American exile ideology (emphasis mine). Two other major cohorts swiftly followed—all of them middle- or upper-class, highly educated, and professional—before the poorer, less skilled Marielitos arrived in 1980. According to this narrative, moreover, Cuban Americans lean right: They vote Republican, since ousting Castro's regime is the primary factor that motivates their politics, and also since they're well-to-do and want to protect the wealth they brought with them or earned, once on Floridian soil, through their industry and thrift.

But this narrative erases an earlier succession of small waves of nineteenth-century Cuban immigrants—not political exiles, but people who came to the United States in search of work, like economic immigrants who come from Mexico and Central and South America today. By the 1890s, half the population of Key West—Cayo Hueso, the Isle of Bones—was Cuban, including mi familia, who had begun emigrating there from Cuba in the 1870s. Over the decades before Fidel Castro came to power, the Rolo and then the Castro family ran the Spanish-language printing press on the island. My family belonged to a working-class community of skilled and unskilled laborers, and its ties to Cuba were strong. National Airlines, for which my father would eventually work as a skycap, ticket agent, and then manager, ran flights to Havana from 1946 to 1961. Before Castro's revolution, my grandparents went back regularly to reconnect with relatives.

But Cayo Hueso is a small island, its Cuban history a small history that has mostly been erased from our national memory by the dramatic convulsions of the revolution, the Bay of Pigs, the Cuban Missile Crisis, little Elián and Janet Reno. Key West's own status in the public imagination, like the status of most Caribbean islands, is simply that of resort playground.

Class

Between 1959 and 1979, most of the Cubans who came to Florida were well-to-do, middle- or upper-class people frustrated with the Communist takeover, and they were welcomed here as good capitalists. Within their cultural productions here in the United States since then, Cuba shimmers like a lost Eden of servants, mansions, pleasure, and beauty. It's a vision that wealth-loving Americans have been all too happy to endorse. Carlos Eire's memoir *Waiting for Snow in Havana*, for example, which won the National Book Award, opens with his family members referring to themselves as French royalty while they frolic among their heirloom furniture and porcelain, unaware of the impending revolution. Mary Urrutia Randelman's cookbook *Memories of a Cuban Kitchen* is laced with photos of her family's 1500-acre tobacco plantation, their 14,000-acre cattle ranch (granted by the King of Spain), members of her family at the Havana Yacht Club, and her laughing parents, sailing off Varadero beach. In her detective novels, Carolina Garcia-Aguilera deploys the common cultural stereotype of the Miami Cuban, dunking buttered Cuban toast in his coffee, bemoaning his exile twenty years after the fact, his yacht pointed toward Havana, ready to go as soon as the radio proclaims good news. In her recent autobiographical one-woman play *Rum & Coke*, Carmen Peláez waxes nostalgic about her family's lost wealth and privilege. I sat in the audience wanting to puke, wondering, *Is this the only story Cubans know how to tell? I can't connect with these people.*

Neither can my aunt, my only relative (out of dozens) who still remains on the island. As a librarian at Key West High, she can barely afford to live there, now that it's been chopped into resorts for the wealthy. All of our other relatives have moved north.

When I was in grad school in Texas, I asked her why she didn't move to Miami.

"Ugh," she said, "Too many Cubans."

At the time, full of youthful hubris and new paradigms from Ethnic Studies, I diagnosed her with a sad case of internalized racism. Later I learned that, like my father did, and like I do, she leans left politically, and that "Cubans," to her, signifies the right-wing Cubans that dominate the news, the post-1959 Cubans—angry, well-to-do, horn-honking, and proud of their passion—and not the Key West Cubans she grew up with, not her family and friends. The dominant-media coverage has erased her story—even to her. To be clear, I am here dismissing neither the stereotypes of Cubans in the United States nor the groups of real, complex people such images represent. Their sorrows are real. Rather, I wish to resist and complicate the monolithic image that writers from the Cuban immigrant community keep delivering to a US public eager to have the desirability of capitalism affirmed. While an elegiac, exilic narrative of a lost paradise of wealth and privilege works for rich or once-rich people, it doesn't work for my people. Yet we're still Cuban American.

My family members are all a little socialist, honestly, but not in a very articulate way. We're mostly poor people, workers, cleaners of other people's houses, grocery checkers, cops. Ranchos and servants don't really do it for us. We'd like economic justice, yeah, but we don't quite know what to do about it; we're not exactly reading Marx and Engels on the weekend. We're just kind of skeptical of the capitalist metanarrative, the way most poor workers are.

We're sure not waxing nostalgic for a Cuba where we were only poorer, where none of my great-aunts bought dresses at El Encanto.

We weren't part of El Movimiento. We lack a political identity. "I'm just a Conch," says my aunt, referring to the term for Key West natives. With property values on the island the way they are, there are almost no Conchs left.

Nostalgia

A conch shell sits on my altar. My dad gave it to me. (I never called him Apá; he made us use English at home—another source of Latino identity, busted.) He used to dive for conchs as a boy. He used to shimmy up coconut palms and throw the coconuts down. When we were children, he'd crack them open and let us drink the sweet, thin milk.

He committed suicide in 2002. I still wonder what part loneliness played. For decades, he pursued the American Dream, moving wherever the job required, working to assimilate, laughing off the way white people compared him to Ricky Ricardo: Miami, London, West Virginia, a man with only a high school education trying to play in the white-collar world with just his silver tongue and smarts. It worked for a while, until his age caught up with him and suddenly every entry-level applicant had a degree, and he watched his career spiral away as he sank from a small-time airline executive to a collection agent to a census-taker, walking door-to-door in rural West Virginia, watching out for dogs.

His suicide ruptures the myth. Latinos, history tells us, don't kill themselves. They nobly sacrifice and organize like Chávez or take up arms like Tijerina. They're heroes, like Pancho Villa and Emiliano Zapata. Call them Joaquín. They labor and sacrifice; they boss their wives and children; they endure for the sake of familia, for dignidad. They do not go gentle into that good night.

But my dad did. No macho, he washed dishes and fried eggs and died alone in his Chevy.

Tidy, my stepmother said. The bullet hole was barely noticeable. He died with his eyes closed. He looked sad, she said, as if he'd been sleeping and was having a sad, sad dream.

God

Latinos are Catholic, or so goes the narrative, and Latinas are particularly devout. Our hair is choked with the smoke of copal and candles, our homes plastered with images of saints and la Virgen and the sacred heart of Jesus.

But my abuela in Key West, with her seventh-grade education and four kids and exhaustion (plus a slew of the neighbors' children to watch for extra money), opened her door on Elizabeth Street one day to a Jehovah's Witness, and boy, didn't it all sound good: paradise on Earth, starting any minute now (as soon as Jehovah wipes out the wicked—and you know Aunt Poni's gonna get it, the way she carries on), and everybody getting a big, nice house with a landscaped lawn like in the pictures in the *Watchtower*, and all your kids behaving for once, and no racism, and everybody with enough to eat and new clothes and equal in the eyes of the Lord. Just like that, she threw off generations of Catholicism and orishas and dragged her kids out of Mass and straight to the Kingdom Hall, and that's how they grew up. My Aunt Lettie even married an elder. My dad, who'd been an altar boy, gave talks from the stage about Jehovah, and when he married a pretty National Airlines stewardess, they held the ceremony in the Key West Kingdom Hall.

My brother and I grew up not with saints and candles, not with Oshún and Yemayá, but with a squeaky-clean Jesus, dreaming of the tigers we'd have for pets (as soon as Armageddon hurried up and got here) and preaching door-to-door.

I left the Witnesses at fifteen. As an adult, I tried the Catholic Church, but higher education had already excised my tolerance for dogma, so I settled, like many academics, into a secular agnosticism, spiritual-but-not-religious. I might chant, meditate, and pray—but not to anyone. Why I felt the need for a rosary, which dangles over my desk, or why I mutter the Hail Mary when planes take off is anyone's guess.

On the wall by my desk brood images of the Virgin: la Virgen de Guadalupe, Cuba's Virgen de la Caridad del Cobre, and Spain's black Virgin of Montserrat. But they weren't the ones I prayed to growing up.

Looks

I have brown hair, brown eyes, and light skin. Growing up, it was always, "Ay, qué linda," and, "You look just like your father." My aunts are light-skinned, too. Mi prima Jeri has blue eyes, and when she gets highlights, the pale streaks look natural. In Miami, where people know that Cubans span the color wheel from black to blond, it's not an issue.

But heritage doesn't always translate visually. Here in Nebraska, I was waiting outside the yoga studio the other day. A guy from my class was also waiting: Larry Mota, a Chicano. He asked how things were going.

I told him how happy I was with the Latino studies class I'm teaching this semester, and he drew back in surprise.

"No disrespect," he said, "but what qualifies you to teach Latino studies?"

Other than a PhD? I wondered. But I explained my background.

"Oh. Oh, sorry. I know some Cubans," he said, "and you don't look Cuban."

Then I pointed out that if he takes Latino studies seriously as an intellectual discipline, identity shouldn't be a prerequisite. No one asks a Shakespeare scholar if he or she is a male British playwright from the sixteenth century. He laughed and conceded the point.

I often forget about my appearance, but I know that to people like Larry I don't look Latina, and my spoken English has only the bland, mongrelized sound of frequent moves among disparate places—Florida, England, West Virginia, Texas, the Midwest—so there's no accent to indicate ethnicity. With my latinidad so muted, I sometimes wonder if I should work harder at staging it, in order to signal both my solidarity con otras Latinas and my difference from the mainstream. But what would that entail? Big silver hoops in my ears? Red lip-stick? Snug skirts and a salsa sway? The polka-dotted halter dresses and head wraps that one visually ambiguous cubana friend chooses to wear? But I resent all the jungle exoticism that's foisted on Latinas, from J. Lo on down, so why would I invoke it? For Latinas, performing our gendered ethnic identity always seems to include the notion of heat, spice, a tasty sensuality offered up for consumption.

As a writer, I've always felt like a thinking subject. As a feminist, I've never longed to be an object. The watcher, not the watched. Why should I go around declaring my ethnic identity all the time, as if the whole world were a customs agent, inspecting me?

Blood

But it's more complicated than that, even, because when I tell Larry Mota, "Oh, my family's Cuban," the fact is, I'm passing.

In 1967, when the attorney told my infertile parents (who paid a thousand dollars for the legal right to take me home) that I was a Latina baby, they believed him. Growing up, so did I. Given that the adoption took place in Miami, we all presumed I was probably cubana, or maybe dominicana or colombiana. To fill in the gaps that my closed adoption left, I invented elaborate scenarios: My Catholic schoolgirl mother, unable to destroy her child of passion, sang like María in *West Side Story* to my devoted but star-crossed sire, pleading down in the street below like some vato Romeo. Sobbing her farewells in Spanish, she relinquished me reluctantly to the nuns.

I was sure that one day I would find her, meet her. To prepare, I read US Latina literature—from all cultures, just to be sure: Sandra Cisneros, Julia Alvarez, Esmeralda Santiago, Isabel Allende, Judith Ortiz Cofer, Lorna Dee Cervantes, Marjorie Agosín. *Each one of these stories*, I would think, *could be my mother's*. For each, I opened a space in my heart.

In this way, my identity crystallized during adolescence and young adult-hood into a kind of pan-Latina formation that was and remains deeply personal, deeply felt.

As any adoptee can tell you, meeting one's birth mother is strange and intense for all sorts of reasons. When I was twenty-six, I met mine, a nice Midwestern lady of Irish, French, and Swedish descent. (Like many Americans, she also claims Cherokee heritage, and it seems plausible, since most of her relatives live in Oklahoma and tell the same story about an ancestor walking the Trail of Tears. My maternal grandmother was a wasp-waisted girl with dark hair and big dark eyes.) My birth mother had taken buses to Miami for the pregnancy and birth, so no one in her hometown of Rockford, Illinois would know.

I wasn't Latina at all.

In one sudden yank of the rug, I felt my family and identity severed from me. I didn't know where to stand. I didn't want anyone to accuse me of being a faker, a trespasser, a poser, a claimer of things not mine.

For about ten years, I claimed nothing.

Now

At forty-one, when I say I'm Latina, it's a shortcut. It's true, and it gets you quickly to what I want you to know, but it's a falsification too, a simplification, a smoothing over of layers of complication, deconstruction, loss; of chronic self-interrogation, multiple erasures, and years of painful reconstruction. A delicate, tentative claim I stake.

Ethnicity is complicated, and everyone has an opinion. During my mid-thirties, it was an African American friend who kept prodding me, shaking her head. "You're not white," she kept saying. "I don't know what you are, but you sure aren't white."

Later, I told a half-Latina, half-white friend about it. "What's wrong with white?" she snapped. "I hate that attitude."

Sometimes I just wanted to disappear.

Today I write from a small place, a complicated island with a history that's almost been lost. I write from a place of clear lip balm and jeans, of a PhD but no love for academia, of no talent in the kitchen (and thus no *Like Water for Chocolate* imitations, no homages to my grandmother's perfect garlic roast pork). I write from a keen and pissed-off class awareness and the streaming juice of very few mangoes.

Don't get me wrong: I like mangoes just fine, and key limes, and avocadoes straight from the tree, verdad, but I write with a prickly awareness of the easy appetite among mainstream readers for a romanticized, exoticized version of latinidad—a simplified, delicious version I could purvey, a version that would pleasure and sell.

But I don't want to help readers "eat the other," in the words of bell hooks. I don't want to teach you how to dance salsa or spoon you my grandmother's flan—and I sure as hell don't want to perform my sexual badness and write about big, dark nipples and violence for the upper-middle-class, educated white people who read the *New Yorker* and listen to NPR. Providing a delectable frisson of dark, sexy danger is not my literary goal.

Academic Latino studies and ethnic studies programs have done much to articulate—even privilege—the experience and idea of border-crossing. Hybridity's hip, and we've all been schooled to admire the supple complexities of liminality. Yet borders still abound, and the risk of crossing them is the same risk it has always been: invisibility, erasure, obliteration. There's solidarity in numbers; there's psychic safety in fitting the stereotypes. Readers and publishers know where to slot you, and when national book distribution boils down, as it does, to thirty seconds of negotiation between your publisher's marketing rep and the Barnes & Noble guy with his laptop open, checking sales figures of past books like yours, it helps if you're simple to sum up.

What happens when a Latina not only doesn't look the part but also doesn't write the part? What happens to Latina writers who cross not only boundaries of nation and culture in their lives but also borders of genre and

subject matter in their work? When the content and style of Latina literary productions confound market expectations and publishers' ready-made packaging
plans, what happens to those manuscripts? What about experimental work that
editors believe will baffle Latino y Latina book buyers, whom they believe to be
less educated and thus less capable of reading complicated work? Híjole.

For me, all the myths have come undone. I don't fit. I don't fit, and that's
okay, and that's where I write from: that jagged, smashed place of edges and
fragments and grief, of feeling lost, of perilous freedom. I extract small fragile
bones from the sand, dust them off with my brush, and build strange, urgent
new structures, knowing too well how small my island is, how vast and rising
the sea.

10

Aesthetics and Theme
Time and Place (with an Afterword on Polemics)
STEVEN CORDOVA

The poems I write are largely set in New York City after the advent of HIV, by which I mean both the period when being infected was a "death sentence," and the happier if equally conflicted period since then when high-tech drugs have rendered HIV infection a "manageable" disease. New York City is an epicenter of the epidemic, and New York City is my second home. My first home—the city where I grew up—is San Antonio, Texas. I was a recent college graduate, only twenty-two years old, when I left Texas. And since I'm now forty-four, my life is divided into equal parts: one part San Antonio of the past, one part New York City of the present; one part pre- and one part post-"death sentence." This biographical information, along with the fact that I myself am HIV-positive and gay, are aspects of my poems that may seem to render them outside the perceived aesthetics and themes of Latino literature. But I will argue that just the opposite is true. The aesthetics and themes of my poems are largely the same as those of Latino literature. I have only changed the setting.

Trying to define both the aesthetics and the themes of Latino literature is what I was up to one summer night in the mid-1990s when I purchased *After Aztlan: Latino Poets of the Nineties*, an anthology edited by Ray Gonzalez. I'd been writing poetry for only a few years, but my commitment to the life was growing with the enthusiasm only a newcomer can evince. I read poetry at night. I read poetry first thing in the morning. I "workshopped" my poems with teachers and mentors—even with my friends—whenever and wherever they would let me. So we can assume I was asking myself—more and more—as I read and as I wrote—what it was I had to say, how I would find my voice.

Opening *After Aztlan* again, all these years later, I find it contains a good number of narrative poems. And indeed, as I have gone on reading and writing, attending countless poetry readings, signing up for writers' retreats and quite a few writers' conferences, I have noted that the use of narration is one aesthetic of Latino poetry. The narrator of this kind of narrative Latino poem begins by zeroing in on a particular set of people living at a particular time and—need I say it?—at a particular place. This cast of characters is thus made up of the speaker's family and immediate community. His or her community is, in the final effect, characterized by its ethnicity. I have found this focus on community to be one theme of Latino literature.

The theme of community is one exemplified by Francisco Alarcón's "In a Neighborhood in Los Angeles," one of the poems I read in *After Aztlan*. "I learned / Spanish," the poem begins, from my grandma

mijito
don't cry
she'd tell me

the mornings
when my parents
would leave

to work
at the fish
canneries.[1]

The time and the place I began to write poetry only served to reinforce the aes-
thetic of narrative clarity I was later to encounter in *After Aztlan*. The time: the
early 1990s. The place: a poetry class for people with AIDS organized by a New
York City nonprofit that I worked for—the Gay Men's Health Crisis (GMHC).
In the years leading up to my employment at GMHC—my twenties—I'd been
deeply involved with the activist group ACT UP (the AIDS Coalition to Unleash
Power). GMHC offered a host of services to PWAs. A PWA is a Person with
AIDS. And PWA was one of the many acronyms you heard a lot, those days.
There was HIV and AIDS, of course, but there was also AZT and AL72—the
names we gave to largely ineffective elixirs. There was the acronym ACT UP,
and there were many more.

I became friendly with the volunteer who led the GMHC poetry class
some time before I actually started attending the class. I thought of her, conde-
scendingly, as "the nice lady who teaches the poetry class." But before the nice
lady went to work with her students, we'd chat—usually about the books she
was clutching under her bare arm. We began exchanging hugs, displays of affec-
tion being not uncommon in nonprofit settings and, in particular, in settings
like GMHC where everyone—ill or not—was under duress, in need of comfort.
That nice lady actually turned out to be Rachel Hadas, a poet, an essayist, and a
longtime professor at Rutgers University. *The Empty Bed* and *The Double Legacy:
Reflection on a Pair of Deaths*—Rachel's 1995 collections of poems and essays—
would relate the grief of losing her mother to the grief of losing GMHC students.

So, consistent with her artistic trajectory at the time, Rachel's class
attracted students. Not only that, Faber and Faber published an anthology of
the class's poems, 1991's *Unending Dialogue: Voices from an AIDS Poetry Workshop*,
along with an introduction and a closing set of remarks and poems by Rachel.
Some time after the release of the seminal anthology, though, Rachel took a
break from the hard work of volunteering. Many of her students, James and

Glenn, Charles, and Tony, had died, or were dying, and she had her family at home and her students at Rutgers to attend to. When she returned to GMHC, there had been a good deal of staff turnover. New staff members didn't know who Rachel was. They didn't know what she'd accomplished. More disconcerting, GMHC clients didn't seem to be interested. I'd walk by the "classroom" next to the reception desk and see Rachel sitting alone at an open folding table, writing, and habitually tucking a lock of blond hair behind her ear.

I became Rachel's first student her second time around, but not because I wanted to write poetry. I think I dared to walk through the classroom door because I'd read a lot of fiction and always thought that, when I finally did get around to being creative, I would write prose. Rachel's class seemed as good a place as any to get started on a Great American Novel. And it seemed, more importantly, like the right thing to do. Then, as quickly as my first class, my ambitions were turned toward poetry. Rachel and I were the only two people present, and we read a poem she'd recently written, laying a single copy of it on the table before us. It was a one-page poem about visiting her mother's grave. I liked it and—as soon as she was through reading it—I pointed to the line break where the poem took a turn from description to introspection, from details about nature described in sylvan terms to an expression of grief. "Ah, you're a good reader," Rachel said.

If Rachel had asked, "Well, how much poetry have you read, Steven?" I wouldn't have been able to say for certain. "Oh, some poems by the Romantics in an undergrad college course," I might have answered (and I know I would have added, "The professor who taught the class was pretentious and silly. I didn't pay much attention"). Given my inexperience with poetry, Rachel's acknowledgment that I could read a poem well came as a surprise to me. The fact that the poem was written in contemporary language, and that it was about grief, helped. The word "grief," like the Tower-of-Babel acronyms and the rhythm of the chants we grew hoarse shouting at ACT UP demonstrations, was another thing you heard a lot, those days. GMHC, along with many sister organizations, private therapists, and an often embarrassing extended family of opportunists and well-meaning quacks, conducted all kinds of forums for grief—individual therapy and group therapy, mostly for people who'd lost someone, or in too many cases, too many someones, to AIDS. More than often, the grievers were themselves PWAs.

Soon—far too soon, from my selfish perspective—other students came along; Rachel's class, I noted, was not a therapeutic setting, at least not in the emotional or the psychological sense. It wasn't a place where people with AIDS went to "talk about" what they were "going through." Rachel was a sympathetic person—Rachel still is a sympathetic person—so, naturally, she put a premium on subject matter that addressed the matter at hand. The matter at hand was, after all, nothing less than life and death. And life, one death at a time and sometimes more than one death at a time, seemed to be slipping away from us.

Addressing, then, the weighty content of our poems, Rachel's first remark was often something like, "So, you're saying the experience you're having is like this other experience you've also had?" Or, running her hands through her hair, thinking out loud, she'd say, "Let me see if I've got this right; you're saying that this is like that and that that means this?" So, in that sense—in that literary sense, in that philosophical and, yes, even in that metaphysical sense—Rachel's GMHC class was a therapeutic setting: Everyone in the room was dying and/or experiencing the dying of others, and through our writing we were trying, individually and collectively, to be clear about the dramatic events we felt it was absolutely up to us to record. We were trying to be clear, in particular, about any analogies, about any similes or any metaphors we used to move our narratives along and give our stories meaning. Forms—traditional forms like sonnets and villanelles, along with forms we made up ourselves—helped the overall project because form is a kind of ornament handed down to us from the past. Form gave our poems—so often full of disturbing, jarring content—a sense of beauty.

Which brings me back to my argument that my aesthetic and my themes are not really all that much different from those of the narrative poems I read in *After Aztlan*. Like many *After Aztlan* poems, many of my own pay homage to a community—a family, of sorts—that has survived even as it has not wholly survived an epidemic (the results of an outer force, HIV, which we couldn't change); an epidemic that only served to exacerbate a long history of oppression (the results of an inner force we were trying to change). Indeed, gay, lesbian, bisexual, and transgender people often point out that because our own families and communities reject us, or are temporarily or permanently estranged from us after we disclose our sexuality or our true genders, we make a family of our friends. Our friends become our mentors. Our friends become our siblings. This is one theme, one phenomenon that unifies our lives. Only, unity is not always that easy, not always that simple or harmonious. In fact, trying to get along can be tough sometimes, even polemical.

And thus, not surprisingly, both Latino and AIDS poetry have their share of polemics. Take, for instance, Francisco Alarcón's "Letter to America":

> America
> understand
>
> we are
> the insides
> of your body
>
> our faces
> reflect
> your future[2]

This kind of posturing, in which a monolithic "we" argues with an equally monolithic "you"—the "you" being "America" in Alarcón's case—was not something Rachel or my subsequent teachers encouraged. I was advised, instead, to reach for more "universal truths," which I slowly grew to interpret as a phrase that refers to experiences we all have—regardless of our ethnic or sexual or social group. I interpreted universal truths to mean, I suppose, our feelings—happiness and anger, fear and shame, and shades thereof. Nevertheless, neither polemical writing nor polemical human relationships were excluded from my poetic education. One Saturday morning, for instance, a group of Rachel's GMHC students and I attended a seminar Rachel organized at the request of Poets House. I still remember, in particular, how Rachel shared with us a newly drafted poem, "Arguments of Silence." "Arguments of Silence" calls into question ACT UP's signature slogan, "Silence = Death." "Silence = Death" was meant as a call to arms. It meant that if you were silent, then drug companies would not test drugs to counter HIV infection. It meant that if you were silent, the FDA would not approve treatments fast enough to save lives. Hateful, discriminatory policies would come to pass—in private companies and at every level of government. Humane policies would not. Humane policies would, in fact, go down. Knowing that I'd been involved in ACT UP, and proud of her new poem, Rachel said, "Steven, what do you think ACT UP would think of this poem?" Sipping at my coffee, I said, "I don't know, Rachel. ACT UP is made up of a lot of people. Do you think we agree with each other all the time?" "Point well taken," Rachel conceded as she glanced down at the table, then back up at us. But in truth—and as Rachel's glance probably suggested—the important point was actually made on me.

The point was this: it's our poetic responsibility to challenge any idea we judge to be in some way specious even when that idea is espoused by a beloved institution. Challenge it because we disagree with it; or because we think there is a larger, more universal truth running through it; or because, in challenging the idea, we hope to build on it and arrive at a fresh point of view. (One lesson I absorbed from Rachel is that a poem, in many ways, is a fresh point of view.)

Now, we can begin to compare "Letter to America" to "Arguments of Silence." "Arguments" begins with the consolatory

> I salute you, friends, who would not button
> your lips. But kept them, chapped and bloody, open;
>
> who refused to huddle caged as in contagion,
> forced to find your balance as from between
>
> the horns of the dilemma how to live
> at once outside and inside of your bodies
>
> and dance and balance not struck dumb by fear,
> your voice a thread, your proper labyrinth's clue.[3]

But then the polemicist at the center of the poem goes on to challenge the slogan so fiercely embraced by Rachel's "friends" in ACT UP. Silence, she argues, doesn't equal death. It doesn't equal death because "Only in the charged silence after death / are certain voices heard."[4] And the poem's concluding arguments drive home the point.

> True, wives and husbands, children and their parents
>
> know without speaking what is wished or meant—
> the curse of family life, and the reward.
>
> Habit, telepathy, passion:
> nothing exempts us from our chatty birthright.
>
> The danger's hardly tyranny by silence.
> It's hard to shut us up while we draw breath.
>
> If anything can guarantee our silence
> death can. But silence doesn't equal death.[5]

I think Rachel's "Arguments of Silence" affected the way that I engage in polemics, to whatever extent I do, more than Francisco Alarcón's "Letter to America." At first glance, that may seem ironic. Alarcón is after all the only gay male poet included in *After Aztlan*, and probably the first gay Latino poet I'd read, period. However, at second glance, by virtue of her work at GMHC, by virtue of her friendship with the gay poet James Merrill and her deep admiration for gay poets dead and living—Constantine Cavafy and Thom Gunn, to name two—Rachel is part of the gay community. Add all that virtue to the fact that by the time I started to write—in Rachel's class—I'd lived in New York City—a gay Mecca—for about a decade. I'd been propelled to "the City" by my sexuality, and compelled to stay by my ever-growing, ever-changing network of friends (and by what never seemed like enough sexual partners).

My gay identification, then, is not a betrayal of one part of myself—my Latino-ness, if you will. It is, rather, an acceptance of another part of myself—my sexuality, my gayness, my HIV status. I'm a Latino poet. Of course I'm a Latino poet. But like all people, when it comes to the different parts of my identity, I am not one or the other. I am one and the other. I am more than and, on bad days, less than the sum of my parts.

Notes
1. Ray Gonzalez, ed., *After Aztlan: Latino Poets of the Nineties* (Boston: David R. Godine, 1992), 3.
2. Ibid., 10.
3. Rachel Hadas, *The Empty Bed* (Hanover and London: Wesleyan University Press, 1995), 75.
4. Ibid., 74.
5. Ibid., 74–76.

11

What We Write About When We Write About Gangs
Daniel Chacón

I wish I had been at Fresno City College that afternoon when all those gang members showed up. I can imagine students jumping out of their way or stopping to watch them, like they were seeing circus people coming into town, walking down Main Street to set up their tents. The gangbangers walked with fists clenched, and they hardly looked at anyone, just looked straight ahead, as if all this was normal, as if they had a right to walk through campus, down the tree-lined path that led to the Student Union. Yet there was a clear consciousness on their part that they were a spectacle, that just being who they were, just being how they were, they were watched; watched, maybe they believed, like celebrities, like Chicano hip-hop stars and their entourage of men and boys. Some were tall, some low to the ground, built like shacks; a few of them were fat, and a few were as fit as athletes. One boy had delicate features, his skin so pale, like baby powder, but even he looked deadly, wearing a bright red Bulldog cap with a white cloth underneath that hung down to his shoulders like an Arabic headdress. One man had sunken eyes, like he was already dead, sadly addicted to the product he sold. They all wore some kind of red, with Fresno State Bulldog T-shirts, Fresno State Bulldog caps, bulldogs tattooed on their necks.

The campus police were there that day, guys with radios and guns, who stood on the steps of buildings or in doorways, or stood near the trunks of trees, their hands on their hips, like they were ready for the draw. A few cop cars were parked on the lawn, doors open.

You could tell the bangers weren't students. They ranged in age from teenagers to men in their forties They didn't have books or laptop computers, yet they were walking somewhere, led by my little brother, Kenneth R. Chacón, who was jumped in at fourteen and who became a college professor at twenty-nine. He could still look like a cholo gangbanger, even as he wore button-down short-sleeved shirts, because you could see the tattoo on his arm, *NSF*, identifying him with the bangers he was now leading. He often shaved his head. Today he wears wire-framed glasses and looks like a young intellectual, a handsome Latino professor, but if you could see him without a shirt, you would see the giant bulldog tattooed on his back; if you knew about his past, you would have no trouble picturing him as one of the men he led to that forum he had organized about gang awareness.

"We're going over here," he said to them, pointing across the campus. He kind of walked like they walked, barely bending his knees, his arms hanging down his sides, and slow, as if afraid of nothing, not even time.

"A lot of people showed up," he told me on the phone, him in Fresno, me in El Paso. "I let them say whatever they wanted. They just told their stories. Some of them cried."

Perhaps what my brother told me stirred my imagination, so much that I can't seem to get bangers out of my fiction. They always show up somehow, without an invitation from me, in stories, in novels, and now in this essay. Leave me alone, I want to say. I want to brush them off my shoulders like pantry moths, but they keep coming back.

That might have been what made me interesting to the other students when I was an MFA candidate at the University of Oregon: that I wrote about gangs, about urban violence. Many of my classmates were writing about what they considered middle-class families (we'd call them rich people), John Updike–like stories about adultery and regret. The people of color in the program mostly wrote about identity, their middle-class characters preoccupied with their sense of American-ness, where they belonged in the great salad bowl.

The now-dead Andrés Montoya, who was also in the program, and I wrote about Fresno. If you have read his first book, *The Iceworker Sings and Other Poems*, you know that death is everywhere, as are gangs, the crazy life, la locura.

I was working on my thesis, a novel called "Saint Martin in the Fields," about a college political science professor who gets addicted to crack and, as a result, begins to interact with the dark side of Fresno, the crack dealers, the junkies, and, yes, the gangbangers. He becomes friends with the people in the cracks of the city, the Cockroach People. He listens to their stories, and at a certain point we're not sure if the professor is seeking crack because of his addiction to the chemicals or because of his addiction to the darkness of the streets, the death, the violence—this world where tonight he could be standing next to a junkie named Maya who tomorrow he'll find out is dead.

Many of the students in the MFA program were from Ivy League colleges, but the rest of us were from Fresno. In my first year at Oregon, in a program that accepted six poets a year, four of us were from Fresno, including Andrés Montoya. All of the Fresno students, except for me, were poets with strong letters of recommendation from Philip Levine. I was a fiction writer. As I think of it now, I see that we all seemed to write about death. One woman from Fresno wrote a poem about her father, who each morning would start the day with reading the obituaries in the newspaper, saying the names of the dead out loud.

Maybe the appearance of gangs and gang imagery in my work is related to Fresno.

People have wondered why so many great poets and writers come out of Fresno, and the conventional answer is because of Philip Levine. He brought so much culture with him when he moved into Saroyan's Fresno, including good poets who followed him there and native poets who studied under him, like Gary Soto and Omar Salinas. Some poets stayed in Fresno just to be near Levine, and they all learned from him and from each other. I think this is a legitimate answer, but what is true on one level may not be the only truth.

According to physicists and mystics, there are many realities. Kabbalah tells us that what we see in this natural world, understood by our sensory awareness, is only about one percent of true reality. The Many Worlds interpretation in theoretical physics pretty much says the same thing. What we experience as reality is such a tiny fraction of all the possibilities that make up the reality of the multiverse. All perspectives are true, and all of them are false.

Like Rushdie writes in *The Satanic Verses*, "There once was, and there once was not."

It is, and it isn't.

I'm making sense in this essay, and I'm full of shit in this essay.

The reality depends on the reality of the observer.

Philip Levine is the reason why there are so many good writers from Fresno, but there would be good writers from Fresno even if Levine had never come to town.

People from Fresno are good writers because death is everywhere; whether or not you know any of the people who are killed, their spirits are everywhere in the city, and death is a main artery of the creative flow.

What⁈⁈

That's a ridiculous idea!

That was my reaction when a student in an undergraduate fiction workshop told the class why he didn't like literary fiction. "It's just about the dead and death and dying."

In front of the class, I stood, scandalized by his comment, my hand on my chest, *What⁈⁈*

Years later, when I was walking with a dead woman on the streets of Buenos Aires at three in the morning, I laughed to remember the student's comment. He was right, I explained to my dead friend. The next day, the dead woman appeared as a new character in the novel I was working on. I couldn't keep her out. I could at best not allow her to entirely take over the language.

"The dead," writes Wislawa Szymborska, "don't know any more than we do."

Sometimes they don't even know they're dead. They aren't the way Hollywood often makes them out to be, all-knowing angelic beings, god-like in their abilities to help us, so it seemed unwise to assume that the dead woman I met in the city was a master of novelistic form and to let her voice take over the work. One of the skills we develop as writers is to know how much to let into the work, how much to allow spirits to fight against the evolving form of our work. This is what Lorca meant when he spoke of the duende that fights the form of a poem. We want to let some of it in, we want to let it happen, that fight against form, because perfect form lacks tension. In the best fictional landscapes, the fabric of reality pulses with energies that threaten to rip it open, like in Toni Morrison's *Jazz*, or all of her novels, where many of the main characters are dead.

The dead have long been a source of demonic inspiration in works of literature.

Lorca writes, "Where death is possible, the duende is there."

Where someone dies, so their spirits remain for a time, older Mexicans will tell you.

People are energy, people are vessels of energy, and so when we die, our energy doesn't disappear—that would violate a basic law of physics—rather it is converted into other energy.

If someone is being murdered by gangbangers, surrounded by them, knifed and kicked and filled with bullets, the victim, right before death, will most likely feel intense levels of rage, hatred, fear. When they die, the energy from those strong feelings stays around.

Recently, when I was visiting my brother's family in Fresno, a kid in junior high was beaten to death by classmates, little bangers, who had surrounded him on the schoolyard after class and beat him senseless, breathless. That fear and maybe rage, the desire to lash back at his killers, stayed in the schoolyard, clung to other minds.

According to Emanuel Swedenborg, the archetypal mystic, the dead, immediately after dying, don't know they're dead. This is not an idea new or unique to him—it's practically a tenet of mysticism on death, from the Tibetan Book of the Dead to folkloric narratives. Swedenborg says the spirit of the newly dead finds like spirits (read: similar energies), and they cling to the hosts. In fact, they think they are their living hosts. Dead spirits who feel rage and hatred will cling to living people who also feel rage and hatred, maybe, yes, a gang member, maybe the very gangbanger who killed him. Feelings, even of rage, become thoughts, and the living host thinks they are his thoughts. Perhaps someone not usually violent has a violent thought, and at that moment a spirit of the dead with violent energy enters him or her and stays there for a while, giving him or her more violent thoughts. Perhaps that's what is meant by being taken over by demons, or allowing demons inside of you; you allow the dead for a time to take over your being, but because those thoughts may be fleeting, uncharacteristic of the living host, when the feeling passes, the spirit of the dead might need to find another host, maybe jumping from one to another like Frogger crossing the stream, hopping from rock to rock.

For a city of its size in the United States, Fresno is a violent place.

Ever since I was a kid growing up in Fresno, I was around people who suffered violent deaths. I remember when I was seven years old, going to the corner grocery store, Sanchez Market, with my cousins to see the blood on the sidewalk where, the night before, some Mexican illegal was jumped and knifed and killed by three men. I remember my own friend Carl with sixteen knife wounds in his torso, jumped by bangers as he was walking home from a party along his own street. I remember my father carrying a gun in the glove compartment when he went out drinking. There didn't seem to be anything weird about this. I assumed this was normal until, at twenty-nine years old, I was accepted into the University of Oregon and studied with people who didn't have the same experience. I remember Montoya and I went to an outdoor concert in Eugene, thousands of people drinking and smoking pot and listening to rock music, and we were amazed that there wasn't a single knifing or shooting, not even a shouting match.

Recently, I returned to Fresno as an adult, having lived away for almost twenty years. I was the visiting writer in the Fresno State MFA program. One afternoon I was walking through campus; behind me were two sorority girls, blondes with bright faces. It was the day after Halloween. One was saying to the other, "Yeah, I went to that party last night where that guy was shot."

The other girl didn't say, "Really? A guy was shot!"

She just nodded her head, as if to say, "Oh that party. I went to the other one."

It was no big deal.

My first day back as the visiting writer, I couldn't get on the campus, because it was cordoned off on all sides by the police. Some Hmong gang members had robbed a bank, and when the cops showed up, they didn't give up; they jumped into their car and the cops chased them. The bangers shot out of the windows like gangsters in the movies, and as they passed a crowded apartment complex across from the university, innocent bystanders were sprayed with bullets.

I try not to write about gangs, but they keep coming out of the language, slipping through the cellar doors and boarded up windows that face the alley of my imagination.

I tried to write a novel about an artist, Victor, a boy with exceptional talent as a painter, who in the end goes off to study in Paris where he meets a Moroccan girl, falls in love, and they have a daughter, an Arab-tina. I wanted it to be about ways of seeing as developed by artists. I wanted it to be about passion for the image. I wanted it to be about Victor's relationship with his wife and daughter. It didn't turn out to be anything like what I wanted.

As I wrote the novel, guided by voice and image, Víctor wondered why everyone thought he was in a gang. Maybe, he thought, he had some gang spirit within him, maybe his dead father was a gangbanger and his mother had kept it from him, maybe he had it in his blood, some hidden part of him that loved violence. So in a certain sequence he ends up sinking so deeply into the gang world, the street life (yes, like my crack-addicted professor in "Saint Martin in the Fields"), that images become phantasmagoric, and he might see in slow motion a fist coming at his face, or he might feel the jaw of a boy crack open on his fist.

Several years ago I tried to read Cormac McCarthy's *Blood Meridian*. There was a battle scene that is etched like a stone carving in my memory's cave, a surreal blur of faces and bloody body parts shooting at me, an axe cracks open a head, a spear pierces a rectum. After that scene, the entire book led me to so many other slaughters that I couldn't finish reading it. It requires some sort of agreement to go into a world like that. I figured I couldn't go into that landscape without it affecting me. In true life, I've always resisted that world. In true life I hate violence; I have never been in a fight. It's true. I have never been beaten up and have never beaten up anyone, and the worst violence that usually happened in my fiction before I created Victor was a push fight or a shouting match. But usually it comes out as pretty tame adolescent gang imagery. That's as dark as it gets. In many ways, the fact that gangs appear in my work could be an organic way for my soul to express the darkness of that violence that I have always been around. Maybe it has to come out, and since I'm unwilling to go into as much darkness as McCarthy, my soul finds ways.

Unfortunately my unconscious way of expressing the darkness is kind of trite, yes?

So stereotypical.

Stories about gangs are, like, so 1980s. Who wants to hear about cholos?

Don't Chicanos have anything better to write about?

I remember a white woman asking me if I always wrote about "Hispanics." Pretty much, I said. She looked at me sadly, like a white liberal looking at a little barrio kid she wanted to help but couldn't, and she said, "Oh, that's too bad. I hope someday you can grow out of that."

Well, maybe someday I can go beyond writing about gangs.

Besides, haven't all the great books on gangs already been written, *George Washington Valdez*, *Spidertown*, and perhaps the most significant one, *La Vida Loca: Gang Days in LA* by Luis J. Rodriguez, an El Paso/Juárez native. It came out while I was an MFA student at U of O. We Chicanos counted the days before that book came out with Curbstone Press. Among four of us, we could only afford one hardback copy that went around, all of us impatiently waiting our turn to read it.

But nobody seems to want to read about gangs and cholos anymore, especially editors and agents.

Another story about gangs?

¡Ay, caramba!

¡Arriba! ¡Arriba!

How trite!

We are the new Chicano/as, the xicana/os, we are children of technology, we have Facebook pages and web pages, we carry ¡Phones, we have a black president, for God's sake. The past we embrace in imagery is not of gangs. That's been done.

In a newspaper cartoon by José Antonio Burciaga, the panel shows a white couple in a museum of art, where Chicano art is displayed. The couple is looking up at a life-sized sculpture of a pachuco, like an image from a José Montoya drawing. The white man, looking up at the statue disapprovingly, says to the woman, "I prefer the Post Pachuco Renaissance."

Well, the Post Pachuco Renaissance has come and gone.

The cholo, son of the pachuco, might be the victim of that, the unwanted child of xicana/o literature.

Across the street from our apartments in Sunset Heights, downtown El

Paso, there is a house that has been cut up into five small, low-rent apartments. In one of them lives a cholo with his mother. He is a tough-looking young man, wearing those white tank-top undershirts and baggy pants. He drives a lowrider, which he jumps all the time as he soars down the street on the hill toward his house. He cranks up the sentimental oldies music, with lyrics like, "Earth angel, won't you be mine?"

In front of his house are some healthy rose bushes, yellow, red, and pink, always blooming and beautiful. The cholo seems to be the only one who takes care of them. In the evening, he comes out in his tank-top undershirt and baggy shorts; he waters the bushes, clips them, and he rakes around them, removing any garbage that might have blown underneath them. As he waters his roses, I feel for him, I feel for myself.

Poor, unwanted cholo!

I will never write about you.

El Paso is one of the safest cities in the country.

The city is larger than Fresno, poorer than Fresno, and over 80 percent of the population is like me—Mexicano, Chicano, Hispanic, and a bunch of cholos.

And even though this place is so safe, from my balcony I see Ciudad Juárez. It's so close I can make out a strip mall and see the cars pull into the parking lots. I see the old buses rattle up and down the poorly paved residential roads. It's so close to our apartments that we can see the bridge where people cross to get to the other side. And the violence in Juárez makes Fresno look like a garden party.

First it was the women, so many of them murdered and raped; out my office window at the university, I have a view of the desert mountains of Juárez, where many of the bodies of the women were found, many of the bones, many body parts without the body. Sometimes just clothes were found, a bloody dress, torn jeans, white tennis shoes that had belonged to Juan Felipe Herrera's yellow-robed girl.

We hope that today the murders of women have stopped, but now, as I'm writing these words, there is a drug war in progress. There have been so many murders that the city is occupied by the Mexican Army, thousands of troops patrolling the streets in army trucks, all the young Indian soldiers carrying rifles. The army hasn't stopped the war; they just made it more visibly obvious. Two weekends ago, twenty-two people were murdered gangland style, one of them a professor at the university, and last weekend sixteen people were killed, including patients at a drug rehab center, where gunmen stormed in with automatic rifles and shot everyone in sight, killing whoever was there.

This is an everyday thing, and my interaction with Juárez is not just visual, not something I see from my balcony or through the windows of my air-conditioned office. Anyone who lives in El Paso, who really lives in El Paso, interacts every day with Juárez. Every day we cross la línea, we cross the line. We cross to go to the pharmacies, to go to school, to go to work, to go shopping at discount clothes stores in downtown. In any given parking lot in El Paso, the mall,

Wal-Mart, Best Buy, the multiplex movie theaters, up to half of the license plates are from Juárez.

With the drug wars, the gangs are much more powerful than they are in Fresno, and they don't simply kill each other. No one is safe. Children are killed, old people are killed, police are killed by the dozens each week; even the soldiers are afraid, yet people from Juárez continue to function and much of their business is on this side of the line. Middle-class Juárez teenagers go to private high schools on this side of the line. On this side of the line they attend classes at El Paso Community College and UTEP. There are rich Juarenses in Mercedes SUVs, and there are Juárez women who carry shopping bags of cleaning supplies across the line and clean our houses once a week for twenty-five dollars. And everyone knows someone who was murdered, threatened, or has seen a murder. Everyone knows someone who saw a massacre or witnessed a carjacking, and everyone is at most two degrees of separation from someone who is dead. Death is everywhere. From where I stand on my balcony, I can hear gunshots, see the smoke of burning buildings. But the people still function. They still go to school.

This energy, this energy, this energy.

Every time I hear another friend or neighbor talk about how the violence in Juárez reached them, the stories fall from the front page of the *El Paso Times* into reality. The dead cling to people in Juárez, their sweaters, the creases in their pants, or they drip their last drops of blood onto the sidewalks and someone walking by picks them up on the soles of their shoes and walks with them across the line onto the sidewalks of El Paso, where a woman working in a tall office building takes them on the tips of her heels, into her office, and for some reason, as she looks out the window onto the twin cities, her thoughts turn to fearful things, turn to rage, turn to hatred, and she doesn't understand why. In an essay, Rigoberto Gonzalez says that most Chicano writers come from El Paso and Fresno. I know why.

When I moved to El Paso, I lived a few blocks away from Coffin Street, where Cormac McCarthy was living at the time and where he wrote many of his novels. His was a dark little house with no windows, like a stone fortress, and as I passed by I wondered what he was like when he wrote dark things like *Blood Meridian*, where was he during those times, what was it like to be around him, to every day enter that bloody landscape? I used to shake my head as I walked past his house and say to myself, "Poor guy, having to go there."

But now I realize that living here, living there, we all go there, one way or another.

I have a novel that wants to be written, but I don't want to write it; I've been resisting for so long. I don't want to go there. I don't want to release that much (gulp!) evil into my work. But maybe I have to. Maybe if I allow myself to go inside of there, I will quit pretending the voices of the murdered are not screaming at me to release them, release them into my work, into my language; and maybe the gangs will quit appearing in my stories; and maybe my characters, in trying to love, won't end up punching everybody; maybe I need to go down into the depths of hell in order to come back with some souls that want to be freed from there.

"It was great," my brother told me about the event he organized at Fresno City College. "I mean, these were the hardest bangers around, man. Some people were scared there would be a fight or something, but these guys just wanted to tell their stories."

I remember a gang member telling about his first day in Fresno, when he was six years old, having moved there with his family into some apartments on the Eastside, the poor side. He was outside playing when he saw a paleta man pushing his popsicle cart, a little one on wheels, yelling, "¡Paletas! ¡Tengo paletas!"

The little boy watched the man, maybe happy to see him, maybe thinking this new place wouldn't be so bad, when four kids, twelve or thirteen years old, surrounded the paleta man. They started picking on him, pushing him, demanding free popsicles. One of the kids pulled out a club and hit the man in the knees, and when he fell to the ground in pain, the kids kicked him all over his body and head until he was bloody and couldn't do much more than squirm. Then the boys raided his box full of paletas, got as many popsicles as they could hold, got his money, and ran off laughing, the new boy standing there staring at the lifeless body as the spirit of the dead man rose out of the corpse.

He became a gang member.

I became a writer.

Either way, we need to tell our stories.

12

Latte No!
Notes on a (Late) Latino Awakening
Urayoán Noel

As I write this, I'm staring out the window of an apartment overlooking Ipanema Beach in Rio de Janeiro, where I have been presenting at the Latin American Studies Association conference. It's morning, and the beach, for once, is empty. In the distance, I can see the variegated topographies of three islands, and I'm returned to my own condition of islandness.

I guess I'm considered an "urban poet" (Def Poetry? Baudelaire?) inasmuch as so many of my poems deal with the physical and spiritual noise of New York City, but I've always thought of mine as a city in transit, scored in the back and forth between San Juan and NYC. In my latest book of (mostly Spanish) poetry, *Boringkén* (2008), I try for a performative poetics both baroque and hologramic, writing from and against the intersections of those two cities: a suitably "stateless" poetics, beyond the strictures of nation-state and statement. None of this is exactly new (think of Víctor Hernández Cruz, a poet of both "Airoplain" and Mainland). Still, the literal is plain. Give me littorals on planes!

Such a stateless poetics is inevitably shaped by my background growing up in San Juan as the only child of an Anglo father from Northern California and a Puerto Rican mother. Traveling through my dad's native topographies gave me a sense of American expanse (The sequoias! The redwoods! The Dairy Queens!), while my mom would tell me stories of her growing up watching the blitzkrieg urbanizing of San Juan in the early 1960s, as fincas gave way, seemingly overnight, to strip malls and chain stores (the island full of Burger Kings so eloquently dissed in Miguel Algarín's classic poem "A Mongo Affair").

Growing up on the island, I was both repulsed and fascinated by the contrast between the urban core and suburban sprawl of San Juan (I walked and bussed both from an early age), by the fact that an island so rich in natural beauty would go out of its way to ape the cement gallerias of the mainland in a sort of New-Jersey-of-the-Mind. My first publication, an artist book of mostly Spanish poems, *Las flores del mall* (2000), was an attempt to chart these landscapes and mindscapes. In some more recent poems on Puerto Rico, I have addressed this Costco-ing of the island in terms of sedimentation, à la Robert Smithson's essay on the "monuments" of Passaic, New Jersey. Back in the nineties though, I was all about the *décima*, a traditional rhymed Spanish form I began to use ironically, fueled by the island poet Joserramón Melendes's landmark 1976 collection *Desimos désimas*. Inherently performative, the décima allowed me to fuse the oral and the high literary, the topical and the arcane, with a postpunk edge, and I began performing these around San Juan circa 1997–98.

When I went to Stanford for my MA in 1998, I pursued this performance kick, doing (not very successful) "avant-stand-up" (don't ask!), inspired by early Steve Martin, Andy Kaufman, and my grandfather's jokes and singsongy refrains. I also did a couple of open mikes and even a slam at, of all places, the legendary, though then unknown to me, La Peña Cultural Center in Berkeley. (I did some décimas and of course was eliminated for going over the three-minute limit. I have not slammed since.) Thanks to a hip senior-year teacher (¡gracias, Mr. Plúguez!), I was already somewhat aware of the Nuyorican Poets, having read Pedro Pietri's "Puerto Rican Obituary" on the island, but it was while browsing the stacks at the Stanford library that I began getting into the work of Tato Laviera and Víctor Hernández Cruz. (Ironically, soon after I would discover there was a personal connection all along: my dad's friend and colleague at the University of Puerto Rico was Eugene V. Mohr, who wrote one of the earliest studies of Nuyorican literature.) Of course, there was a performance poetry and open mike scene in Puerto Rico in the 1990s, but I could never quite figure out how to fit my décimas and stand-up and singsongs, my nervous energy and conceptual shtick ambitions, into the parameters of "spoken-word."

Frustrated by my lack of academic focus and unsure how to link the poems and the punchlines, I left Stanford in 1999 and moved in with some friends (later my bandmates and currently my collaborators in the Spanic Attack arts collective) in East Williamsburg, Brooklyn. My first job in New York City was at Boricua College, where my next-door colleague was Nuyorican poet Nancy Mercado, then an editor of *Long Shot* magazine. Nancy and the great folks at the late, lamented *Long Shot* gave a number of emerging Rican poets, myself included, some of our first publication credits. Nancy also introduced me to the scene, and within a month of meeting her, I had been to the Nuyorican Poets and had seen Pedro Pietri read.

Like so many before and since, I can say with certainty that it was Pietri who showed me the way. Here was the epic poet of the Puerto Rican diaspora, mining the singsongs and the punchlines (I later found out he too had dabbled in stand-up early on). Against geographical determinism, Pietri understood Puerto Rico as a mindscape, in and as performance, as what he called, in ElPuertoRicanEmbassy.org, his web collaboration with visual artist Adál Maldonado, a "conceptual territory." (*Noricua*, Spanic Attack's ongoing performance collaboration with Edwin Torres, is heavily indebted to Pietri's conceptualist take on Puerto/Nuyo Rican identity.) For Pietri, it was about neither mere print poetry nor mere spoken-word, but rather about a provisional in-between, about a mishmash of bodies and voices, always messy, always inclusive, always in transit. Watching Pietri read and reading with Pietri taught me what poetry could be, idealistically, at its best, as a public culture, as a way to rethink the terms of belonging.

It was about at this point that I started to see beyond my own islandness, beyond the self-doubt and self-irony that comes with being from what Jamaica Kincaid describes as a "small place." In Pietri's downtown cosmopolitanism, in the AmeRícan vistas of Tato Laviera, in the dislocations and synesthesia of Víctor Hernández Cruz, in the embodied crossings of Sandra María Esteves, in the glossolalias of Edwin Torres, I saw a better way of understanding myself as Puerto Rican, beyond the strip malls and the false consciousness, beyond the internalized colonial self-hatred, beyond the othering of the non-white, the non-straight, and the diasporic that has characterized island Puerto Rican official culture.

Laviera was a regular at a weekly open mike I hosted in El Barrio (aka East Harlem) circa 2002–2003. Watching his joyful, in-your-face performances, I learned a lot about the need to bring the audience into the performance, even if it meant sacrificing the downtown poet's carefully constructed sense of cool. I was also impressed by his ability to speak to multiple (sometimes competing) constituencies at once: young and old, islanders and mainlanders, street poets and academics. Lastly, I picked up on his nuanced multicultural sensibility, one that understood Nuyorican poetics not as solitary but as always linked, always attuned (e.g., to African American and Chicano/a poetries). Soon I began to see myself as similarly attuned, and I began to take myself seriously as a (cough) "Latino" poet.

For a long time, terms like "Hispanic" and "Latino" had seemed to me either demographic contrivances for another senseless census (the largest minority!) or else marketing terms designed to tap into a profitable niche (see Arlene Dávila's *Latinos, Inc.*). Scholarly attempts at theorizing these terms seemed to me hopelessly passive, frustratingly metaphysical, as in Ilán Stavans's *The Hispanic Condition* (see Juan Flores's essay "Life off the Hyphen" for a famous critique along these lines). Hanging out in the downtown NYC poetry scene, however, I began to see a more heuristic, constructive rationale for keeping "Latino" in circulation: the term's very catch-all quality could, like NYC, bring disparate poetics and politics together.

I remember meeting poets Mónica de la Torre and Rodrigo Toscano around the same time in 2003, shortly after beginning my PhD in Spanish at NYU, and thinking about how funny it was to think of them both as US Latino poets. Despite their shared experimental sensibility, Toscano's borderlands Marxism and de la Torre's quirky take on Latin American vanguardism are as different as their hometowns of Mexico City and San Diego, but a reading of the two as avant-garde Latino poets could bridge el D.F. and la frontera, post-language and the post-vanguardias, Toscano's Brecht and de la Torre's Oulipo. By this time, my manuscript "Kool Logic/La lógica kool" was under contract with Bilingual Press. Seeing the great work done by independent presses and journals devoted to Latino/a literature, Bilingual Press chief among them, further sensitized me to Latino cultural work resistant to the mass marketing apparatus. I had begun to realize that "Latino" is, if not quite simply what you make of it, then at least about breadth, which is one reason I was so happy to join Bilingual's eclectic poetry list, one that ranges from Alurista to Gustavo Pérez Firmat.

By the time of my second year at NYU, I had switched my research focus from early twentieth-century Latin American poetry to contemporary Latino/a poetry. I had come to appreciate "Latino," understood in a broad, elastic sense, at once as a subcultural identity (think of the long-standing oppression of Chicanos and Nuyoricans in the United States), a multicultural identity (an ethnic-American one that is "on the hyphen," to use Pérez Firmat's term), and a transcultural identity (think of borderland and diaspora, of the transnational movement of bodies and cultures). Approaching the study of Latino literature this way, I could pivot between the local, the national, and the transnational, splitting the difference between island and mainland.

I still have substantive doubts about the viability of the Latino tent, particularly as it relates to class, race, and sexual and gender difference. At its most unspecific, a term like "Latino" is merely generic, just a shelf at Barnes & Noble. A vague, unquestioned conception of "Latino" risks simply reproducing social hierarchies. If "Latino" is to mean more than a lone shelf in the back ("Border Studies" at Borders) or an overpriced chain-store café con leche ("Latte, no foam"), individual stories must matter (one reason I'm happy to be contributing to this volume).

So must bodies. Before Judith Butler and the heyday of performativity, Gloria Anzaldúa's *Borderlands/La Frontera* framed an identity politics around the complexities of embodiment, a project expanded upon in such recent scholarly works as Lázaro Lima's *The Latino Body*. My own writings on Latino/a poetry, on and off the page, take seriously these critical concerns. One reason performance matters so much to me is that it helps me understand the quirks of my own body (something I am very much aware of since having been diagnosed with epilepsy as a child) in relation to other bodies, other vocabularies. Performance can be funny, painful, polemical, and self-reflexive all at once, in a way poetry rarely is; it can serve as a fitful score of eccentric Latino/a bodies (I'm thinking of John Leguizamo's *Freak*, or of the simultaneously fierce and quirky avant-drag of Nina Flowers).

Of course, our stories are also shaped by institutional contexts, whether countercultural (as in the rise of the Nuyorican Poets I) or elite (as in doctoral studies at high-powered research schools like NYU, where Latino Studies scholars like me are trained). Some of my favorite contemporary Latino/a performance poems riff savvily and self-reflexively on institutional contexts, and on the tensions and contradictions of a public culture of poetry that teeters uneasily between commodity and community. Witness Willie Perdomo's ironic account of his own slam-era celebrity in "Spotlight at the Nuyorican Poets Café," or Emanuel Xavier's "The Death of Art," a witty and passionate riposte to high-culture slam-haters like Harold Bloom that is nuanced enough to not let poetry readings off the hook: the poet protagonist says he can only tolerate "half an hour of spoken word before I start tuning out" and even admits to using poetry readings for hooking up (a pragmatic proposition, I would say).

Both poems send up the excesses and the tired commercialism of the public culture of poetry in the (post-)slam era, yet neither gives up on community; rather they insist on the importance of the shared word, on the body's truth, on the turnings and crossings of our competing and complementary languages. As somebody who writes about performance poetry, I'm sometimes asked how I "feel" about slams, Def Poetry, and the rest of the ubiquitous apparatus of a marketable spoken-word culture. Steering clear of either heartfelt apologia or outright dismissal, I refer those who ask to poems like Perdomo's or Xavier's.

Ultimately, perhaps the term "Latino" matters to me precisely because it's so messed up. Like Perdomo's or Xavier's poetry reading, it's a place where everything clashes: authentic and inauthentic modes of publicness, poiesis and polis, our eccentric bodies and the institutional and market forces that make our bodies "properly" legible (as Latino/a). Performance poetry is important, and not just as a supplement to a print text, or as a stepping stone to an acting, modeling, or rapping career, inasmuch as it makes us rethink what counts as legible by confronting us with poetry's messy resonances off the page.

I came to New York City ten years ago looking for community (always an only child, I guess), my overactive, occasionally misfiring neurons looking for a target, seeking out some mainland in my mainframe. These are not demands traditionally made of poetry, yet these are, however unreasonable, the demands I made of it: poetry as the shared language of our idiosyncrasies, as babel/babble and as lingua franca, like the city itself.

In liberal societies, identity politics is supposed to be tacit (you're free to be Latino/a, or whatever, on your own time, so long as you keep the terms of deliberation intact). In the wake of my slow Latino awakening, I prefer to think in terms of a Hi-Density Politics (the title of my new manuscript) attuned to the tangle of the city and its brainscape, where our quirks and our failings, our frailties and our misfiring gray matter, can matter in something like a public way, where "our" and "we" are a function of eccentric voices and movements, always provisional, ultimately shared.

It's two weeks later and I'm back from Brazil, sitting in El Molino Rojo, a hole-in-the-wall restaurant in the shadow of Yankee Stadium. It's one of those caribeño joints where you can't tell if it's Dominican or Puerto Rican. It's been an unusually cold and wet start to the summer. As I sip a café con leche ("cortadito," of course), I wonder: Why would anybody pay Starbucks prices when you can get this for a dollar? To say nothing of those annoying indie/hipster home-roasted places! (Maybe in this economy, and as Starbucks continues to falter, one-dollar café con leche will become the next big thing. Latino = Latté no! You can keep the foam.)

Immediately, my amped-up synapses go into synesthetic overdrive: a slide show: (1) the burnt taste of a Starbucks latte; (2) the subtle aroma of Brazilian coffee; (3) the foam of the crashing Ipanema waves; (4) that beach with all the cacti on the South coast of Puerto Rico; (5) me as a child, foaming at the mouth at my grandparents' house; (6) the unplaceable Spanish accent of my grandmotherly waitress (seemingly Caribbean, but . . .); (7) the jumble of brown bodies on 161st Street.

It strikes me that any Latino identity worth claiming must make room for these myriad sensoria, these relations, these coordinates. My own Latino awakening came late. Or rather, it's still happening. Like this city. This brain. This heart. Me late.

13

"I Don't Write About Cuba"
HELENA MESA

1

"You got it wrong," my father said. I'd returned to the Midwest and the Rust Belt, this time to south-central Michigan, and my father had driven out from Pittsburgh to help me move in. After three days of unpacking and helping in the way my economist father knows how to help—polish brass doorknobs, hang pictures on the wall, do a few minor repairs—we were about to say goodbye. I was sitting on the edge of his hotel bed, he was about to realize he'd lost his watch in my unfamiliar apartment, and we were both about to travel seventeen miles (each way) down a dark stretch of I-94 to retrieve his watch so he could leave in the morning.

"You got it wrong." My father was reading my poems for the first time in ten years. Looking intent, he said, "Madrid is in the center of the country." He waited for a reaction, and when I looked puzzled, he continued, "You wrote: 'The father who left on a boat full of nuns and priests heading for Madrid.' Madrid doesn't have a port. The boat docked in Galicia." The truth is, my father left Cuba on the last boat commissioned by the Spanish government to evacuate clergy; his good friend obtained for him, my father, passage on the boat after weeks in hiding, after a night when his counterrevolutionary publications almost landed him in jail, if not worse. These details are not in the poem.

Truth is, my father was heading to Madrid by way of Galicia. To me, the change is metaphoric of his true destination, but to my father, if his story is to be told, it should be accurate, which means the details of the narrative must be factually precise. He doesn't deal in metaphor, or he doesn't like to think so, and the idea of transformation, of metaphor as a physical movement, one of transference, is insignificant to him when alluding to his personal story.

It was in the dark, driving back to fetch his watch, in silence because we couldn't agree on a radio station, that he murmured, "And after we docked, the boat caught fire and sank." I waited. My father is not one to talk about his departure from Cuba. In childhood, I thought nuns and priests were players in all Cuban-exile narratives. I hadn't yet learned he was an atheist, which explained his weekly nap through every Sunday Mass. I hadn't yet heard a plethora of departure stories from other Cubans. Thus his story resounded like a myth—something extraordinarily ordinary, something fantastic, something vague and barely believable. But from my father, I've learned to wait for the unexpected, for the unknown, and so again, I waited, until he said, "That was one of three times I almost died when trying to escape." And what struck me, more than the near-death experiences, was that my sixty-nine-year-old father suddenly realized, for the first time, a truth about leaving Cuba: Something saved him, and what that something was is indefinable, inexplicable, especially to a non-believer. And it scared him.

2

When I think about Cuban American poetry, I often think about the desire to "get it right." I think of identity politics. I think about political poetry draped in an elegiac tone. I think of lyrics exploring place through memory and the imagi-nation. I think about narratives that capture a sense of displacement and exile, that often rock the speaker between the two shores of loss and longing. And of a rupture in time, where speakers long for an era and a landscape that no longer exist, and in some cases, where the next generation longs for a place she has never seen. In Rafael Campo's essay "The Solitary Star: Finding a Cuban Home in Poetry," he writes: "All my life, I have been told that Cuba no longer exists as a place, and yet it remains the intensely evocative destination, consciously or unconsciously, of my family's every story, every argument, every move and action. Cuba is at once all that was lost and everything that is remembered but cannot be spoken of, and yet of course is."[1] Cuban American poetry is full of narratives rooted in this paradox, and voice after voice holds memories of place and experience, not just to "get it right," but to remember and, in some cases, to fill the absence.

Take, for example, Silvia Curbelo's "The Lake Has Swallowed the Whole Sky." The poem captures the dreaminess of displacement in lines such as:

> We wake up a hundred times and
> don't know where we are . . .

The speaker, a communal we, both wakes into confusion, not knowing where she stands, and exists in a metaphoric sleep reminiscent of death. The "we" exists and lives "Asleep // at the wheel." Curbelo posits the familiar metaphor for a jarring experience, suggesting how the speaker lives in a foreign place by rote or without thought. Implicit within the statement "asleep at the wheel" is the danger of an accident, that living without a sense of awareness or immediacy can wreck you. Later in the poem, she writes:

> The way
>
> the rose gives up its stem and
> floats completely, without history.
>
> In the end every road leads
> to water. What is left of a garden

is the dream, an alphabet of longing.
The shadow of the girl. Perfume.[2]

Like the rose, to rupture a sense of being, to be detached from what roots you to the ground, is to progress without history; it's that derailment or break from the past (or a homeland) that often characterizes Cuban American poetry, whether that of exiled Cubans now living in the United States, or that of the following generation who seek a sense of family history and personal identity. One could argue that what remains is doubly removed—not the distant garden, but the dream of the garden, and of an alphabet that doesn't necessarily construct language or syntax. Likewise, we see the shadow of the girl (instead of the girl herself) and imagine the perfume left behind, two intangibles that will quickly dissipate and leave yet another void.

But exile dislocates more than the self. That is, if we remove place, we also disrupt time, thus creating multiple timelines: that of memory; that of the exile living in her new locale; that of Cuba moving forward without the exile's presence; and, in this case, a stasis resulting from the Cuban Embargo and a poor economy. In "Primos," or "Cousins," Sandra Castillo shows the rupture of time through a photograph; she writes:

> Trapped by geography,
> you lean against a Ford Fairlane,
> an odd, left-over '50s we never knew,
> out of time, out of sequence.

Later, in the same poem, we see the speaker staring into the photograph, trying to bridge the gap, her concentration so deep she no longer hears her aunt speaking to her. Castillo writes:

> I hold you a long time,
> and though Tía Hilda is mouthing words,
> spinning sentences into the aftertaste of absence,
> it is today,
> and water surrounds us, separates us,
> moves between us,
> her ambient voice, our home sky.[3]

She desires a connection, but like many Cuban poets, the memory is elusive, especially for writers who either left Cuba at a young age or were born outside Cuba and grew up in Miami, a place of verisimilitude. Miami says: This is Havana, this is so far from Havana. Some neighborhoods eerily resemble the homeland, while rushing forward in an American landscape that inherently suggests what is lacking, what is lost.

Of course, I am only touching on the range of Cuban American poetry published since the revolution, but I would be negligent if I didn't mention the importance of political poetry. Ricardo Pau-Llosa's "Conscience" quarrels with a Nelson Mandela speech given in 1990, wherein the activist states: "There is one thing where that country [Castro's Cuba] stands out head and shoulders above all the rest—that is in its love for human rights and liberty." In response, Pau-Llosa writes:

> Another flight from Cuba
> has brought former political prisoners.
> One is being interviewed on the radio.
> He tells how adolescent boys who get caught
> writing anti-government graffiti
> are brought to the cells
> where the common prisoners are kept.[4]

The poem continues to chronicle the boys' suffering—the sounds of being beaten, the suggestion of rape—before ending: "Sometimes the guards join in. / Mostly they just watch." The understatement and bluntness of the final two lines leave the reader cold, force us to question what we know or can't know about the people still living in Cuba.

3

But I don't write about Cuba.

I was born in Pittsburgh to Cuban parents. One photograph shows me wearing a pink-and-yellow-eared Mickey Mouse hat. Another photograph shows me standing in snow so deep I might disappear into the white landscape. Each summer in childhood, my parents loaded our wood-paneled station wagon and drove the three and a half days south to Hialeah, where my grandmothers and aunts lived. My memories of this trip consist of eating Dairy Queen, sleeping on motel floors, and singing along to ABBA in Spanish, the only tape all five of us could tolerate. (In fact, I was a teenager when I first discovered that ABBA was not Cuban, but Swedish.) For my parents, our arrival was a homecoming, but for my sisters and I, Hialeah was the beginning of renegotiations; my father's work required that he travel throughout the summer, and so my grandmother dutifully raised us for three months out of the year. My grandmother couldn't speak English, and I refused to speak Spanish to her (or to anyone) until I was five years old and suddenly aware that I was both hungry and incapable of communicating. I have never been to Cuba, although my sister claims that I once said, "If I ever go to Cuba, I'll kneel down and kiss the ground." I do not remember saying this.

Perhaps when I say I don't write about Cuba, I should say, I don't write about Cuba directly.

Only four poems in *Horse Dance Underwater* reference the trek

Cubans—family or otherwise—take when migrating to the United States. And when I consider how Cuba appears within these poems, I don't find a homeland or nostalgia, but a portrait of my father, particularly my desire to comfort a loss that I do not possess. The literal absence of Cuba as a theme may very well speak of the distance between my father and me, in addition to the disjuncture between his past and my own. Moreover, the way in which the poems obscure any references to my family's emigration only further suggests that leaving Cuba is a metaphor for my relationship to my father—the distance between us, the distance between his experiences and my own. And what may be more odd is that my father's story—my practical, logical, economist father, the one who dwells in facts and statistics—his story becomes a mechanism through which I distance (and legitimize) intimate and private themes such as solitude, death, and melancholy.

For example, one poem examines the loss and oppression I imagine my father felt when first living in a landscape that was not Cuban, but landlocked, frozen, and gray. His loss "starts with blue fire, the heat / deep in his bones, spreading to lungs / filled with hornets. Skies were charcoal / beds left to die of their own accord." While deeply lyrical, the poem moves from a newspaper announcing a sunken ship to a street where no one watches to a room we can recognize as a home filled with ordinary things—hot water pipes, books, and guitars. To me, the poem nods to his escape from Cuba, his blacklisted name, his near-death, but the nod is a private nod, not readily available to the reader. When I titled the poem "Gusano"—which literally translates into "a worm," but has become a Cuban term for "a traitor, a Cuban émigré"—I was thinking of Robert Lowell's *Life Studies and For the Union Dead*, specifically Lowell's impulse to draw on more historical or public subjects as a way to justify more private and personal poems, such as his "Waking in the Blue" and "Home After Three Months Away." Similarly, many of the poems in *Horse Dance Underwater* anchor themselves in recent history, in landscape, moving outward to marginalized figures like migrant laborers, prostitutes in the late 1800s, the sick. My hope is that the poems fuse the personal subject (the loss, the abandoned places, the search for more) with something beyond a readily identifiable speaker or experience; in other words, I hope to blur the line between the personal and the public, as the two are so rarely fixed or easily defined. For instance, one poem moves from a Puerto Rican legend where women defend San Juan ("Braids of Water Too Swollen to Bear"), to the desire to comfort a stranger ("Tonight, No Sleep"), to a poem that examines loss:

Mechanics of Early Autumn
Migrant workers pick late tomatoes,
the rows half-tidy, the last before the men
pack and move on, leaving beehives
half-fallen from a tractor, combs empty.
Lilac fails yellowing grass. Steeples finger

the hammocked sky, insignificant rebellions
you would say, simple details like cracks in a mug
cast as sadness. Glaze cracks, china chips,
the day is not unraveling. And still
on the drive, leaves raise their silver hems
to walk through puddles not yet formed.[5]

Similarly, a series of poems about female saints questions whether or not having a vision is truly a vision or merely a form of mental illness, the aftereffect
of anorexia, especially as, early on, these women's visions could lead either to
power or to accusations of "devil's work":

Notes on a Saint: Deirdre, Brigid of Munster
d. 570

So tranquil, she let a beetle devour her side;
townsmen said it grew hog-sized and roamed
the halls in fear of her steady gaze. After
they walked wide circles around her house,
the path a grooved orbit. She wrote letters
to her mother: *An animal sleeps in my mind,*
fur thick and mangled, then stuffed the notes
inside her mattress. Townsmen said she lived
on manna, though at night her abdomen
puffed with air and tree sap, a round hump.
In the spring they brought her the blind:
two parents, a priest. She could do more, they knew,
left stones outside her door: three smooth offers
for something taken and missed. *Is it real?*
Will it ever wake? A girl asked if her hands
bled at night, if they tasted of iron stakes—her eyes
wistful, as only a girl's could be, her stink
dumb, like sour milk. She told the girl to leave,
walk until she could no farther, and settle, there,
a true penance. *It curls tighter. To breathe,*
a chore. For days the river fought its banks,
the air was a broth. Leaves shook rain
and as she waited for the drops to burn her veil,
fireflies dawned, their light a mortal light
that left her dizzy and sick, the animal large and foul.[6]

4

W. S. Merwin ends "For the Anniversary of My Death" with the lines:

> As today writing after three days of rain
> Hearing the wren sing and the falling cease
> And bowing not knowing to what[7]

Years ago, when I first read those lines, I was left breathless. No, each time I read that last line—"And bowing not knowing to what"—I am breathless. It speaks to that ineffable, unknown force that arrested my father in a car speeding along I-94 in south-central Michigan. It speaks to the willingness to bend time—the insistence on the present moment; the anniversary for what has not occurred, but will occur, a marker for death that we pass each year; the end of three days of rain; the time spent in a chair, putting language to paper; and the bowing that not only occurs within this moment, but continues. The honoring of the thing beyond us all.

It is that bowing to something both familiar and unknown that, as poets, we face each time we write. It's something we see in Pablo Medina's "The Exile," where the man returns to a past suspended in time: "The year had neither ended nor begun." Sensory images—the cane fields, smokehouse, orange—all fill the man's imagination and become first a song, and then the river, symbolic of the past that summons his return: "Will you be with me?" But the call to join the past can only lead to death, and as much as the man longs to reenter, he cannot. Medina writes:

> There were stones all over the yard smelling of time.
> He picked a few, threw them down the well
> and listened to the water swallowing.
>
> It made him smaller. He walked out the gate
> and closed it behind him, wiped the sweat from his
> eyes, felt his feet settling on the road.[8]

It's a road I think we hope for, a path to find our way through unfamiliar land-scapes, to grasp language, and perhaps—for the exile, for Cubans like my father, and for some Cuban American writers—perhaps it's a heightened sensibility related to that of the Romantic poets: a geography of imagination and its undu-lations through memory. But I am not sure that this thing is particular to any one type of writer. My father may still listen to the water swallowing, but more often than not, he allows his Cuba to grow smaller. With that in mind, it only seems right that I, too, should throw my own stones or stumble in my own way. Regardless, neither of us is willing to submit to that river asking, "Will you be with me?"

Notes

1. Rafael Campo, "The Solitary Star: Finding a Cuban Home in Poetry," in *Open House: Writers Redefine Home,* edited by Mark Doty (St. Paul: Graywolf Press, 2003), 138.

2. Silvia Curbelo, *The Secret History of Water* (Tallahassee: Anhinga Press, 1997), 70.

3. Sandra M. Castillo, *My Father Sings, to My Embarrassment* (Buffalo: White Pine Press, 2002), 74–75.

4. Ricardo Pau-Llosa, *Cuba* (Pittsburgh: Carnegie Mellon UP, 1993), 86.

5. First published in *Pleiades* 28.2 (Spring 2008): 129.

6. First published in *Bat City Review* (Spring 2007): 160.

7. W. S. Merwin, *The Lice* (New York: Atheneum, 1967), 58.

8. Pablo Medina, *Arching into the Afterlife* (Tempe: Bilingual Press, 1991), 79.

14

The Child in the House

Gina Franco

Out of so many possible conditions, just this for you and that for me.

—Walter Pater, "The Child in the House"

In narrative, beginnings and ends tether middles together only nominally. It is the same as saying we were always in a middle way. Or that in every genesis there hangs an exodus. Or in every origin a tendency. So that any beginning might be solely an accident put into the service of ends, as much as it then becomes—maybe erroneously—a study of power, and of matter, as well as a dear tangible spot, at last, in which to rest one's head.

—A beginning: an early memory, say, where there is only the child in the yard of the house. This child squatting below the shade of the swamp cooler in this wet-earth smell of wood wool pads and condensation. With one bare foot sliding into this puddle of green algae. With both hands smoothing the runoff and the paint chips from the underside of the cooler. Which is suspended above her head, somehow, from the wall behind her. She places her palms against the lower vents where she can touch the pads with her fingertips. The air is hot and water trickles over her wrists. She feels the sun in the part in her hair, which is good, because she thinks God lives in the sun.

Though today she is tired of thinking of God, for today she understands he is everywhere heavy. She has seen his face in the frame at the bottom of her mother's drawer, below the white bras with their thick wilting cups, and his skin is gray as underwater light. He wears a wreath of barbed wire on his head, and blood runs from his brow in rivulets down his cheeks, his neck, into the boundary of the frame, though she studied his face and could find no visible wounds. The eyes in his head are turned upward so that the whites seem to stare blindly ahead, or so that it seems he cannot lift his head far enough upwards to receive an impending blow. And this is odd because she thought he'd be gazing down at her and her mother in her mother's room, so she asks who is he looking at? And her mother turns from her folding to say, he is looking at his Father. She closes the drawer on the face in the frame, in which the child understands that God's face is a face of waiting, and in which she remembers she understands having to wait, though she cannot remember if she understands why it is fathers that must be waited on, if so.

Now she crouches in the shadow of the machine that hangs from the wall above her and feels water drip onto her scalp. She thinks of this shadow as a room in her one-roomed house, the one her father would build for her in the depths of the river. She would live there on her own. He would teach her to swim underwater as he did, skimming the bottom of the riverbed like a fish, and sometimes he would drop stones by her underwater window to announce his visit—azurite, quartz, pyrite from the mine—which she would shelve in the girders of her house. She talks to him below the whine of the fan that whirls on its axle, which in the story is the sound of rushing water, the sound of the departing rivers of the earth rushing to the sea and elsewhere. All the days in the house were the same day. It was a place where nothing comes next.

> *The carpenter stretches a line, he marks it out with a pencil; he fashions it with planes, and marks it with a compass; he shapes it into the figure of a man, with the beauty of a man, to dwell in a house.*
> —Isaiah 44:13

And so if I ask: where does poetry begin for me? If I am to reach into the thorns and take hold of the crown—that place where the tree divides itself indefinitely away from itself, either skyward or earthbound, branching and rooting by halves into infinity—I must acknowledge that I have not discovered a source, but merely a point of dissension, and that somehow, for me, knowing is always posited through divisiveness, in the beginning. I tap the tree. But I seem to have only a sticky-milky duality at hand, which separates readily into this or that thing: right from left, light from dark, north from south, soul from body, spirit from letter. You from me.

—In opposition, distance.

And there is (for me) a very deep wound in these distances, what is either a fantasy space to fill, or a dialectical breach that renounces any possible unity where unity begins to reek of assimilation and of uniformity, or where unification reeks of subjection and of law: mind over matter, man over woman, father over mother, white over brown, rich over poor . . . me over you . . .

The view that suggests that such polarities always feed by a matter of preference into hierarchical structures is not only compelling, but also seems frighteningly intuitive. It is like watching the subconscious mind as it overshadows consciousness from its invisible exile—which I can watch only in retrospect. The same view tells me that, like it or not, American, English-speaking, I am a consequence of Western Eurocentric thought, a post-Enlightenment baby born to urge dualism into hierarchical action. For even if I think I believe in unity, I am hung up on difference. That is, the differences I would make are marked by a logic of otherness, which all too often becomes a logic of power.

Further: that when I think of unity, I am inclined to confuse it with abstraction—with the making of the ideological, the statistical, the generic—which works toward ignoring concrete, distinct reality: the unique reality of individuals. This is erasure. It is the spirit of conquest and of annihilation. It is self-interested, but I have often confused it with—and blamed it on—the interests of the good of (my) culture. I would go so far as to say that abstraction is always already a political animal, for it continuously stakes claims on community.

Though in actuality, to be effective, abstraction must oppose community, for its media must be highly selective.

Thus I have grown wary of abstraction, for it prefers itself to anything else, is too willing to be vicious to be truly interested in kind-ness, and yet I am unable to live without it, for it is inextricable from the work of words.

—As the wood from the tree.

Like most art in its most utilitarian modes, poetry bears our distances for us, if only momentarily and artificially. Art is a ruse, yes, but at its very best it doesn't pretend to be otherwise, or at least it doesn't pretend to be essential, even when I beg it to be. It has long been necessary (for me) to salvage poetry from its idealizations, the giant abstract shadow-forms the child did once expect it to shelter—beauty, goodness, truth, oneness—which, properly speaking, are the dwelling places of the person, not because they do not reside within art (they can), but because in terms of putting things in order, I am not for art; art is for me. That is, it is easy to want to believe in words, but it is just as easy to see that, in themselves, as a starting place, words are idle.

At first, we were children of the earth, and the earth was filled with both sorrow and consolation. Matter was not God, but the language of God, which made all of earth potentially sacramental and transient, all of it a vastly beautiful and vastly dying multiplicity of signs pointing beyond itself toward the prolific, desiring utterance of the ineffable. Matter was then also the language of expressive prayer—not a superstitious invocation of cause and effect as is often assumed, but an artistic, concrete, evocative manifestation of hope—offered by one who exists, radically, as both body and soul.

That was long ago, mostly before my parents and I were born, though some relics remain in our homes. Now, in my mother's house, across the room from where I sit, a prayer candle burns next to a glass of water on the wood-stove. Folded beneath the glass of water are scraps of paper filled with her loose handwriting, magnified in the bottom of the clear glass. And though I haven't read them, I know they are prayers, some for my brother, and probably some for me. I know the most urgent of these are written in Spanish, my mother's child-hood language, a language her husband and children do not share with her, and which she reserves for privacy and dreams. The rest are written in English, the language of formal supplication.

The candle itself is covered in the grim, complex, traditional iconography of Christian mortality—the skull, serpent, and apple at the base of the crucifix, a field of flames in the background, and in the frame, the scourging post, the burial shroud, the sword and the lance, the rooster, the ladder, and the corn plant. On the back is the novena prayer to Justo Juez, the Just Judge, a plea for protection against injustice which asks that if the supplicant cannot be spared from injustice, let injustice be brought into the wounds of the immolated Christ whose sufferings restore justice to humanity.

And a glass of water: the most elemental of offerings, a drink for the dying Son who cried out in thirst, offered in language that invites the infinite to sip from the finite and to nail itself again to the world.

This is the true purpose of religious symbolism (and why the symbol is itself symbolized by the tabernacle, the marriage tent, the temple, or the body): to house the encounter between humanity and God. Unlike a poetic symbol, which diffuses its object to arrive at a concept, and which is in effect a self-reflexive system of textual referents, the religious symbol sees itself as the meeting place of paradox, where unity and duality coexist—and commune—where matter and meaning are one, and where corruption literally reaches into perfection and is touched.

Yet, as a more literary sense of language has eclipsed and transformed what was once commonly understood of religious symbolism and allegory, entire languages within our languages have been lost, entire arts. This is not just the loss of an art for art's sake, where the house is built solely for the sake of the house, but also the loss of what a house is, or at least what it might have once been.

Stargo, Arizona: copper was in it, and so was our home. The house was avocado green, stucco plastered over chicken wire and tar paper, like the other houses. It squatted in the middle of a square dirt yard, and though the five rooms were too spare to be cramped, in them the furniture was awkward, as though the house never meant to have a family of three eat at a table or sit on a couch across from a television. The ceilings were low and the house was dark, but in summer, late afternoon, patches of sunlight on the floor made the house seem intimate rather than small.

The outside walls of the house were everywhere pocked, especially along the flanks where I scratched away wide strips of paint and exposed the brittle white undercoat. I sat on the cement stoop where the kitchen led out to a narrow side gate to a shared gravel driveway. The yard was hemmed on three sides by a wire fence that wore an uneven spray of silver paint, as did the clothesline behind the house, as did the cinderblock jammed into the holes in the backyard fence. Where the fence uprooted itself from the cement base, the scalloped wire thrust its silver-veined tendrils into the hard light and gleamed, and I scratched at the paint there too, making silver dust for the faces flaking up from the side of the house. The paint was visionary. There were paths in it, and fields to mine. There were holes like clouds taking shape. The world for the making was suspended in it; I had only to decide what that meant.

> *What cannot be said above all must not be silenced, but written.*
> *Myself, I am a man of speech, I have never had anything to write.*
> *When I have something to say I say it or say it to myself, basta. You*
> *are the only one to understand why it really was necessary that I write*
> *exactly the opposite, as concerns axiomatics, of what I desire, what I*
> *know my desire to be, in other words you: living speech, presence itself,*
> *proximity, the proper, the guard, etc. I have necessarily written upside*
> *down—and in order to surrender to Necessity.*
> —Jacques Derrida, "Envois"

The making of signification in Western thought is so closely bound up with the history of Christianity that to speak of language—and everything made of language—as though it has survived and might finally shirk the influence of logocentrism is very difficult. It is very difficult to secularize a system of signification that was born and raised in the house of the early church, though I can understand why (in the name of freedom) it seems necessary. One way to revise our understanding of language is to shift the center of gravity away from the significance of signs (which may point to nothing of significance) and onto signs themselves (which may only point to other signs). The most adamant of our literary critical minds have written about this problem with great intricacy, but obviously not without using the same tools and the same materials that were used to build the father's house, and not without risking the kind of devastation to meaning that exposes on either side of the wake those extremes we accuse each other of indulging—a hands-off cynicism on one side, or a tightfisted fundamentalism on the other—and that are too easily paired off (to my mind), left and right, with American politics. I sometimes (secretly) believe we have embarked on nothing more than a religion of signs.

I understand these are thornier questions than I can allow here, and that I am being fast and crass in my generalizations, but I mean it only speculatively, and I mean that it is strange to reflect on my relationship to poetry—and to what defines Latino poetry—in this environment, as I perceive it. I mean "strange" in the sense of estranged and extraneous, for I see in American culture an imperative, a vital need to identify and dismantle the oppressor while I might still be able to hold him accountable; and yet, I am left wielding my swords at abstractions (history, was it? or government? or religion? or patriarchy?) that point ever back toward self-alienation. I mean that even the feminist in me believes I might have persecuted fatherhood into oblivion—with motherhood following closely behind. I mean that we seem already stripped of that common ground between us which allows us, as people, to speak of "our" culture.

Culture as we understand it has become nebulous territory, especially on entering the divide between subjectivity and the fluctuating collective landscapes we call tradition, community, and language. It seems that culture becomes an authority wherever standardization—a category or a type—is substituted for individual experience. In that moment, culture enforces a generic relationship to identity—an orthodox sameness—between us, which efficiently elides our internal diversities, and not for the sake of the community, but for the sake of the community's identity. Which seems backward to me. But which is one practical consequence of privileging signs over significance. Or in preferring what to whom. In the pressure to identify who we think we are, we leave behind whoever falls from the net beyond the frame.

Our house was built, like the other houses, against the face of a steep rise that company shovels had carved into a pyramid of narrow streets and precipitous dead ends, so that nearly all the yards in back ended with a soft avalanche of shale that was suspended in rock bolts and wire mesh. And these piles of fallen rock were everywhere at the base of things, where we walked, where we drove. Fallen rock lined the road from the lowlands in Clifton six miles away to the flats of New Morenci and East Plantsite to the winding climb toward Old Morenci, Stargo, and the three open pits of the mine. Fallen rock clogged our passageways after rainstorms and flash floods; it floated in the netting of the Clifton-Morenci tunnel.

It had something in common with the mounds of ore that rode the conveyor belts across the sky over the mine road to the crushers to be pulverized, to the concentrators for extraction, to the smelters for refining. It had something else in common with us, the generations descended from mining camp tents and tiny settlements that grew from prospectors' sluice boxes, New York money, and the heavily recruited skills of Mexican rock-pick miners. My father's grandfather was one of the ones who walked from Mexico, his lungs already filled with silica dust when he arrived, built his three-roomed house on the land he was given on the cliff face, and married. While they saved money to build, while they laid precarious foundations and nailed found wood on their time off from the mine, they lived in grottos they hollowed into the cliffs behind their unbuilt homes. They whitewashed their cave walls and shaved mouths into their ceilings for stove pipes. They kicked loose rock from the clay, hammered railroad ties into makeshift steps, and scaled the thin steep trails, up and down, from their camps on the crags above the river to the underground shafts where the digging was done.

It seems inevitable that such a restless, determined longing for home would flow into the work of turning up cornerstones and laying down brick. But the ones who made of the minescape a breathtaking maw (ribboned in all the mineral colors of earth) were also the ones who bulldozed towns in the search for higher grade ore deposits and more efficient methods of extraction. The mines swallowed up Metcalf, the Coronado Trail, Old Morenci, and eventually Stargo, where the house I lived in was. Where I had been sitting on the stoop in the yard making holes in the side of the house.

So it was: the mines yawned into colossal graduated shelves cut into the rock. Our neighborhood rimmed the berms mounting a small peak. The houses below us sank into the tiered gulf behind Center Market and swam in smelter smoke most mornings when we woke with our lungs full of sulfur and a white haze clouding our rooms. The smoke was heavy and drifted downward, settling on those who lived in the lowest basins. We had an expression for that part of town: "Where do you live?" "We live in The Hole."

My father and mother, my aunt, uncle, and cousins, my cousins' cousins, their aunts and uncles, my godmother: we lived in the stucco company houses on the hill in Stargo until I was four, when those houses were vacated, condemned, and leveled for mining, and the tenant miners were relocated to "New" Morenci. Until then, between the fathers' work shifts, we climbed the poured concrete steps that bridged the levels of our neighborhood streets, walking up and down the earth with our mothers as our fathers walked the radius of the mine and as the mine wives looked to other mine wives for solace. Sunday, the day of outings, the wives dressed us girls (for we were all girls) in lace and velvet, piled us into somebody's wagon, scolded us into sitting on the pews during Mass, and promised us treats from the company store where we went shopping for groceries, after.

> *Soon spreads the dismal shade*
> *Of Mystery over his head*
> —William Blake, "The Human Abstract"

Solidity: there are lapses I can't account for, a terror that arises from a breach between belonging and self-determination, and that is so profoundly hushed in the generations before me that from their tight-lipped anger I arrived at my own silences and anonymities without recognizing them for many years. Why my parents wouldn't teach us Spanish. Why my father changed his name from Carlos to Charlie. Why my mother and father divorced. Why we were no longer Catholic. Most of this life I have forgotten, would rather forget, for on the other side of "why" is a toiling homogenizing blankness that, from the inside out, wills itself into our living structures, subverting them, organizing them, institutionalizing them, and reifying them. What succeeds is a white-walled edifice, a windowless, room-less, formless composition that erects itself like a billboard in plain view so that there is nothing else left to see. Whiteness is the most insidious of monolithic abstractions, and as far as I know it remains uninhabitable, by anyone.

Later, much later, I would come to understand that for very difficult and elusive reasons, Latino writing seemed at first to belong to someone else. And that another literary tradition seemingly far from my own—British, nineteenth-century, Protestant—would always feel more familiar to me. I still cannot quite touch these grounds. They are just out of reach. I have instead a parallel I keep turning over, a set of memories that bear some resemblance (and perhaps an abiding connection) to the experience of having lost a place of origin. Or of watching it sink without seeing it happen.

—The desert sinking beneath a sea.

—The way it felt when we went to the little Pentecostal church for some years, and solidity began to slip away. Though not all at once. I remember the scrape of metal chairs on white tile and the glossy white paint of the brick walls. The hulking upright piano in the corner; its yellowing wooden keys. I remember the pastor's white belt, the way he tucked his guitar pick into his buckle, and that all the women wore pantyhose, even me. I remember my mother's large-print King James Bible, keyed with gold tabs to the books I had been required to memorize—their order, as well as some measure of their contents—and I remember the pastor's daughter had eyes the color of trees and that I wanted eyes that color, too. I remember that eventually, in the tedium of so many days spent in church (Tuesday, Wednesday, Friday, Saturday evenings, and all day Sunday), there was nothing left to look at: no crucifix or cross, no pictures or symbols, no candles, ornaments, windows, or altar. No art besides music, and only gospel music at that.

—And beneath the negation of graven images, I remember the deeply submerged horror of matter and of body: the idols of flesh (no jewelry, no mirrors in the bathrooms, no physical contact between members of the opposite sex) that are the source of damnation, if indulged.

—And above the carnal vanities of earth, the pursuit of personal charisms, transcendent gifts of spirit, which felt to me awash in subjectivity—healings, tongues, prophesies, and once a man who claimed to be able to see out of his glass eye—that were yet experiences raised up within the self, and that one can only live to tell about . . . .

—And I remember: it is just as possible to sacrifice signs to significance, that this is the particular aptitude of self: to fend off the hostility of change, loss, and decay, whatever the cost, for my own sake.

—Here I am.

I remember that in my mind Isaac was a small child when his father walked him up the mountain, bound him to the altar, and drew his knife. Isaac was a child because I was a child: Isaac's father laid the wood for the holocaust on Isaac's shoulders, he laid the wood in order, he laid his son on the wood of the altar and drew his knife.

The angel's final intervention didn't interest me. The child's mind, Isaac's mind, understood perfectly well by then that the angel intervened too late. What is laid down by then brought Kierkegaard to his knees in Fear and Trembling; how it is laid down brought Auerbach to expose it as a work of tyrannical realism. Terror on one hand, beauty on the other. But it remains a poetry that works greatly on the mind (a ram caught in a thicket by the horns) not just because it is terrible or beautiful—even ordinary things can be one or both—but because it binds you to Isaac and because for Isaac there is no closure. For Isaac and for you there are nations: forfeitures of mythic proportions. Everything under the sun you assume about the roles of fathers and children—and of love—for an instant goes up in flame. "Where is the lamb for a burnt offering?" What is at stake? Even the child's mind (especially the child's mind) responds: I am. Everything I think I am is at stake.

15

A Meditation on the Experience and Aesthetics of the Other Rican

BLAS FALCONER

There used to be a time when the Puerto Rican experience was the experience of the people on the island; then it became the experience of people in New York City. Now it is the experience of people like me, who started out in New Jersey, and now I am in Georgia and it is a different reality.

—Judith Ortiz Cofer[1]

My father, John Howard Falconer, of German-Scottish descent, is the son of a milkman. He grew up in Erie, Pennsylvania. He ate pork chops and sauerkraut for dinner. My mother, the daughter of a successful businessman, was born in Salinas, Puerto Rico, a small fishing village on the southern side of the island, and could see the ocean from her kitchen, the mountains from her back yard. They met in Silver Spring, Maryland—at the swimming pool of an apartment complex. My father worked as an engineer for IBM, and my mother translated Cuban radio transmissions for the CIA in the sixties. She has never been able to keep a secret.

I spent most of my childhood in Reston, Virginia, thirty minutes outside of Washington, D.C. My parents' best friends were just like them—European American husbands with Puerto Rican wives: Terry and Eduvíjise, Tom and Emílse, John and Dominga. Each family had three children and we all lived within a mile of one another. Our mothers spoke to us in Spanish, and our fathers spoke to us in English. In the summer, we roasted a pig on the front yard of our suburban house. The neighbors slowed down as they passed; they drew the curtains. On Christmas we caroled. We ate lechón. We drank coquito. Some of us looked more like our mothers. Some of us spoke Spanish.

At Hunters Woods Elementary School, no one had ever heard of the name Blas, but back in Puerto Rico, I could point to the plot of land where my great-great-grandmother lived—a stone's throw from my great-grandmother's home—now, also, a field of yellow grass—across the street from where my grandmother lived with my grandfather Papi Blas, my uncle tío Blas, and later his son Blasito, and his son Blasito. Walking down the street in my bare feet, I was often stopped and asked: ¿De quién eres? I could just as easily have been my aunt's or my uncle's—until I opened my mouth.

In Virginia, I was sometimes told what great fortune my mother had to marry my father, who must have pulled her up from certain squalor. When I corrected them, their faces turned from pity to incredulity to anger, the stereotypical table turned on its side with all the rice and beans.

My mother's parents taught us to savor every bite, to eat until we were full, and then to order dessert. My father's parents, having lived through the great depression, made us decide what we wanted to eat before opening the refrigerator door, so we wouldn't let all the cold air out.

In sixth grade social studies, Mrs. Sawyer told the class about immigrants in New York, and how there were, in fact, entire communities living together, speaking Spanish or Italian or Polish. I went home and asked my mother if we could move there.

West Side Story was my favorite film. My father bought me the soundtrack for my twelfth birthday, and before long I danced down the hall, singing, snapping my fingers. The story didn't seem so farfetched to me, a Puerto Rican girl falling in love with an American boy.

My first boyfriend, Vicente Torres, was born in Puerto Rico and raised in the Bronx with his two younger sisters. When he spoke of New York, he said, "Government cheese and ketchup." He said, "A mother who never learned English," but still thought Puerto Rico a beautiful wasteland compared to life in New York in the seventies. His mother had come in search of prosperity. My mother had come despite it.

Juan Flores identifies four recurring subjects in Nuyorican poetry—simplified here: discrimination, an idealization of Puerto Rico, an acceptance of home on the mainland, and, finally, an identification with members of other marginalized communities.[2] "Flores does not consider the mind-set of Puerto Ricans living outside the five boroughs of New York."[3] As I read this in the Nashville Public Library, I sank into my chair. In spite of my "unique" upbringing, he could have been describing the arc of my own book of poems. Discrimination: pages 4 and 19. The Edenic island: pages 6 and 18. Tennessee as my new home? Pages 43 and 59. An identification with members of other marginalized communities: 21 and 58.

Reading the work of Other Ricans, Rane Arroyo, for example, I also see similar themes. Sometimes, as in the case of Judith Ortiz Cofer, the author complicates or challenges these themes. So, often, when addressing issues of identity, the subjects are the same in part, I'm sure, because we do draw on many of the same sources: the imagery of Puerto Rico—so different from the landscapes of home, whether New York or Virginia or Georgia or Chicago—the history of the island, the politics of colonization and identity.

Some might say that the traditional lines of the mainland Puerto Rican poet emerge from two poets in particular. When my grandmother was a young girl, still in school, she knew the poet Julia de Burgos. My grandmother was an Independent, too, and inspired by de Burgos's fierce patriotism. As influential as she might have been to my work, the stories of Julia de Burgos, the politics, the spirit, inspired me as a young man more than anything else. In college I read William Carlos Williams and fell in love with his clear and simple diction, his precise images, but I admired Whitman and Eliot, Frost and Plath, just as much.

I envy Nuyorican poets, who have a clear foundation from which to write a unique Puerto Rican perspective. As the movement evolves, these poets might write in opposition to this tradition the way one might write in opposition to the long tradition of the sonnet, but there is a specific place to begin from and to return to, against which to push, and to further.

Bob Holman invokes the muse in *Aloud*, an anthology of Nuyorican verse, saying that the book is a "SHOUT," the poems a "contact sport,"[4] but when I pick up the pen, the voice I hear is a whisper. I want to slow down, to draw out the line. Miguel Algarín writes, "The language of poetry is now associated with the great mass of people who are suffering the scathing effects of living so densely together."[5] But I stomped through the creeks of Virginia in winter. I took piano lessons. I fell in love with the boy across the street.

One only needs to read the linguistically innovative poetry of Víctor Hernández Cruz, or the traditionally formal poems of Uruyoán Noel, to see that there is no definitive style to Nuyorican poetry. Nevertheless, the aesthetics of the Nuyorican movement are often largely defined by the presence of a Puerto Rican community, one where information is passed from person to person, daily, by word of mouth, where people might become emboldened by others in similar circumstances. William Luis says, "The Nuyorican poet became the prophet of the Hispanic and Latino communities . . . writ[ing] for a majority and provid[ing] a coherent understanding of the marginal and isolated conditions under which their neighbors live."[6] By way of Ishmael Reed's *From Totems to Hip-Hop*: Nicolas Kanellos says,

> The Nuyorican writers created a style and ideology that
> dominates urban Hispanic writing today: working-class,
> unapologetic, and proud of its lack of schooling and
> polish—a threat not only to mainstream literature and
> the academy, but also with its insistence on its outlaw
> and street culture elements, to mainstream society. . . . In
> capturing the sights and sounds of their "urban pastoral,"
> it was an easy and natural step to cultivating bilingual
> poetry, capturing the bilingual-bicultural reality that sur-
> rounded them, and reintroducing their works into the
> communities through the virtuosity that live performance
> demands of folk culture.[7]

Often this translates to short end-stopped lines, which punctuate each phrase. It translates to taut language, pronounced alliteration, rhyme, rhythm, and repetition—an influence of the drum-driven plenas—and code-switching: "de que I know, Yo si sé / backnforth here soy de aquí" ("Nideaquínidealla").[8] Here, Tato Laviera is writing to a community fluent in code-switching. This linguistic choice establishes a likeness with the audience, a sign of sameness.

Judith Ortiz Cofer says, "I couldn't write in Spanglish if I wanted to, because I never spoke it. I can't write like Pedro Pietri, because I did not grow up in the streets of New York and I did not learn to speak it . . . . When I read the work of the Nuyorican poets, I relish it; I teach it, I love it, I am delighted by it, but I can't write like they do."[9] How then does Cofer, how do other Puerto Ricans living outside of large Puerto Rican communities, articulate the themes outlined by Flores?

In "First Job: The Southern Sweets Sandwich Shop and Bakery," Cofer writes,

> If they [the patrons] presume I am Pocahontas
> at the palace, there only to amuse their royal selves,
> I tell them, smiling sweetly, to try the mierda,
> which is especially good that day.[10]

Spanish is a sign of her "otherness" and her means of challenging the status quo, as she suggests that the customers eat mierda, or shit; she pretends to play the part, but in fact, it is also her way of repudiating the customers' "marginalization." Cofer charms the slow talkers and empowers herself with her "otherness," but her subversive measures are done in secret, subtly, and thus are articulated by the embedded rhyme in a longer line, the downplayed repetition, enjambment, and varied meter. The political emerges slowly and less explicitly through the recounting and the understanding of a distant memory. She tells all the truth, but tells it slant.

Rane Arroyo says that Emily Dickinson has been a strong influence, though his methods of telling the truth at a slant are different from Cofer's.[11] Arroyo's "Dream Starring Andy Garcia"[12] relies on popular culture to offer the reader familiar footing, but the quasi-surreal imagery (another influence) of the dream offers a brief glimpse into the unique psyche of the speaker. Together they articulate the experience of the private individual, isolated in the larger context.

In large part, the poem of the Other Rican is shaped by the absence of a large Puerto Rican community and often identifies, however loosely, with individuals of another marginalized community. For example, Cofer makes an imperfect connection with the Native American figure, the Southern woman, and, in other poems, Biblical women so present in the Bible Belt. Perhaps Rane Arroyo expresses this best in "Write What You Know" when he writes, "I knew the Mexican waiters who cursed [the patrons] / every time they smiled under the parachutes of / fragile mustaches. We were and weren't strangers" and

> I know that my beloved
> Hardy Boys may never recognize me
> from other migrant workers while solving
> *The Mystery of the Lost Muchacho.*
> I'm waving to them: here I am, here I am.
> Hombres, how many more clues do you need?[13]

Again, there is no one aesthetic, but I see several similarities: In these poems, the tone is one of meditation as opposed to oration. The poems ask questions, sometimes implied, that can't be answered, offer a puzzle that cannot be solved, as if they were an exploration to discover, to understand, as opposed to a means of imparting knowledge. The poems reveal the mind as it discovers, and so the speakers come from a position of uncertainty, imbalance, of openness. These poetic devices become a way to describe a personal experience, and the emphasis is placed on the relationship between the writer and the memory or subject, more than the relationship between the writer and the reader. When Spanish enters the poem, it is often done because it is part of the memory, not because it is the language of the reader or the audience.

Having moved around much of my life, I see that my relationship between home (Virginia, Pennsylvania, Maryland, Hungary, Texas, New Mexico, Tennessee) and Puerto Rico has always been in flux. In spite of my father and my upbringing in Virginia, I identify myself as Puerto Rican, and I am often defining/redefining my relationship to the island, my family, other Puerto Ricans, non–Puerto Ricans—creating a constellation of similarities and differences. I often want my poems to reflect these concerns. However, I see that my newer poems address Puerto Rico less explicitly. There is even a conspicuous absence of the Puerto Rican landscape. The draw to write about such subjects and family is waning, and in its place, I'm writing about my life where I live. One poem, "The Battle of Nashville," first tentatively draws a comparison between the speaker and members of the civil rights movement. Second, the speaker identifies himself as a gay man in a relationship in a potentially hostile place. Third, the poem makes reference to Civil War soldiers. In all three cases there is a clear identification with the "other," and in all three cases, the marginalized are fighting for their place in the world. I suppose that writing about the civil rights movement in Nashville, the Civil War soldiers, a gay relationship, becomes a means of writing the Other Rican experience.

In the past, my poems often used the landscape, the history, the stories of Puerto Rico to convey experiences that have nothing to do with Puerto Rico. I have often said that the poem "The Given Account: Puerto Rico 1510," inspired by the first documented murder in Puerto Rico, is as much about a failed relationship between two men as it is about the legend. My poem "Dead Reckoning" describes a failed ferry ride to the island, but it also conveys my initial fears of moving to Tennessee. Now I find myself drawing on aspects of Tennessee to articulate my relationship with Puerto Rico. After all, the lens through which I contemplate any subject has been shaped, specifically, by my history as a Puerto Rican growing up in Virginia, living in Nashville, and in that sense, will always reflect who I am and where I've come from—wherever that may be.

Notes
1. Judith Ortiz Cofer, "The Infinite Variety of the Puerto Rican Reality." Interview with Rafael Ocasio. *Callaloo* 17.3 (1994): 730–42.

2. Juan Flores, *Divided Borders: Essays on Puerto Rican Identity* (Houston: Arte Público Press, 1993), 182–95.

3. William Luis, *Dance Between Two Cultures* (Nashville: Vanderbilt University Press, 1997), 38.

4. Bob Holman, "Invocation," foreword to *Aloud: Voices from the Nuyorican Poets Café* (New York: Henry Holt and Company, 1994), 1.

5. Miguel Algarín, introduction to *Aloud*, 12.

6. Luis, *Dance Between Two Cultures*, 40.

7. Ishmael Reed, *From Totems to Hip-Hop* (New York: Da Capo Press, 2002), 352.

8. Tato Laviera, "Nideaquínidealla," *Afro-Hispanic Review* 25, no. 2 (2006): 173.

9. Ortiz Cofer, "The Infinite Variety," 734.

10. Judith Ortiz Cofer, "First Job: The Southern Sweets Sandwich Shop and Bakery" in *A Love Story Beginning in Spanish* (Athens: University of Georgia Press, 2005), 25.

11. Rane Arroyo, "Interview with Rane Arroyo," 2005. http://www.cervenabarvapress .com/arroyointerview.htm (accessed 30 January 2008).

12. Rane Arroyo, "Dream Starring Andy Garcia" in *Home Movies of Narcissus* (Tucson: University of Arizona Press, 2002), 13.

13. Rane Arroyo, "Write What You Know," in *Home Movies of Narcissus* (Tucson: University of Arizona Press, 2002), 68.

16

Curative Poetics

MARIA MELENDEZ

He's about to give it to me. I'm locked in a dim, closet-sized room in Berkeley with a man in his twenties. I'm ten years old. He's lit incense and invited me to sit in a corner while he turns to an altar behind him and sways a little, chanting under his breath. My father has explained to me that this man will give me my mantra, my sacred syllable. He's said that after the man does this chanting, he'll turn to me and say it—then I'm to repeat it.

My father was in Vietnam in the early seventies as an MP, missing out on the stateside movimiento for Chicano liberation, trying to keep his soul intact "in country." He'd left a Catholic seminary program and joined the Navy to avoid getting drafted into the Army and, he'd hoped, to avoid getting sent directly to 'Nam. The enlistment gamble didn't pay off. The year he served as Military Police in Vietnam came at a point in the war when hardly any sense of meaning or mission remained to be dredged from the wet soil. When he returned to the States and started a family with my mother, he was, and remains, a man who scans the faces of those around him for signs of treachery, a man deeply aware of his need for some inner peace.

For awhile, he found scraps of that peace in Transcendental Meditation, and, hearing the studies floating around about the overall physiological benefits of meditation, he thought it would be a healthy addition to my life. What I remember most about our trips to the Berkeley meditation center are the routine mini-mart stops we made on the thirty-minute drive back home—he'd usually buy me a little jug of strawberry milk.

But deeper lessons remained, subconsciously, including implications about the structured powers of sound. During my initiation, when the young TM instructor turned back to me saying the mantra again and again, making a coaxing wheel of his hands to urge me to join in, I believed he was giving me something useful, as my mother might be given a new embroidery needle or measuring spoon by a neighbor. Preparation classes had taught me that repeating this mantra in my head (and, by my extension, imagining the sound inside me) would clear my mind and bring me deep calm. Over the next few months of daily practice, these things felt true. When I eventually gave up TM as a teen, it wasn't because I found the sound failing, but because I mistook calmness for weakness, for complacency. In the manner of adolescent fires, I wanted to shed everything that remotely suggested passivity, and jettisoned the practice of sitting quietly for twenty minutes a day.

Revisiting that period with an idle troll through the Google pool of opinions, I learn that some ex–TM practitioners claim that one's "personal"

mantra—supposedly so sacred that it's never to be repeated to another person—
is actually selected by the teacher from a formulaic "mantra table," which offers
four or five choices based on the initiate's age and gender. OK. So maybe the
sacred syllable wasn't specially tuned to the spiritual frequency of me, one Maria
T. Melendez, but was instead generalized for "female, 9–13." While it makes
me feel a little duped for how I regarded the nature of the sound as "personal,"
contemplating a systematized mantra table doesn't take any sheen off the fundamental idea that a sound can do real work upon the mind-body. A decrease
in stress hormone amounts and lower blood pressure continue to be two of the
well-documented physical changes wrought by meditation; in my experience of
TM, the sound-work of the mantra itself executed much of my movement into a
calmer state.

What are the poetic applications of the powers inherent in sounds? María
Sabina provided one answer to this question in her role as Mazatec healer.
During the 1950s, ethnomycologist R. Gordon Wasson documented her work as
a channel of sacred chants (many of them proclamatory in tone, self-celebrating
and self-expanding) meant to heal the sick. Describing her sacred articulations
as originating with the little mushroom "children" she ingested prior to a healing ceremony (in the way healers from her southern Mexican region had done
for generations), Sabina provided sounds that healed through her chanting. The
English translations of these chants (recorded by Álvaro Estrada and translated
by Henry Munn) have a number of properties easily recognizable as poetic,
including their use of rhythmic anaphora and vivid imagery. As a healer-poet
whose life and work bears a complex relationship to English, Spanish, and indigenous Mazatec "audiences" (listeners and readers), I look to María Sabina as one
of the cornerstone poets of the Americas:

> Because I can swim in the immense
> Because I can swim in all forms
> Because I am the launch woman
> Because I am the sacred opossum
> Because I am the Lord opossum
>
> I am the woman Book that is beneath the water, says
> I am the woman of the populous town, says
> I am the shepherdess who is beneath the water, says
> I am the woman who shepherds the immense, says
> I am a shepherdess and I come with my shepherd, says
> —from *María Sabina: Her Life and Chants*

A number of ancient societies demonstrate, as María Sabina's chants do, a
well-defined social and/or medicinal function for poetry and for verbal forms
resembling what readers today know as poetry. I listen for links between those
well-defined functions and the role of poetry in the tangled social webs I work

in. Listen hard. After all, no amount of socially sanctioned "proficiency" in poetry will increase the likelihood of someone banging on my door in the middle of the night and begging me to come work my words over the body of a sick loved one. No one's life, it seems, depends on what I do. So what's the point?

Soul-saving. That's one answer, one clear function poetry preserves in the contemporary United States. But before we move into a realm that can feel, at least in its rhetoric, disembodied and ethereal, let's take one last look (empirical, no less!) at poetry's effects on our pitiable mortal coil.

A team of European physiologists has recently proven cardiorespiratory benefits associated with the recitation of hexametric verse. Basically, they found that reciting poetry written in hexameter has the desirable medical outcome of creating greater synchronization in "stability and coherence" between the speaker's heart and breathing rates. Put more poetically, reciting hexameter brings your heart and your breath into harmony, a process that allows both to work more efficiently and healthfully in your body. Eureka! Here's hard evidence of the good poetry can do in the world. I can't help but feel joy and, embarrassingly, some relief at this scientific validation for what ancient societies, and my gut-level experience, have already shown about health-inducing verbiage: it exists.

As for saving the soul, I've found that poetry can cure a soul-deep sense of dis-integration.

I live in a doorway
between two rooms. I hear
quiet clicks, cups of black
coffee, *click, click* like facts
budgets, tenure, curriculum,
from careful women in crisp beige
suits, quick beige smiles
that seldom sneak into their eyes.

I peek
in the other room señoras
in faded dresses stir sweet
milk coffee, laughter whirls
with steam from fresh *tamales*
sh, sh, mucho ruido,
they scold one another,
press their lips, trap smiles
in their dark, Mexican eyes.
　　　　　　　　—Pat Mora, "Sonrisas," from *Borders*, 1986

I first read this poem in an undergraduate literature class at Colorado State University, in Fort Collins. As a mixed-race Chicana, I know the doorway Mora speaks of, and I felt attraction and repulsion present in both the "white" and "brown" peoples' rooms. In my cuarto Mexicano, shame and pride jumble together. The racism of his time that my Mexican American father internalized as self-loathing comes through in historic hindsight: during the years before my father entered the Navy, Hispanic soldiers were placed in dangerous military positions at a statistically higher frequency than servicemen of other races. Further back in his own history, my father remembers being hit with a ruler in kindergarten for speaking Spanish and so raised my sister and I speaking English only. But my aunties urged me to learn Spanish, and brought me a sense of cultural continuity and survivance (survival and resistance—Gerald Vizenor's term) through their recipes, some of which (chilaquíles, garnachas, chiles rellenos) both my father and my Anglo mother made in our home. Most of my childhood friends were white, and they, too, helped me shade my ethnic background as a source of both pride and shame: "I wish I had a real culture like you," on the one hand, and "Ugh, those dirty Mexicans . . . but not you, Maria, you're not a real Mexican" on the other.

As for the "white" room Mora evokes in the poem, my father's repeated expressions of disdain and humiliation toward my white mother (something having more to do with his socialization as a man than with their racial differences, I see now) caused my childhood psyche to equate whiteness with a kind of . . . it hurts to admit it . . . disgusting weakness. I remember sitting in Mass at Saint Michael's and feeling hateful toward a little white toddler next to us, gripping the pew with his ugly, applesauce hands. Yet, whiteness was clearly the nature of the places where the best education, jobs, and homes lay, both geographically and conceptually, in my childhood. Not to mention that my mother is a very nice person.

"Sonrisas" recognized, made visible, a psycho-social split in my life that I'd been unable to completely articulate up to that point; it physicalized, through its imagery, my own sense of being frozen between two imperfect worlds, a victim of my own biracial status. (Obviously, I hadn't yet read Du Bois, Anzaldúa, or other great theorists of double consciousness, mestizaje, etc.) When I'd heard that Mora would be reading on campus at CSU, I'd hoped to be able to speak to her about how important "Sonrisas" had been to me. I approached her after the reading, and started expressing how "Sonrisas" really helped me name my own dilemma, my own crippling mental handicap in feeling stuck at an identity halfway point. She didn't buy it. "That doorway is a space of power." Pat Mora looked me right in the eye and gave me this great cold-water cure for the self-pity in which I'd been steaming . . . a young adult bemoaning the tensions in her dual identity. That doorway is a space of power. The poem itself pulses at the core of this curative moment with the simple suggestion of its first line—not "I languish" or "I wither," but "I live in a doorway."

Another threshold poetry swings across, another divide poetry connects (as body tissues reconnect, to heal) is the perceived distance between human and more-than-human beings. Backing out of poetry, for a moment, to words themselves as spell-casting: consider Japanese scientist Masaru Emoto's claims, in *The Hidden Messages in Water*, that simply taping the words "love" and "gratitude" on vessels of water beautifies the nature of that water. The loved and appreciated samples in his studies produced much more elaborate, aesthetically stunning crystals than the verbally depauperate samples housed in bare, unmarked containers.

Sounds kooky, I know. And alluring, poetically. If there's something in my words that can help the material properties of the world around me (and in me—water's my best feature) achieve more radically elegant structures, I'd like to hear about it, imagine about it, art about it. Really, there had better be something that words and sounds actually do in the world, or else why fuss with them so elaborately, as we poets do? As Flannery O'Connor famously said of the Holy Eucharist, "If it's just a symbol, then to hell with it."

A Japanese legend about seventeenth century haiku master Chiyo-ni illustrates a belief in the catalytic power of verse to make (begging Auden's pardon) something happen. Patricia Donegan recounts the legend in *Chiyo-ni: Woman Haiku Master* (Donegan and Ishibashi):

> In Japan there are many beliefs in the power of poetry—
> Chiyo-ni's included. . . . And originally, as in most cultures,
> Japanese poetry in ancient times was religious incantation.
> . . . [T]anka poetry, the precursor to haiku, evolved from
> shamanic chants believed to have the power to move the
> gods and demons. In the Edo period and even today haiku
> poets have maintained that haiku has unusual healing
> powers and helps to prolong life. There are several stories
> about the powers invested in Chiyo-ni's haiku. According
> to one, the governor of Kaga had heard about Chiyo-ni's
> fame. . . . [W]hen he needed to revive his garden's most
> beautiful cherry tree, which was ailing, he invited her to
> the palace. There she spontaneously composed this haiku:
>
> spring will come again—
> without flowers
> you'll be firewood
>
> To no one's surprise, the tree began to bloom again.

The comic nature of Chiyo-ni's direct chiding of the cherry tree invites both a celebration of poetry as lighthearted connective tissue between humans and nature, and a metaphoric reading into the poem's seemingly simple surface. How many of us writers, in those low points of despair and creative weariness, need similar chiding, cajoling, and verbal whipping from our writing buddies to get us back into that saddle and typing again? Bloom, dammit, or you're done for. That's a message I could do with every morning.

Beyond connecting writers and audiences with our own creative abilities and with the creativity of other lives around us, what about poetry's ability to heal the gap many perceive between their own lives and the Creator? Although the incantations of the Mass were my earliest exposure to this verbal intention, the first time I heard a woman from the secular world claim this desire as a sincere impetus for her poetry came in graduate school. Brenda Hillman, a guest on our campus at UC Davis, described her studies of Gnostic philosophy and explained that she felt herself, like the Gnostics, to be a true dualist, someone who felt the human and divine realms to be totally distinct. She went on to say that, for her, poetry was a way of bridging what she called the "loneliness" between humans and the Divine. The idea stayed with me as another of the real, if not empirically measurable, things that poetry can do for those who viscerally feel such a rift.

The capacity to remedy—although not every poem contains this capacity, or intends it—draws my attention often enough as reader and writer that it colors my experience of poetry. Cures for numbness, for despair, for disconnection—they're what I'm after much of the time, going about my business with words. When I write a poem that knows more than I do, and aspires to greater ideals than I daily do, I hope that I'm letting it do some of this restorative work.

17

Cholo de los Hinterlands

CARMEN GIMÉNEZ SMITH

The only equequo I ever owned broke, ironically, while I was moving. I had had my little equequo for over ten years, through graduate school, through several moves, through a divorce, and he finally landed on my son's shelf of precious and curious objects. My son liked the equequo's round belly and the little bits of acquisition that hung from his body: money, an Inca Cola, a red car. The belief was that you could hang a representation of anything you wanted from his body, and you would get it. I liked the equequo's narrative: a little man from the hinterlands comes to the city armed with all he needs to make a life there. My mother told me that he was a talisman like the owls that an aunt collected. I liked the pragmatism of this little figurine. Rather than the vague promises that other amulets offered, this one acknowledged the realities behind our hopes; more specifically, he defined the terms under which this mustachioed traveler would achieve success or wealth. Every one of the material bits that hung from his body was a metonymy for some larger desire we confronted in our migration.

On the other hand, there was the classist, somewhat racist narrative that led to his conception. He was a cholito from the Andes overloaded with the bling of civilization. He was overdressed for the city's party. He would always be the indio with his wide-brimmed hat and his sandals. My mother was intrigued by my interest in the figure. I think, to her, it was a kind of reverence for a culture that she could always contextualize for me, romanticize for me—although she had lived in Peru for only one-third of her life. Her description of life in Peru was part magazine, part family gossip garnered from the hour-long phone calls she made each week, part childhood memories, and part romanticization of the other place she had called home. What home was to me was complicated by what my roots appeared to be to other people around me.

When I was in high school, an enormous suburban school in San Jose, California, a boy who had a locker beneath mine muttered, "Get back on the boat" under his breath while we both pulled books out from our locker. This slur mostly amused me. I thought: my parents came here in a plane, man.

In this case he was reading my identity through the broad hegemony of immigration's otherness. His contempt was as diffuse and ill-defined as my experience. I was the idioms of Peru, Chile, and Argentina, the lomo saltado and the jumbled Catholicism of immigrants. But I also felt the same pressures of class, the alienation prevalent in the suburbs. The same sorts of pressures that created my anxieties were the ones he externalized by attempting to marginalize me. These questions and assumptions did not disappear as I moved through the

academy. I was often confused for a Chicana. My role in social circles was sometimes to decode culinary curiosities (What's a chimichanga? I don't know.), or to
assume an ambassadorship for all of Latin America in any conversation involving
a Latin American country. When I began writing poetry, I was steered toward
the poetry of telling identity and I liked it. I admired the impulse to define, to
say: we are here.

But a big problem for me was that by purely engaging in a description
of otherness, I might be left out of a larger conversation about how poetry can
change, how new ideas are born. In this regard I think a resistance to identity
as a posture in poetry is an innovation in and of itself. I wanted to develop new
strategies for using language. I had stories, but I hoped that they worked to fore-
ground the dynamic possibility of language.

How can I speak generally as a "Latina" when I am really the daughter of a
Peruvian and a peripatetic Argentinian with a German grandmother? This identity is too diffuse, too complicated to reduce into one trajectory, however much
external cultural forces would like to make it. One of the great mythologies of
the American experience is the melting pot, which to me seems like code for
homogenization, for voluntary self-negation. My identity was too eccentric to
codify. My grandmother spoke English with a British-Chilean accent. She spoke
French with a British-Chilean accent too. She dressed like Queen Elizabeth II.
On the other hand my mother, my grandmother's daughter-in-law, was born
from generations of civil servants from Iquique. She loved Brenda Lee and drove
a Karmann Ghia through the streets of Lima. She wore wigs when she lived in
New York in the seventies, laughed at the hippies. How might I reduce this to a
general narrative, a one-size-fits-all Latino poetry?

Although I do like to claim that I have a very clear picture of what I do as
a poet, the truth is I don't. External forces tend to tribalize aesthetics and frame
poetry in political, cultural, and/or gender discourses. These frames can be helpful when imagining the great web of influence and range of conversation that
takes place in poetry. At the same time these distinctions and divisions tend
to polarize and displace. They pigeonhole. I don't identify with any particular
school or movement. I've read widely and picked up strategies and gestures from
lots of different poets.

It is in fact this relationship to language that I feel is the primary engine in
my work. I have a brain trained in Spanish then subsumed by English. When I
read Latinate words in English, I hear the echo of my mother tongue.

In graduate school, I gave a reading, and one of my fellow students told
me my work sounded like it was translation; that observation still resonates for
me because I feel I have the luxury of bridging two languages into a peculiar
argot. Through my friend's lens I extended the notion of translation to include
alternative modes of mediating experience. I have nothing to report that's
peculiar to the way my life went. Bilingualism gives me access to two different
names for objects, two signifiers; I'm also able to access provocative and curious
etymologies. For example, the word *cataratas* means waterfall in Spanish while
cataract, its cognate in English, refers to the clouded eye: I'm alerted to a strange

confluence of seeing and veils of water. In this way I see Latino poets speaking a beautiful polyglot language that most clearly resembles the Babel we've created in this country.

I think that refusing to engage in the traditional manner of telling stories is one way to reconsider how cultural identity becomes manifest in poetry, and a way for unheard stories to be told. But I think that's only one part of a larger mobilization that should be part of redefining how Latino/as participate in the larger conversation about art. I might argue that a move away from traditional narrative identity poetry is a good important step in bringing writers of color into the light of broader neutral consideration. I think it's problematic to define identity qua identity through the narrow scope of telling an "us" as writing. I have thought more about how to speak as a feminist and mother, and these are the identities that I meld into the visceral native idioms of my "identity." This identity is multilingual and millions of years old and rooted in stringent definitions of biology. The power hierarchies that dictate female experience and the experience of the mother are comparable to the imperialist or orientalist systems that attempt, through signs, to define me as a person of color, and these overlaps are the source of my interrogation.

In this regard, I might point to a poet of patria, Cesar Vallejo, who, like the French symbolist Mallarme, stretched the limits of his mother tongue to accommodate a more accurate map of his experience as it was informed by his landscape and by the economic forces that came to shape his rural upbringing. Because of the density of both of these poets' work, they are often cast aside as obtuse, but in my mind, their desire to get at reality through the language itself, through the material that comes to define all of us, is the most realist(ic) work we might see in poetry.

So really, original notions of identity poetry (and for that matter, more generally, poems invested in a devotion to a so-called realism) limit experience to reinforcing notions of being as general truth, and it's really a fakery, a performance, because we now live in a very self-reflexive culture. We are well-versed in cultural parody. We're post being surprised by stratification. Even the most lyric of us can acknowledge the instability of the unified *I*. This is, in part, because of historical and social trends that have literally changed the face of America and, more specifically, art.

I see the myriad approaches, which emerge from an infinite number of particular narratives, that the poets of my generation take on to explore questions around class and identity. Rather than embrace a unified cultural experience of the Other, poets like Rosa Alcala, Sandy Florian, Roberto Harrison, Monica de la Torre, Peter Ramos, and Rodrigo Toscano go to the source texts of these definitions and upend them, reveal them. The lyric gaze is crucial to these postures, but they are not the sole point of entry. Instead of a merely humanist appraisal, their critiques are material and glossy with the vernacular of the equequo/a. Assuming the capricious symbolism of postcapitalist abundance, these poets revel in the shifting values of objects, of words. These poetries are dense with the sign systems that inform our cultural and social ascents and descents. What could be more accurate, more resonant than poetry that emerges from legitimate investigation of the cultural forces that come to inform how we are seen and made?

The equequo gets pinned with the desires of its owner. His currency is only validated if he was given as a gift. In my case, my mother bought it for me at the market because she reveled in the irony that the desires this figurine represented were fulfilled in her new, her second, homeland, and because she was amused at my interest in this self-parodying relic. Ultimately, to me, the equequo comes to mean the object that most closely resembles the systems I struggle through to find the sum total of my identity. Both of us are travelers weighed down with, but eager to possess, abundance.

18

My Emily Gore
Freudian Obsessions, Biculturalism, and Autobiographical Poetry
PETER RAMOS

As those with similar experiences and backgrounds can tell you, growing up biculturally has its disadvantages. There are many, but to sum up the biggest one as simply as possible: it's confusing. Sometimes painfully so. My case is not so different from that of others. My father was born and raised in Venezuela. In 1963 he moved to the United States where he married my mother, a white Anglo-Saxon Protestant "Navy brat" who grew up in Virginia, Paris, and Los Angeles. My father, who has some Lebanese ancestry, also lived in Beirut for a few years, where he learned Arabic and French, the latter the language my mother and father spoke in the house when they didn't want my brother and me to understand them (this backfired eventually). Having experienced the pain and humiliation associated with being a foreigner twice (in Lebanon and here), my father—despite his thick immigrant's accent—neither spoke to us in, nor taught us any, Spanish. And so my brother and I had to learn what we could of it in school and from our Venezuelan cousins.

Eventually I realized there were advantages to such an upbringing. For one thing, it's a nurturing environment for someone who eventually wants to be a writer. Raymond Williams, discussing Modernism and language, makes the point that in the case of an immigrant (and his/her household) who comes from a colonized region to a new metropolis or country, his/her attempts to assimilate the family into the new country's customs and culture begin to undermine and dissolve the immigrant's native tongue: the old language becomes secondary or subordinate to the new one. But this process also allows for—and, in fact, actively produces—strange multilingual combinations in the household, with family members speaking to one another in different languages as well as individuals using different languages in the same sentence. This linguistic, cultural interface or confrontation tends to illuminate the extent to which language itself is a material, to be manipulated in new and often strange ways. Williams reminds us that many famous writers, especially those from the Modern era, came from such a home environment, the kind that produced "an Apollinaire, a Joyce, an Ionesco, [and] a Beckett."[1] We could add to this list Jack Kerouac, William Carlos Williams, and Charles Simic, not to mention Roberto Tejada, Blas Falconer, Gina Franco, Rosa Alcalá and hundreds of other Latino/a writers practicing today.

I take Williams's claim to include at least two other important points regarding this relationship between a (subordinated) immigrant tongue and the new language. The first is that the immigrant tongue, however diluted or marginalized in the new environment, nonetheless bleeds through in ways that call attention to the very pliable nature of language itself. In my adolescence, for example, whenever my father wanted me to feel special guilt for my poor academic performance, he would say, "Your mother and I pay a lot of money for you to go to this school. But a lot!" In Spanish, the conjunction would make sense—a way of emphasizing the first part of the statement. In English, it sounds funny. Such syntactically strange sayings were a source of shame for us, growing up. And yet, they personalize my father; the older I get, the more endearing his awkward language constructions and translations seem.

The second quality produced by this kind of linguistic/cultural confrontation seems more related to the US-born children of immigrants: a keen awareness of the dominant language and culture they have been born into and yet feel somehow partially (and, to them, shamefully) barred from. Julio Marzan describes this phenomenon as it applied to the poet William Carlos Williams, whose mother was Puerto Rican. According to Marzan, Williams chose to be called "Bill" at a young age (and for the rest of his life) as a means of gaining acceptance from his surroundings—those outside of his childhood home, that is—and to avoid being considered "foreign" by the community; it was a kind of persona he took on, a way of being reborn as an Anglo-American. "As that persona," Marzan argues, "the new ego becomes a spokesperson of mainstream values and, of course, its prejudices."[2] In fact, considering that such large numbers of the US population either come from immigrants or are themselves immigrants, Williams's case seems perfectly common. And however ambivalent immigrants or their family members feel about the process of assimilating into US culture—however much guilt, shame, or resentment is involved—the fact remains: assimilation is such a common process, so widely shared by so many US citizens throughout history, it has itself become part of our culture. It's no wonder so many works of American literature—*Goodbye, Columbus*, *The House on Mango Street*, *How the Garcia Girls Lost Their Accent*, to name just a few—have this very process as their central theme. At the level of language, however, the linguistic confrontations that make up the assimilation process engender in immigrants and their children new ways of articulating the American experience.

I certainly wouldn't compare my own poetry to William Carlos Williams's, but by way of addressing some of these issues, I thought I'd focus on the process through which I wrote one of my poems. Here is the poem in its entirety:

The Put-Together Wedding Cake
They've gone to a cocktail party,
gone to Hawaii for pot roast.
Find it on the coffee table, the cake

that is, that is real but glowing
in a living room milder than Heaven.
You've never seen a cake like this—

blue bamboo on icing smooth as wallpaper.
But you must join the pinker

to the darker figurine, plastic hand
in plastic hand. How will you speak for them?
The groom is learning the language, dull-eyed
for remembering what they said: "American the gold
and golden fleece!" The bride thinks of daffodils
which turn into kitchen gloves.

Hers is not gold but white
as an icebox.

I choose this particular poem because it takes up many of the same issues and obsessions that appear in other poems of mine—namely those associated with identity, culture, and language, with what Marzan, referring to William Carlos Williams, would call "poetic sublimations of identity concerns."[3] But I also choose it because the poem is old. I began writing it fifteen years ago, at a crucial point in my life. From here I can clearly see what I was doing when I wrote it, and why; I can connect the language and issues in the poem to my life at that time. But it strikes me that the poem, if it works at all, works in part because I wasn't at all sure at the time what it was about when I began writing it. This is a valuable way to begin a poem, I believe, especially when writing "about" one's life.

In college I used to hear two views about creative writing: (1) write about what you know and (2) write about what you don't know. Apparently, Grace Paley famously said, "Write what you know about what you don't know." But I would reverse this model: "write what you don't know about what you know," or, even, "write toward what you don't know about what you know." The self, then, or one's past, is as good a ground as any for this particular kind of writing method. If the subject toward which you write is mysterious (as it should be) or partly unknown, then the right words, even if they don't seem to be logically connected, will eventually resolve themselves into a pattern, a clear picture. Or, as Allen Ginsberg said, "If the poet's mind is shapely, his art will be shapely."[4] This is to write "inside-out"—as I recently heard it put. Or, as my colleague Ann Colley said, of writing in general: follow your obsessions.

When I entered college, there was quite a precedent for writing poems about one's personal experience, for dredging up one's familial trauma in order to make art of it. Back then, the confessional and deep image poets were still considered relatively contemporary. I was an undergraduate at Goucher College, the place where just thirteen years earlier the poet Anne Sexton performed her final reading on October 3, 1974, the day before she committed suicide. More than Sylvia Plath or Robert Lowell, she seems to embody the aesthetic and cultural qualities of that particular era, many of which were still lingering in the academy when I entered as a freshman. Recently I heard a recording of that reading, Sexton's last: the way she swirled the ice in her glass, the boozy, mild slur in her banter between poems, even the flick of her butane lighter, like a pistol's dry click—these all seemed familiar to me, and I was transported back to my undergraduate years, when literature and philosophy professors still seemed to speak and act as if they were permanently cast in Edward Albee's *Who's Afraid of Virginia Woolf?*

It was a different time. There was still a lingering belief in and subscription to mid-century modernist terms and practices like psychoanalysis, inner-child, the unconscious, as well as a sense that art and poetry were essentially related to such terms and performed the same kinds of work: i.e., psychic healing, recovery of the authentic "self," and a healthy distrust of the overly rational self, all of which seems, from this side of the century, somewhat naïve and ideologically romantic. Language poetry, the darling of poststructuralism and deconstruction, was still not quite institutionalized. And the poetry of identity—at least of Latino/a identity—had not yet fully entered into the public or academic spotlight. Aside from William Carlos Williams, whose Puerto Rican identity was all but invisible at that time, no Latino/a poet was offered in the curriculum. The poets I was reading then—Plath, Sexton, Lowell—although they did write about immediate and distant family members, tended to focus on their eccentric, often blue-blooded New England kin. That such figures were white went without comment or question; race and ethnicity, in their cases, were entirely moot since even the idea of "whiteness" had not yet become a popular critical study.[5] Because my mother's grandmother (whom we called "Nana") was the closest person in my family to fit such a description, it seems no coincidence I wrote so many poems about her, as well as her daughter, my grandmother, Emily Fenn Gore, both born and raised in New England. Sexton herself had and wrote about her own "Nana," her great-aunt, Anna Ladd Dingley, about whom she wrote the poem "Some Foreign Letters." Similarly, Plath wrote about her maternal grandmother in her poem "Point Shirley." In each case the poem's speaker addresses a strong but deceased New England matriarch, and so the connection was all the more appealing to me. I saw my own maternal great-grandmother as playing the same role, occupying a space of legitimate Anglo-American authority, a precedent set by poets such as those I had been reading.

By the time I graduated from college, Freud and Jung had been thrown out of the academy (the former to be returned by Lacan shortly); Derrida was firmly set in the curriculum, and most deep image and confessional poets were quickly fading from sight. But from such poets I learned ways of addressing one's childhood experience and especially trauma through poetry. I understood, from Plath's poems, that the self could be transformed or mythologized and abstracted into something greater than one's personality, or, from Robert Lowell's *Life Studies and For the Union Dead*, that one's persona could be flattened through language into pure surface material—could be made absurd, funny, horrifying, or tragic—could be all these at once. The late Joe Strummer once said, referring to the process of song writing, "no input—no output," and this is true for me, at least for poetry. One must have poets to converse with, and for better or worse, these were my first and probably, therefore, the most influential.

I began the poem "The Put-Together Wedding Cake" in my second year of my MFA, though it did not have its title until later and in fact wasn't complete (if we can say a poem is ever complete) until three years later. Two things should be noted: I was reading lots of T. S. Eliot, Ezra Pound, and William Carlos Williams at the time I began the poem. I'm sure I wouldn't have come to these words without them. And also, my mother and father were about to separate. That I grew up speaking English and associating my native tongue, homeland, and culture with my mother and her family; that I privileged all of these over my father's; that she read to me when I was a child; that language and poetry have always been for me feminine and Northern, compelling but cold, always somehow distant from myself; that all these elements seem related to the poem now (to me at least, and especially from this distance) does not mean they were apparent to me when I wrote it. At the time I was living in Baltimore City, in a rundown apartment, away from my parents, and had gone out in early November to the Charles Theater to see a 1959 black-and-white movie by John Cassavetes called *Shadows,* his first. I was pretty affected by it, and when I got back to my apartment I immediately wrote the following:

> coffee tin pan kettle pot saucer spoon foil wrap plates broiler oven
> stove appliance glass decanter icing wedding cake champagne glass bubbly
> coconut cake frothy gowns girdle latex bra pointed pale pink bosoms
> of the 1950s blue Hawaii blue green sequins

Later in the journal I wrote the following:

> my brother and I break into our grandparents' home, our mother's side
> shouting hysterically in Spanish
> banging dishes in the chrome kitchen, milk white
> our grandmother hated to clean and cook in, breaking glasses
> letting the Chinese prints out of their glass frames
> hurling tea cups we sniff out
> the bedroom, rummage through grandmother's closet
> lifting girdles pink silk foam and latex
> touch her frothy nightgowns grab a fistful of pink dresses
> finger every last sequin

Attracted to and yet somehow essentially alienated from a 1950s Americana (the culture and time I always associated with my mother and her matriarchal line), I felt directly, almost subconsciously, related to it as well. The poet Allen Grossman once said to me, "Write with that part of your mind that doesn't get along." In many ways, I see my strongest poems as language oriented but driven as well by some obsession—the mind wrestling with something, with itself. In the poem as it is now, the speaker's obsessions with such versions of US culture and Americana are transferred to the speaker's father: he seems to blindly, unconsciously strive for the aesthetic and material gain associated with marrying this woman, a US native ("the gold and golden fleece"). But this transference is actually obscuring the extent to which I was trying to gain and use a poetics most closely associated with "authentic" whiteness—privileged poetic speech complete with a description of one's New England pedigree. That I probably felt some guilt and shame in trying to sound like a New England confessional poet, that I was trying to thereby distance myself from my father, his ethnicity, his "awkward" American English—all these probably have some-thing to do with the unconscious aesthetic decision to displace my feelings for my mother's side of the family, with all that it represented, onto the speaker's father's character in the poem.

But these obsessions (pathologies?)—not only the ideas, but the words themselves—move me. That is, the right words, whatever they are, seem to draw me forward, as if I'm not writing the poem so much as being pulled along by it, by something greater than myself. This is probably what the Greeks had in mind with the muses, that wild, strange, and familiar feeling of being inspired by the words themselves.

You'll notice that "I" doesn't appear in the poem above. The poem's action takes place before my birth. It's written in the second person, a list of commands. Who is the speaker talking to? The speaker, in my view, seems to address him or herself, the process in this way mirroring the act of looking back to the inception of the self in order to understand the self. I'm not in this poem, and yet I feel it is in many ways my most autobiographical.

There are all the qualities I mentioned: attraction to yet distance from and resentment toward a mother whose culture is idealized and essentially unavail-able to the speaker—and to the speaker's father as well, reiterating the speaker's own divisions. Though to the poem's credit (if I may), the speaker seems to understand the debilitating conditions of the time and place that act upon this bride—a woman in the culture of the 1950s and '60s—"she thinks of daffodils / which turn into kitchen gloves." In this poem, as in many of my poems, a speaker addresses a time and culture whose effects haunt him or her in the pres-ent, even though that time and culture were there before his or her birth. Clearly I was influenced by the kind of confessional and modernist poets I had been reading since college. But by the time I was composing this poem, I was aware of particular identity concerns that do not generally come up in that kind of poetry. In other words, I tried to take what I could, technically, from the poets of that particular era, even though they did not necessarily take up the same kinds of social/cultural issues I faced.

For the record, I don't really believe in an essentialized Latino/a poetry. That is, I do believe in such a thing as Latino/a poetry, but I don't think its content can or should be circumscribed. "We" are necessarily an impure people, full of ethnic and cultural mixtures, and as such, we should not be limited in our choices—for subject matter or influence—when we write. One way then to make poetry out of our rich, occasionally confusing heterogeneous backgrounds is to be open to all the artistic influences that are available, regardless of where they come from, and to explore those parts of the self that are not quite clear, yet insist somehow. I think of Keats's Negative Capability, a welcoming of the mysterious, or Frost's poem called "The Census Taker" in which the speaker puts his ear to a door in order to hear words he can't quite make out. I still believe there is merit in dedicating part of the artistic process to opening yourself up to the ghosts of your past—cultural, aesthetic, linguistic—those amorphous shadows that linger but haven't (yet) taken clear shape.

Notes

1. Raymond Williams, *Politics of Modernism: Against the New Conformists* (London: Verso, 1989), 78.
2. Julio Marzan, *The Spanish American Roots of William Carlos Williams* (Austin: U of Texas P, 1994), 65.
3. Ibid., 31.
4. Lazlo Géfin. "Ellipsis: The Ideograms of Ginsberg," in *Under Discussion: On the Poetry of Allen Ginsberg*, ed. Lewis Hyde (Ann Arbor: U of Michigan P, 1984), 280.
5. Of the poets mentioned here, only Lowell came from "blue blood," though both Plath and Sexton came from and wrote about New England. And although Plath herself was a first-generation US citizen, she would not have been considered ethnically other-than-white, either then or now. Both poets, furthermore, wrote about relatives who had lived in New England for at least a generation.

19

Fringe Poetics
Gabe Gomez

El Paso, Texas, 1985. The yearly rodeo in El Paso happened in February, a temperate month draped before the searing days of spring and summer, setting the tone for the rest of a predictably uneventful year. Save for the Harlem Globetrotter's yearly pilgrimage, the occasional Pink Floyd Laser Light show or World Famous Lipizzaner Stallions, the first two months of the year in El Paso were the illusionary shtick of a one-trick pony act. To say that El Paso was a quiet town in 1985 is an exercise in redundancy, so it should be no surprise that a rodeo in West Texas was cause for a reasonable amount of pandemonium.

El Paso is a quintessential border town. Attached are its ancillary markings of bicultural character that blanket the idioms, street names, and sensibilities of its population. Its attractiveness remains in the abstract for many native El Pasoans, like myself, who have left, yet reconstruct the memories of this startling collage and confluence of cultures, endlessly trying to accurately capture its madness and beauty within its own city limits, rather than the confluent sums of America and Mexico. In this, the rodeo was a repackaged version of our city and a reminder of our tethers to frontier myths and the ethos of the feral west.

No one was immune to the rodeo's presence. Tickets were sold at 7-Eleven stores, and billboards with an image of a bucking bull and cowboy peppered the streets like a radicalized science fiction, splayed with the kind of biblical struggle only animals can symbolize. It even found its way into elementary school curriculums. It probably didn't help that I attended Lyndon Baines Johnson Elementary School, where our mascot was a maverick embodied in the form of a steer wearing a cowboy hat. So in February 1985, LBJ Elementary held a school-wide art contest. Students who drew the best rodeo scene would win a family pack of rodeo tickets. Blame it on the wonder of youth or an unconscious avengement of cultural hunger, but the thought of scoring free rodeo tickets kicked everyone into a lather. One week later, the winners from each grade were posted in the main entrance hall of the school. . . . I didn't win. My friend Craig and I stood before the winning pictures in disillusionment until we realized a common feature found in all of the winning pictures: rainbow. Be it bucking broncos, steer wrestling, or barrel racing, all of the pictures had, to some extent, a rainbow crowning the scene. Craig ran back to his classroom, applied a three-tiered rainbow to his splotchy amoeba-like image of a snarling bull, and resubmitted his picture for the contest. His picture was up in the main hall by the end of the day.

No amount of hyperbole could adequately hype the fact that this rather uneventful moment would serve as the foundation for my life as a writer. I have spent years staring at those pictures in my memory, mystified by their uniformity and the complacency behind them. Although there are other moments woven throughout my formal literature and creative writing studies that have tempered my ideas about poetry and art, the core of my interest in poetry and experimentation begin with the same sense of unyielding wonder and skepticism I had as a child.

For years I have focused my interests on poetry and art that embodies a restless and searching spirit, work that manifests or evolves from established traditions and motivates further inquiry. Admittedly, it has taken years for my interest in the avant-garde to turn inward and outward to the community of Latino/a writers, where there is no lack of adventurous material. From Harry Gamboa Jr. to Roberto Tejada, a rich history of experimental Latino/a writing exists. My own poetry has led my curiosity to seek out other poets who transcend classifications and capture the fathomless breadth of Latino/a identity.

> **Schoolmate**: So what are you man?
> **Me**: What am I . . . ?
> **Schoolmate**: Yeah, so you Mexican or what?
> **Me**: Yeah, I guess . . .
> **Schoolmate**: So where you born?
> **Me**: Here.
> **Schoolmate**: In El Paso?
> **Me**: Yeah.
> **Schoolmate**: And your parents?
> **Me**: Chihuahua.
> **Schoolmate**: Oh, so you're a Chicano . . .
> **Me**: Yeah, sure, okay . . .

This conversation was replayed verbatim to my mother when I was a kid. She began to speak before I was done. "No, no . . . tu eres Mexicano!" she roared above me. This was my first introduction to the politics of identity as a child. Having grown up in the tiny farming village of Carrizal, Chihuahua, my mother had undoubtedly rehearsed and executed this reply before her new school teachers in the United States or boss at the Newberry Department Store after we moved to El Paso permanently. It was clearly something offensive and perhaps hurtful to her; it was something that she had obviously contended with throughout her life, the nerve still raw from countless confrontations where she felt her own history exposed to stark objectivity with a new set of ideals thrust upon her.

To complicate things even further, we spoke only Spanish in our home. It wasn't a dialect-laden regional Spanish either, but a clean textbook affair that would earn us scowls and corrections at its spontaneous deconstruction. To this day, I have never held an English-speaking conversation with my father. I would sometimes stand in wonder at my parents when they would season their eloquent Spanish with English interjections around certain friends. It was like site-specific art, where the conditions of their surroundings affected the performance of their speech. Still, words like nationalism, immigration, and civil rights had not entered into any of our conversations at home. I suspect it's because we lived in the full immersion of those words and their meanings rather than the abstract ideology realized by distance and time. El Paso was the embodied rather than the romanticized—rare were those moments, in my youth, of self-reflection and pause about our place in the universe as Mexicans.

My siblings and I spent the majority of our childhoods among the places where my parents had grown up. We would spend weekends, summers, and holidays in Chihuahua. Having lived in Juarez, Mexico, until the age of three, I had grown up with two very distinct identities. There was the US version of me, born and educated in Texas, and the Mexican version of me, living in a rural farming town without phones or television. In spite of the fact that much of the work in my first book is centered on this little town, a benefit of these experiences was that, as a child, I never developed an unreasonable idealism about my Mexican roots. There is not a sense of longing or distance between these experiences and my poems. My first cigarette, kiss, and fight happened within those streets and pastures, and every one of those moments remains the clearest among any other memories.

There was no hard separation between my two lives. I completely understood the meaning of "el otro lado" and easily navigated through both worlds, but the idea that I became something "else" when we crossed the border didn't enter my thinking about my home, family, or what would become the content for my poetry. To be sure, becoming someone "else" had been a different experience for my parents, and was nothing like the luxury of reaching the US bridge in a car and saying "American" to the Customs Agent. In a way, my parents sheltered us from questioning our lives in America too deeply. It was simply never discussed beyond the facts about their former lives. There was never any voluntary information, only the wrenching of details prompted, usually, by old photographs. I was thirty-five years old when I discovered that my father was a bracero in California. He picked grapes as a migrant worker in his early twenties, before he learned how to use an arc welder. Countless other stories bobbing on the surface are still waiting to be heard.

Still, the two environments and dual landscapes provided complete freedom for me to simply explore creatively and listen to the world that was exposed through two languages (and countless dialects), food, and music. It is precisely this freedom and a love for language that began to produce poems. The ribbons of words, cadence, and music were the original impetus for my writing to begin. The contrast of both environments created an enormous canvas of ideas that could be extracted and built upon. There were no restrictions, forms, or styles, only decisions about time and place. It made sense to include multiple perspectives in the things that I wrote, but counterintuitive to shape them linearly. So rather than writing "traditional" poems—even though I didn't know them as poems—I strung together small "correspondences" or fragments, each sentence, word, or stanza derived from the preceding fragment, yet independent of each other. These disjointed writings made more sense of the experiences. I began to see my subject, and indeed the world around me, as one would view a sculpture, by examining it from every angle—its characteristics changing with light and time. Naturally, the materials and methods to express these perspectives had to change too if I sought to truly capture my subjects. This was a task beyond my abilities, so once I found out that creative writing was actually an academic discipline, all of my attention and energy fell to poetry.

According to the 2000 US Census, there are over 550,000 people who live in El Paso, and roughly 75 percent of the population is identified as "Hispanic" or "Latino." With such statistics, the correct assumption would be that Latino culture is thoroughly evident and celebrated throughout the city. So it's rather surprising that, in high school, the only tome of required reading from a Latino/a author was—at least in my case—*Bless Me, Ultima* by Rudolfo Anaya. I'm hopeful that the decision-makers at the El Paso Independent School District have improved these odds by now. Anaya's book admittedly turned me off from Latino writing for years. To this day, I labor through its pages. For better or worse, the book became a template in my mind for all Latino/a literature, and it wasn't alone. Films, visual art, commercials, and after-school specials were marked by the same characters, forced accents, and hyperbolic dilemmas. This wasn't my parents' feigned Spanglish. These characterizations were choreographed, forced, and sadly laughable. As much as I would like to list other Latino/a writers as influences on my poetry when I was a teenager, there simply weren't any that were central to my life. It was Wallace Stevens who seized my attention completely. As an overweight, bilingual sixteen-year-old who listened endlessly to Joy Division and rambled incoherently into sketchbooks, these lines,

> I do not know which to prefer,
> The beauty of inflections
> Or the beauty of innuendoes,
> The blackbird whistling
> Or just after

from Stevens's "Thirteen Ways of Looking at a Blackbird," pierced through me like lightning. It wasn't until a lit course in college that I was exposed to a full dose of Latino writing. Unfortunately, my distaste only escalated from there. I found the majority of Latino/a writing predictable, overtly sentimental, awash with static scenarios and vapid interior/exterior struggles of identity; I too resented the bravado of cultural nationalism, but mostly rejected its general failure to capture the brilliance and complexities of a vast and panoramic community.

But then there was Cherríe. . . .

Cherríe Moraga was teaching playwriting at Saint Mary's College of California when I arrived there for graduate school in 1998. The playwriting department faculty had a series of readings from their works in progress, and one evening Moraga read a draft of what would eventually become *Who Killed Yolanda Saldivar?* The play is a fictionalized account of the woman convicted for the murder of singer Selena Quintanilla Pérez. It was an epiphanic experience, and one that would vastly change my perceptions of contemporary Latino/a literature. Moraga's writing would come to represent a personal and creative transition in my poetry and unconditionally qualified her as my first influence from the Latino/a writers' community. From the same batch of ingredients as other Latino/a writers, Moraga dove deeply and unapologetically into the nuances of Latino/a culture and exposed its sinew and nerves to the sunlight, unlike anything I had read. Most importantly her work followed form but was unencumbered by its parameters. Her reading, a poetry workshop taught by Lyn Hejinian, and assorted discoveries from Jack Spicer and Robert Duncan set the foundation for my current interest in experimental poetics.

Years later, it was Moraga and Hejinian's work that I gravitated to when I wrote my poem "The Outer Bands." There was simply no other way that I could capture the disparity my wife and I experienced after Hurricane Katrina through traditional poetry. The serial poem compiled from fragments of conversation, media blurbs, speeches, and so on, was the first time my background and history met with my ideas about form. After years of failed attempts, the poem I had always wanted to write finally materialized. Not long after Katrina, I was given a copy of *Pity the Drowned Horses* by Sheryl Luna, a poet born and raised in El Paso. In her poems, I have found the voice of El Paso that I've waited for my entire life.

Defining the avant-garde is like trying to decipher the meaning of life from a fortune cookie. Still, it is a task worth the frustration, and one recently undertaken by Chon Noriega, Director of the UCLA Chicano Studies Research Center, in his introduction to *Urban Exile: Collected Writing of Harry Gamboa Jr.* When referencing Gamboa's work with his groundbreaking art group Asco, Noriega writes:

> What does the avant-garde look and sound like when it blooms outside of the hothouse of the bourgeoisie? What does social protest against racism look and sound like when articulated outside a realist code? For a Chicano working class avant-grade group raised in the barrio, assimilated to American mass culture, and making discourse the object of its social protest, the answer is simple: it looks like both and neither; and it sounds the same, but different.

Noriega suggests that Gamboa's methods are perhaps less representative than his Latino contemporaries, but are ultimately of equal grounding. He suggests that Gamboa's career, which began in the form of "blowouts"—demonstrations against racist policies at his high school that evolved into writing, performance, installation, and site-specific work—runs parallel and is ultimately tethered to race and class and immersed within a larger media construct of Latino experience in America. But what it also infers is a tenuous relationship between subject and form. Gamboa's art, made from similar angst, injustice, and forced assimilation, is the source for many of our own stories, poems, and performances—but his, as Noriega suggests, was recontextualized and presented simultaneously with his need to search for new methods of expression.

Experimental art is a fringe activity, an alternative act shadowing its larger counterpart. In spite of our cultural ubiquity, there still remains the uniformity of our exterior perceptions, that we are all one community rather than a spidering network. To be sure, Latino/a literature would not be as varied if it did not inherently contain a sense of innovation, but it is those writers who push and seek to reinvent that will ultimately reclaim the understanding of the Latino/a experience in America, rainbows and all.

20

La Página Roja
Lucha Corpi

I was born in Jáltipan, a small tropical town in Veracruz. I started the first grade at age four. At age six, I could read well enough. My father asked that I read the daily news to him to keep my skills up. At the time, the regional newspaper had a separate crime page—la página roja. It was a loose page so parents could easily remove it to keep children from reading it. My father let me select readings from any page, except of course la página roja. He dutifully removed it, folded it and put it in his shirt pocket to dispose of later. Since there was no threat of punishment, I was not deterred from finding and reading the red page at every opportunity. The red page covered crime from accidents to murders, brawls in the zona roja (red light zone), white slavery, and gambling. Although I didn't know exactly what prostitution and gambling were all about, I surmised they were serious social and moral offenses but not necessarily illegal. The sale of minors or adult women to houses of ill-repute and the use of a human being as a wager, however, were felonies as grave as homicide.

Both my grandfathers gambled away their property in card games. Not surprisingly, we were all lectured on the evils of gaming. Ironically, every week, my father played the national lottery. The nuances in criminal law and my father's own behavior eluded my grasp then. But I suspected that prostitution and gambling were among "the sins of the flesh" the town priest cautioned everyone against, pointing his index finger to the sky. "But you must ward off the sins of the mind for they are indeed more insidious than the sins of the flesh," he admonished.

"More than anyone, he surely knows the flesh is weak," my grandmother used to tell my aunt. To me, she would say, "Don't let any man, including the priest, get to that little turtle between your legs." But I was more concerned with my sins. I was not only disobeying my father by reading the red page, I was also committing an insidious sin of the mind. I would say a few Hail Marys just in case and make a mental note to ask the priest about the meaning of it all on my first confession, in a year. Waiting for clarification, I continued enjoying the red page but began to tire of reading about brawls, brothels, knifings, shootings, and accidents, in all their gory but repetitive details.

Instead, I became intrigued by crimes that involved duplicity and premeditation—"intelligence." One became my favorite, the case of Ema, the wife of Luis, an abusive, lecherous man. Desperate, Ema attempted to poison Luis by mixing in his huevos rancheros a large amount of a highly toxic powder made of ground cashew nut shells. Ema was an amateur murderer and left a trail of clues for the gendarmes investigating the case. Evidence piled against her.

1. Cleaning the wood stove, her maid found several shell pieces
   mixed in the ashes. She found this unusual. Her mistress
   Ema had often expressed her dislike for the fruit and
   the nut of the cashew. Town folks knew the shell of the
   cashew nut was highly toxic.
2. Although Ema asked the maid to make breakfast for her husband, she herself prepared the sauce. The maid noticed it
   was unusually thick and lighter in color.
3. Ema sent the maid on an errand but remained at home while
   her husband had breakfast, perhaps to make sure he died,
   "or out of a perverse, morbid desire to see her husband
   squirm in agony," the newspaper reporter speculated.

The following night, all the women in my family sat in the breezeway, as it was their custom to do after supper. The men were at the square talking, singing, or playing games. "Lesson one," my grandmother warned. "Be far away from him when he ingests the poison. And for God's sake, resist the sweet desire to watch him squirm!"

"Ema just didn't know how to do it right," my aunt remarked. "She should have put the deadliest of coral snakes in his underwear drawer. He reaches for his calzones and ZAS, he's history. After all, those snakes wander into houses and their poison is quick and lethal."

"Maybe she wanted to be caught," an older female cousin suggested. "Or maybe she just reached her limit and was desperate enough," another cousin said.

"No," my aunt rebutted. "She knew what she was doing. The sad part is that Luis didn't die, but the poison left him insane."

"Huh! The poison didn't make him go crazy. Terror did. A warning to abusive and lecherous husbands," my grandmother said loudly. I later learned she intended her comment for her son-in-law, resting in the next room and sus- pected of having a mistress.

"I just don't believe that he's truly insane," my mother stated. The women agreed.

I never heard my father comment on the case, but I didn't dare ask for his opinion about this or any other murder, lest I confess reading la página roja.

Whether the almost-murdered man was mad or not, there was no trial. The judge simply sentenced Ema to take care of her invalid husband for life. The whole town became her prison, town folks her guards watching her every move. Ema would never be able to make another attempt on her husband's life, never be free of him. No one was surprised when this unrepentant wife hanged herself from a beam in her living room. About a year later, my grandmother showed my mother a social note in the paper. Ema's insane husband had made a miraculous recovery and was about to marry a wealthy widow in a neighboring port city. Weeks after Luis married the rich widow, in an article in la página roja I read that Luis had been arrested for beating a prostitute to death for no apparent reason.

After supper that evening, my mother joined my grandmother in the breezeway. My grandmother sat in her favorite chair, and I on her lap. No one seemed very eager to talk. Then unexpectedly my mother said, "He'll probably get off, free. No scandal. Not a day in jail. Widow Lara will see to it. Money talks."

"And Ema hanged herself! Tell me, who's the real criminal?" My grandmother said and added, "There is no justice in this world."

As I rested my head on my grandmother's chest, all I could hear was her heart pounding against flesh and bone.

Since the publication of Edgar Allan Poe's *The Purloined Letter*, the detective story has changed little. It is a plot-driven long or short story, leaving room for little more than the solution of the crime. The challenge—the precise art—for any crime writer is in finding ways to offer much more than just the unraveling of the plot, bringing to justice those who have broken the law, and restoring, finally, the social order.

Chicana/Chicano crime fiction may follow some, many, or all of the conventions, traditions, and structural demands of the genre. But it breaks away from them in the treatment of Chicana/Chicano themes and the development of characters steeped and deeply rooted in the culture. Thematically, our crime novels fit perfectly within the confines of Chicana/Chicano literature, exploring themes such as:

1. Spirituality, religion, and the struggle between good and evil.
2. The re-interpretation of legend and myth.
3. The search for justice and socioeconomic equality, human and civil rights.
4. The history of the Mexican people in Mexico and in the United States.
5. The cultural and linguistic wealth in the various and distinctive Chicano communities in the Southwest.
6. The border and La Migra.
7. Sexism, homophobia and racism, and other gender and gender-preference issues within the culture and in the larger context of a multicultural United States.

Chicana/Chicano detective fiction offers in some cases the best vehicle to explore many of these subjects in a direct, although sometimes shocking, manner. It reflects the reality of ordinary people, like us, who find themselves in the midst of strife, violence, and injustice, to which they have perhaps become oblivious, or that they feel powerless to change. Guided by the detective's moral-ethical compass, crime fiction offers a way to engage emotionally and work through those moral-ethical dilemmas. In the process, our perception of the world about us changes, and the possibility of obtaining justice for ourselves, as for others, becomes a more tenable objective.

Some well-known Latin American male writers have penned at least one mystery novel, perhaps intrigued by the possibilities of sociopolitical commentary offered by the genre, or perhaps for the simple reason that crafting a detective novel or a thriller is good discipline for any writer. But the fact is that in Latin American as in Spanish literature the noir novel has been until recently the exception—an oddity.

In Mexico, for decades before Paco Ignacio Taibo II began to gain recognition for his very popular detective fiction series and made the writing of crime fiction legitimate, Luis Spota had the dubious honor of being the only Mexican crime fiction writer. In Cuba as in Spain the number of crime fiction writers has quadrupled in the last decade. But for the most part, the writers of crime fiction in these countries are men.

In 1985, Rolando Hinojosa's *Partners in Crime* was published as part of Hinojosa's series, *Klail City Death Trips*. Rafe Buenrostro, a policeman, became the second Chicano detective in Chicano and US mainstream crime fiction. A year later, *The Little Death* by Michael Nava was issued and we met Henry Rios, a gay attorney. These two remarkable novels, however, marked the beginning of a new cycle in Chicano/Chicana narrative—crime fiction, but more specifically the police procedural or private detective novel. Hinojosa's second police procedural, *Ask a Policeman*, was published fifteen years later because, for him, crime fiction is only a thread in the fabric of his larger literary work on Belken County. Conversely, Nava published eight Henry Rios detective novels until he decided to retire Rios a few years ago.

Other Chicano/Chicana authors followed after Hinojosa and Nava. In 1992, Rudolfo Anaya introduced Sonny Baca, a professional PI, in his novel *Albuquerque*. Baca is the protagonist in four detective novels by Anaya, one for each of the seasons. Also in 1992, Arte Público Press issued my first detective novel, *Eulogy for a Brown Angel*, and Gloria Damasco, presumably the first Chicana detective in US literature, stormed out onto the crime scene. To date, I have written four Gloria Damasco novels, the latest, *Death at Solstice*, out in 2009. In 1993, Manuel Ramos published his first crime novel, *The Ballad of Rocky Ruiz*, introducing Luis Móntez who, like Nava's Rios, is also an attorney. Ramos's Móntez series includes five novels.

Hinojosa, Nava, Anaya, Ramos, and I form the structure on which contemporary Chicano/Chicana crime fiction rests. It's said that Hinojosa and Nava are the grandfathers, and Anaya and Ramos the fathers of the Chicano mystery genre. From 1992 until 2005, when Alicia Gaspar de Alba published *Desert Blood: The Juárez Murders*, I was the only Chicana writing and publishing detective novels. I suppose that in the genre hierarchy or crime genealogy, I would be considered the grandmother and Alicia would then be the mother. But I've never heard anyone in the male establishment, Chicano or mainstream, talk about us Chicanas in such terms.

A quick look at the Sisters in Crime or the Mystery Writers of America directory is sufficient proof that in the United States nearly half of published crime fiction writers are women. But the same is not true in the production or publication of Chicano/Chicana crime fiction. Of roughly twenty writers only four are Chicanas. In a group of about twenty-five, five Latinas are published authors of crime fiction.

From time to time during my seventeen years as the only Chicana detective-fiction writer, while at a reading or a signing other Chicanas and Latinas have confessed their secret desire to write detective fiction someday. To date, with the exception of Gaspar de Alba's *Desert Blood: The Juárez Murders*, and more recently the anthology *Hit List: The Best of Latino Mystery,* featuring the work of four other Chicana mystery authors, I have seen few tangible results. And I have often asked myself why; what keeps Chicanas (and Latinas as well) from writing and/or publishing crime fiction?

Seeking answers, I began to take a look at my own upbringing, my experiences as a girl growing up. I developed a taste for murder and mayhem while secretly reading la página roja. Later, my family and I moved to San Luis Potosí in Central Mexico. There, I found myself in the midst of a super-conservative Catholic community where women, young or old, who dared to read crime novels were punished or became social outcasts. Some women did read them pero a escondidas, always making sure their secret was safe if they confided in anyone. Mexico in the fifties and early sixties seems long ago but, although the rules have been relaxed and it is no longer such a crime for Mexican women to read crime novels, the majority of them still don't read them, let alone write them.

I remember a conversation I had with Sandra Cisneros after my two novels *Eulogy for a Brown Angel* and *Cactus Blood* were published. "I haven't read any of your novels, because I don't like reading that kind of novel," she remarked. I did not give her comment great importance. There are things I will not ask my friends to do for me—like reading or liking my work, attending my presentations, or even buying my books. Love takes precedence over crime. But what Sandra said became relevant when I read an interview with Rolando Hinojosa. In it, he mentions that he read many crime fiction authors to learn the craft before he wrote his police procedurals. Like him, I also read many mystery novels and authors' essays on the writing of crime fiction before I wrote *Eulogy*. If anyone is going to break the rules and conventions—and break them I do—we must know first what they are and what the cost, personally and professionally, will be.

Every road taken in my search for the reason Chicanas do not write mysteries kept leading me back to the reading corner. Sin lectura no hay ni escritura ni literatura. Suspecting that I was on to something important, I asked Professor Norma Alarcón, an avid reader of mysteries by women authors, why she thought Chicanas do not write detective or crime fiction. Without the least bit of hesitation, she answered, "Because they do not read them. No les han tomado el gusto. They haven't developed a taste for it."

Since then, I have asked many Chicanas and Latinas the same question. To mention a few, their comments range from "Ugh! Fuchi!! No way" to:

"Ay mujer, es que eso de cargar pistola y andar matando gente."

"Who wants to write about raping and killing?"

"I'm against portraying women constantly as victims. That's why I don't watch the Lifetime channel."

"We're not like men."

I have walked away from conversations on the subject with some major questions to ponder: Do we Chicanas really believe

1. That since violence has to do mainly with testosterone, therefore it has nothing to do with women?
2. That the constant and at times systematic killing of women all over the world, including Mexico and the Chicano microcosm, is real but it is not in good taste to write or talk about it?
3. That in truth women are victims of injustice but it is not okay to seek justice in the public arenas?
4. Or in general, that writing crime fiction is neither feminine nor feminist?

Other comments have to do with either the creative process or the value given to the crime fiction genre. I've been told, for example, "It's very difficult to write that kind of novel because it is so rigid." Or "That's not really a literary novel. It's formulaic."

It's true that crime novels in a series may become formulaic. Ideally, each story stands alone, even when it relies for continuity on the same investigator's point of view. But, in each novel, a distinct set of characters, moral dilemmas, and ethical decisions confront the investigator. Skillfully crafted, each story in a series will be entertaining yet poignant and emotionally engaging, delivered in a language accessible to a variety of readers, with characters portrayed honestly in all their facets, including those who do wrong. It will deal with moral dilemmas, unethical and criminal acts, but it won't be preachy in its approach to what is right and wrong.

Is the job of the literary writer any different from that of the genre writer? The development of a credible plot and characters and adequate descriptions of the place where the story develops are the basic requisites any literary or genre fiction writer must meet. Writers may choose to fracture time, set the story in the midst of a particular era, counterpoint stories within the larger work, use brevity of detail or indulge in complex description, maintain a tight pace or allow characters moments of reflection. But, literary or genre, any writer must answer to the degree necessary five pertinent questions: What? Who? Where? When? Why?

For the crime writer, a sixth question—How?—is paramount, because the investigation of the crime and the quest for justice are the wheels that keep the plot moving and eventually lead, in a full circle, to the motives for the crime and the apprehension or death of its perpetrator.

It's a fallacy that mystery writers make a lot more money than literary authors. So the following comment never fails to make me chuckle: "Maybe, to make money, I'll write a mystery novel someday, but only under a pseudonym."

I do not have the heart to burst these dreamers' bubbles. One crime novel hardly brings in even a five-figure royalty advance, in a very competitive field where you need to establish yourself with at least three mystery novels. I can, however, assure any Chicana who is now contemplating penning a mystery novel that the writing of crime fiction, when one respects one's art, is as legitimate as any other kind of writing; that exposing the machinations of a "justice" system that more often than not stacks the deck against women, especially women of color, is not only alright; it is also a way of obtaining justice for those who won't or can't speak for themselves.

My grandmother died when I was nineteen, two months after I got married and moved to Berkeley, five years before I started writing poems, ten before I began to write stories, and thirty-three before I wrote *Black Widow's Wardrobe*, the story of a woman who, in 1972, kills her abusive husband. Like Ema of the scandal remembered from my youth, Licia, the "black widow" in my novel, is the victim of her abusive husband. She kills him. Extenuating circumstances or not, her own sense of justice demands that she be punished. The legal system agrees with her, but it stacks the deck against her as it did against Ema. Unlike Ema, Licia is legally tried, but by an all-male jury. Convicted, she is sentenced to eighteen years in prison. Upon her release, someone tries to kill her. And Chicana detective Gloria Damasco is hired to find out who and why.

During the investigation, Gloria explores the nature of justice. How absolute a notion is it in the face of discrimination, abuse, or the sociopolitical reality encountered in the system by people—particularly women—of color? How do law and justice interact with or prey upon each other? Is true justice really attainable by all? What role does compassion play in the administering of justice?

In *Eulogy for a Brown Angel*, Gloria Damasco, as a woman of color and a political activist, also seeks answers to those questions. She finds a young child dead during the 1970 National Chicano Moratorium protest march and riot in Los Angeles. Gloria suspects that a Chicano journalist is responsible for the murder of both the child and a young gang member, a possible witness to the deed. LA Homicide Detective Kenyon asks for her help to entrap the suspected Chicano journalist. For the LA detective things are simple; he takes his personal and moral concerns for granted, for in the solution of a crime justice is served and goodness prevails. But for Gloria, there is more at stake than restoring the order upset by the murders. In her words:

> In the summer of 1970 everything any one of us did had
> to be considered according to its political impact on the
> Chicano community. So . . . I supported the unwritten rule
> that forbade Chicanos to go public on any issues that could
> be used to justify discrimination against us. . . . I treaded
> on a quagmire of the conscience . . . accepted as (my)
> right and responsibility the function of making sure that
> justice was dealt equally to everyone. . . . But goodness,

like justice, was only a relative notion, depending on who interpreted or administered it.

Gloria grapples with her conscience, considers dropping the investigation altogether. If she serves as bait for the killer, a Chicano, she will become an outcast in her community, never to be trusted again. But letting the murderer of an innocent child go free is heavier in her conscience. The scales have been tipped. But Gloria ploughs further. She needs to understand the forces that would compel someone to take the life of a child. As Gloria poses the question to me, I also wrestle with my own ethical conflicts as I try to define for myself my own concept of fairness vis-à-vis the nature of justice. In the process, I have come to realizations of great personal value to me, as a woman and a writer:

1. Justice is a living organism, mutating, evolving. Like a poem, it takes substance and form from incongruent elements at various levels of consciousness and subconsciousness. Both poetry and justice, however, are elusive. They both require from us that we stop and listen—acknowledge.
2. Our sense of justice also requires that we act on the knowledge, that we calibrate our conscience with compassion and empathy, for without them there can be no true justice.
3. For me, as a Chicana mystery writer, acting on that knowledge means writing.

At times, when I'm writing, I think of my grandmother and her pronouncement that night, long ago, that there is no justice in this world. I regret I never had a chance to tell her that sometimes I write to bring about justice, even if poetic, or that the pounding of her heart against flesh and bone that evening has become the *Andante Vigoroso* of my heart. But I want to think that she would be proud of Gloria Damasco, and of me, for giving voice to those who can't speak for themselves.

21

Afterword
Latino Identity and the Desiring-Machine
WILLIAM LUIS

Latino (and Latino literature) is a desiring-machine that produces other machines, each with its own flows and interruptions, and exists as a process of production. In *Anti-Oedipus*, Deleuze and Guattari consider the body to be a desiring-machine made up of many machines that are linked in a linear fashion to other machines: the mouth, the breast, the stomach, the intestine, the anus, and so on.[1] The desiring-machines create flows of desire that are also interrupted, producing other currents that flow, each with its own interruption. If for Freud the unconscious is the desiring-machine, for Deleuze and Guattari the social-machine complements the desiring-machine, and one cannot produce without the other, just as parents are the product of society, laws, and repressions.

Latino is a desiring-machine that generates other machines; these are terms that reproduce the same signifier with different and varying meanings. In *Dance Between Two Cultures*, I considered Latino as a manifestation of the Cuban American, Puerto Rican American, and Dominican American literary, cultural, and historical experiences.[2] In this and subsequent works, I propose that Latinos are born or raised and educated in the United States and write mainly in English. Latinos and Latino literature are linked to, but also interrupted by, Hispanic writings. For me, writers born or raised and educated in a Spanish-speaking country, nurtured in their national culture, who later migrate to and live in the United States, are Hispanics. Once in the adopted country, Hispanics continue to maintain a close relationship to their culture of origin and write mainly in Spanish. There is a significant difference between Hispanics and Latinos, and I do not consider these terms to be synonymous or interchangeable. Rather, like desiring-machines, they are linked in a linear manner to each other, for each has been subjected to different historical and cultural forces, particularly during the crucial developmental years, and marked by the society in which they live. US culture, education, politics, society, and race relations mold those reared in the United States, and Latinos feel more comfortable in the dominant culture and write in English. This positionality does not preclude Latinos from becoming Hispanics, especially if they live in or return to a dominant Spanish-speaking environment, or Hispanics from becoming Latinos, above all if they take up the Latino cause.

My approach to Hispanic and Latino literatures is directly related to my research, first as the contributing editor of the Hispanic Caribbean section to the *Handbook of Latin American Studies*, and second as an invited scholar to author a chapter on "Latin American (Hispanic Caribbean) Literature Written in the United States" for the *Cambridge History of Latin American Literature*.[3] My assigned responsibilities for the Hispanic Division of the Library of Congress included reading everything written by and about the Spanish Caribbean and reviewing those works considered to be of permanent value. In this capacity, I came across Caribbean authors who wrote about their country from their place of origin. There were others, however, in significant number, who described similar events about the same geographic space, but authored their works from the United States. These two groups of writers, whether living at home or abroad, conceived their subject matter in their national language, Spanish, for a Spanish-speaking audience. Though they were all Caribbean writers, those who lived abroad injected into their literature an additional element, consciously or unconsciously, that referred to the time, place, and culture of the nation from which they wrote.[4]

While researching my contribution to the *Cambridge History of Latin American Literature*, I encountered another group of Caribbean writers and works. Like the earlier ones, this group also wrote about the Spanish Caribbean from the United States. But unlike the authors who envisaged their works in Spanish, the language of the adopted country of these most recent writers appeared to consume their literary expressions. They invariably mixed the history and culture of their parents' country of origin with that of the adopted one, and some even dared to combine or fuse the two languages, the latter producing what is commonly known as Spanglish. This linguistic and cultural hybrid space was familiar to me during my formative years in New York City, as friends, neighbors, acquaintances, and strangers crossed linguistic, cultural, ethnic, and racial boundaries. The Lower East Side of my youth was a cultural palimpsest, layered first with Jewish culture from Eastern Europe and later with communities of African Americans, Puerto Ricans and, on the western boundary, Chinese. None was erased, each lived side-by-side; some even built on earlier ones. At that time, I stumbled upon a different kind of writer and book, one not recognized as part of the high school curriculum: Víctor Hernández Cruz's *Papo Got His Gun* (1966). As a college student, I discovered Piri Thomas's *Down These Mean Streets* (1967), followed closely the activities of the Young Lords Party, and heard Pedro Pietri recite his groundbreaking poem, "Puerto Rican Obituary" (1971). Some of these and other writings would become foundational works of Latino literature.[5]

My research suggested that though large numbers of Caribbean immigrants arrived in the United States after World War II—Puerto Ricans seeking work as a consequence of the failure of Operation Bootstrap, Cubans fleeing the Castro takeover of Cuba, and Dominicans escaping the consequences of the Trujillo dictatorship and the US invasion of 1965—there was indeed a long-standing Hispanic and Latino tradition traceable to the early nineteenth century. This other, alternate history highlights the lives of Cubans and Puerto Ricans who worked, organized, and fought for their country's independence against Spain, but did so from the United States. As their situation became more permanent, these authors documented the culture of the country from which they wrote. Their works were of particular interest to me, since many of these nineteenth-century writers, considered foundational authors of their country's literature, wrote about events in their country not from a national space but from their country of residence. I soon realized that the so-called national literature of these and other countries might have been influenced by the culture and place of writing. It became evident that Cuban writers like Félix Valera, José María Heredia, José Martí, and Cirilo Villaverde incorporated US images, concepts, and traditions into their writings, and that Puerto Rican authors like Eugenio María de Hostos, Manuel Zeno Gandía, Arturo Alfono Schomburg, and Jesús Colón were also impacted by events on the mainland. Schomburg and Colón, two Afro-Puerto Ricans, were exposed to another experience: the racial discrimination known to their African American counterparts.

The ideas I proposed about foundational fictions differed considerably from the more traditional approaches of other critics, which do not take into account the time, place, and culture of the place of writing, factors that invariably influenced how authors conceived of events back home. However, I was equally fascinated by the literary constructs of works composed in English. This other literature, with authors writing about their parents' culture and place of residence, dismantles the idea of fixed boundaries even more and contributes, like any other literature, to that country's development of a national narrative. This is a concept that many Puerto Ricans from the island at first vehemently rejected but are now more willing to consider, and that Dominicans also, from their national space, are more eager to embrace. After all, this aspect of the "national" literature is reaching a broader and more diverse audience. This is the case with Dominican American writers like Julia Álvarez and Junot Díaz.[6] Since these voices are expressed in the language of the dominant culture, English, they also destabilize the classifications of US literature, thus forcing readers to reconsider its foundational construction, which incorporates cities and regions inhabited by people of Hispanic descent. Writers like Martí and Villaverde wrote in Spanish and English, while still others like William Carlos Williams and Jesús Colón, more in tune with an English-speaking audience, weaved island and resident images into their literary language. Their works fused different geographic, linguistic, and cultural spaces, all into the same text.[7]

The confusion as to whether to use the term *Hispanic* or *Latino* is compounded by the terms themselves, whether we use them in Spanish or English, since these words have different meanings in each language. English and Spanish speakers tend to mix Hispanic with *hispano* and Latino with *latino*, and vice versa. When a speaker enunciates one of these terms, he or she may be alluding to a particular meaning in one language, while the listener may be considering a different linguistic referent. In Spanish, hispano invokes Spain and the Iberian Peninsula, and *hispanoamericano* refers to someone who resides in a Spanish-speaking country of the Americas. However, in the United States, Hispanic has been accepted to identify people of Spanish descent, regardless of country of origin or time of arrival, and includes those who have long lost their accents. For a newly arrived immigrant or exile, the term is imprecise, since this Spanish-speaker identifies not with the broad sounding and all-inclusive Hispanic, but with his or her country of origin or national identity. So, someone from Peru or Argentina or Colombia does not consider him/herself to be Hispanic, but Peruvian, Argentinean, or Colombian, respectively. However, with the passage of time, this immigrant or exile may be drawn to wider concerns in the adopted country that affect the same language speakers.

A similar indistinctness occurs with Latino. In Spanish the word latino is related to *latín*, Latin, the root of all Romance languages, and is used in compound terms such as *Latinoamérica* to identify a country or region whose language derives from Latin. Consequently, when native Spanish-speakers employ the term in Spanish, they refer to Latin, but also Romanian, French, Italian, Catalan, Spanish, and Portuguese. When mentioning Latin America, inevitably these linguistic speakers include countries where French, Spanish, or Portuguese is spoken. So, the term *latinidad*, which has moved quickly into the English language, in Spanish alludes to a condition associated with Spain, Latin-based countries, and their corresponding languages.

In English, Latino is commonly misused as a synonym for Hispanic to identify people of Hispanic descent, regardless of their family nationality of origin, their individual self-identification, or the length or location of their residence in the United States. Yet often, when identity is revealed, our characterization of the speaker is altered. For example, when referring to a Latino or Hispanic of Colombian descent, we tend to ask questions about origin and national space, but may in fact discover that he or she was born in the United States and is more grounded in US culture than previously imagined. Latino and Hispanic have become catchall terms that can encompass anyone, from someone who speaks Spanish and is associated with Hispanic culture to someone who is dominant in English and barely recalls his parents' or grandparents' country of origin. For some English and Spanish speakers, Hispanic is more cultural while Latino invokes positionalities related to politics, class, race, gender and so on. Latino identity, in a manner of speaking, refers to a subaltern condition within US society and environment, which some Cuban Americans from the 1.5-generation reject.[8] These other Latinos consider themselves to be Cubans, with little in common with other minority groups.

Language and culture play important roles in the lives of Hispanics and Latinos and influence how we should consider or evaluate their condition. Those who are fluent in Spanish for the most part tend to be closer to their parents' country, language, and cultural origins, and travel with some regularity, if possible, to their country of origin. This, of course, is not the case with exiles, like Cubans, who cannot or will not return to the island they abandoned. The Miami community however has, in some respects, become a national space abroad. Hispanic writers who author books in Spanish write for a Spanish-speaking audience living mainly in countries where Spanish is the national language, even though the United States has become the second largest Spanish-speaking country in the world. And a Latino in Spanish is not the same as his linguistic counterpart in the United States. US Latinos write in English for primarily English-dominant readers. The tendency is to homogenize or essentialize identity and reduce it to its lowest denominator, perhaps reflecting nation-building projects of the nineteenth century. The term Latino within the United States context, however, conveys interconnectedness with other national, racial, linguistic, and gender groups and issues that go beyond any singular concern or identity. Culture, politics, race, gender, and sexual orientation are certainly important factors that cannot be limited to any one particular culture or identity. Latinos tend to look beyond their national or Hispanic background and connect to other marginalized groups, whether or not they come from the same country or region, the same social or economic class, are of different races or genders, speak fluent or broken Spanish, or can only write in English.

I have argued that Latino is more appropriately a Spanglish term, which mixes English and Spanish; it uses an English word with Spanish pronunciation. Latin was the more common term Latinos used in the New York City of my childhood, in the decade of the sixties, to designate their situation on the mainland. As the term evolved, the word Latin was articulated and pronounced with a final Spanish *o*.[9] So, the English *Latin* became the Spanglish *Latino*. The word Latin appears in Pietri's original "The Puerto Rican Obituary." Toward the end of the poem, the poetic voice affirms his characters' identity:

> If only they
> Had used the white
> Supremacy bibles
> For toilet paper purpose
> And made their *Latin* Souls
> The only religion of their race. [My emphasis.][10]

In a subsequent version of the poem, Pietri changes Latin for latino, and restructures the lines as follows:

> If only they
> Had used the white supremacy bibles
> For toilet paper purpose and make their *latino* souls
> The only religion of their race. [My emphasis.]

Let us recall that Juan, Miguel, Milagros, Olga, and Manuel worked hard, abandoned their distinctiveness, and dreamt about the American Dream, only to encounter rejection and death. However, there is redemption in accepting their identity. Though Pietri provides words of salvation for his characters and readers, the poem is written mostly in English, for an English-dominant audience.

As I mentioned, the English Latin is pronounced in Spanish, thus producing the term Latin(o). Latino is a hybrid word that connotes its own condition and the multicultural experience of people of Hispanic descent, who reside in the United States, and whose parents' culture of origin is no longer the overriding element of their identity as it was for their ancestors. While Latinos still retain a metonymic relationship with their parents' culture—foods, songs, pictures, and other artifacts—they accept the culture, politics, and economic way of life in the adopted country, which is also their country, and these fuse with their own beliefs, which, in turn, impacts the dominant culture.

The Hispanic machine is connected to the Latino machines, which produce their own flows and interruptions. Though US newscasters, politicians, and even a large part of the US population are presently obsessed with illegal immigration and the fence along the US–Mexico border, Hispanics and Latinos have long social, cultural, and literary histories in the United States that belong to both the culture of origin and that of the adopted country. If we summarily review the Cuban and Puerto Rican print culture of the nineteenth and early twentieth centuries, we find descriptive journal titles that reveal their particular intent. For example, in the New York of the early nineteenth century, Father Félix Valera contributed to the religious beliefs of his country of residence by publishing, in the first half of the nineteenth century, *The Protestant Abridger and Annotator*, *The New York Catholic Register*, and *The Catholic Expositor and Literary Magazine*. After Villaverde escaped from a Havana prison and fled to the United States in the middle of the same century, in various stages of his life he edited *La América*, *Frank Leslie's Magazine*, *El Avisador Hispano Americano*, *La Ilustración Americana*, *El Espejo*, and *El Tribunal Cubano*. José Martí, who like many of his fellow countrymen lived almost as long in the United States as he did in Cuba, wrote from his country of residence, in the latter part of the century, the chronicles "Cartas de Nueva York; o, escenas norteamericanas" ("Letters from New York or Scenes from North America") for newspapers in Buenos Aires and Mexico. He also contributed to New York's *La América*, and NYC newspapers like the *Hour* and the *Sun*. While Martí and Villaverde were writing their works, Enrique Piñero was editor of *La Revolución*, of the Puerto Rican Republican Committee in New York, the same one on which Eugenio María de Hostos, who also published his own short-lived *La Voz de Puerto Rico,* collaborated. These and other writers contributed to the emerging literature and national culture of their country of origin and of residence.

In the early twentieth century, I am drawn to the weekly *Gráfico*, because of its early use of the word Hispanic. Ramón la Villa published *Gráfico* in New York City with the subtitle "Semanario defensor de la raza hispana" (Weekly Defender of the Hispanic Race); his mission was to expose the injustices committed against Hispanics, regardless of national origin, thereby recognizing the existence of a Spanish-speaking community that went beyond national boundaries. Shortly after its creation, Adolfo Rodríguez became proprietor and editor. He subtitled the periodical "Semanario defensa de la colonia hispano americana" (Weekly Defense of Hispanic American Community), thus alluding to a similarity between Hispanic and Spanish Americans—even though one editor preferred one term to the other—but also appealing to a more specific constituency by exchanging race for community. The Puerto Rican journalist and tobacco roller Bernando Vega became the third owner of the same publication. Under his direction, the journal was known as *Gráfico: Semanario defensor de la raza* (Weekly

Defender of the Race), another title that provides insight into the journal and into the readers being served. Equally important, Vega penned his editorials in Spanish and English, continuing a tradition present in the *Tobacco Worker*, which he coedited during the 1920s. Let us review *Gráfico's* evolving subtitles once again. As we have seen, La Villa refers to a forged identity among Hispanics or Spanish-speakers in New York; Rodríguez reinforces the same idea proposed by La Villa, but also makes clear that the journal focuses on the Spanish American community; Vega omits the linguistic or regional term *Hispano* or *Hispano Americano* and recovers the concept of race, thus suggesting a condition that affects not only Hispanics but other groups as well. Regardless of the changes, each editor kept the verb *defensor* as he "defended" the reader against the social, political, and racial conditions present in New York.[11] Vega's bilingual editorials recognized that members of the Hispanic community spoke Spanish but also read English; this factor alludes to an English-speaking population that identified with and supported the Hispanic community. The latter was emblematic of Vito Marcantonio, the congressman from East Harlem who labored tirelessly on behalf of working New Yorkers. The congressman was known as the defender of Puerto Ricans and other Hispanics.[12]

Latino is a desiring-machine. It speaks to the lives of the largest groups of resident immigrants and exiles living in the United States, but also to those, living in territories incorporated into the greater United States, who consider themselves a part of this country's culture and history. The term Hispanic flows and is interrupted by other Hispanics, and these by Latinos, and Latino is also connected to another Latino, and on to other Latinos, and so on, each referring to other groups that are less populous and even to individuals whose lives and experiences are as significant as those belonging to larger communities, regardless of their reason for leaving their country of origin, traveling to the mainland, residing in a particular city, or accepting a Latino identity. Just as Latinos are linked to other Latinos, Cubans are linked to Puerto Ricans, Dominicans, and Chicanos, for example, living in the United States; Latinos are also connected to Salvadorians, Guatemalans, Colombians; that is, to other Latino signifiers with different and varying identities.

While it may be socially and bureaucratically feasible and culturally manageable (from mainstream society) to group Hispanics and Latinos, for there are similarities linking these groups, there are also significant differences among them that can be traced to their culture of origin, their time of migration, and their place of residence. Equally important, there are disparities among Latino groups, just as there are telling differences between Cubans, Puerto Ricans, and Dominicans. And if Latinos are connected to other Latinos, then Cubans, for example, are connected to other Cubans, as there are notable differences among Cubans in the United States: between those who arrived before Castro's uprising; those who received political exile during the early stages of the Cuban revolution; and those who sought refuge in subsequent years, in particular the Marielitos (1980) and the more recent balseros, who left on make-shift rafts at the start of Cuba's Special Period. These Cubans are linked to other Cubans traveling to the United States from Europe, South America, and other parts of the world. If the time of migration is determined by political and historical factors both at home and abroad, then the geographic area of residence helps to condition the Hispanic and, later, Latino experiences. There are telling distinctions between Cubans who live in Miami, Cubans who live in New York City, and those in other areas like California and the Midwest. The first are more likely to retain their parents' anti-Castro position; the second more willing to integrate themselves into a larger and broader minority landscape that includes their experiences as one group among many others; while the others find themselves isolated in a dominant majority culture. There are even sharp racial distinctions between Cubans of European and African descent. Other Latino machines are prevalent among Puerto Ricans: those who left the island at the turn of the twentieth century and those who departed as a result of Operation Bootstrap; between these economic migrants and their middle- or upper middle-class counterparts who traveled to the United States for totally different reasons, to study at US universities, and between this latter group and others of more humble origins who joined the US armed forces.

The repeating machine Latino takes into account different types of Latinos. There are Latinos of mixed marriages, raised by one Hispanic or Latino parent and another of a different race or culture. Latino also applies to other Latinos, who were raised as non-Latinos but who find identity in the term as it becomes more accepted and meaningful to them. Latino includes those who are not Latino, but who were reared in Latino neighborhoods and identify with Latino issues, and others who have no Latino background but accept a Latino identity. There are Latinos like Alberto Fuguet, who is known to Spanish Americans as the creator of McOndo generation, which rivaled García Márquez's Macondo. Though born in the United States, at a young age he migrated to his parents' native Chile. His most recent novel, *Missing (una invesigación)/Missing (My Uncle's Story)*, written in Spanish, narrates the life of his uncle who went "missing," lost his "roots," and integrated himself into the culture of his adopted country, the United States. The novel includes English expressions.

In a postmodern world, should emphasis on origin still play a central role in our lives? Deleuze and Gautarri's concept of deterritorialization is meaningful here insofar as it dismantles any fixed concept of Latino. It links the Latino terms, allowing them to flow freely, without any specific boundary. Latino implies a continuum of dissipation and change.

Someone may ask: Do all machines, flows, and interruptions produce meaningful and equal relationships? Or, are some machines more significant than others? If Spanish is an operative concept, then how do Spaniards, for example, fit into the concept of Latino identity? Though Latinos speak Spanish, are Spaniards Latinos? For that matter, are Latinos Spaniards? Are Hispanics, in the Spanish sense of the word, Hispanics the same way US culture defines them? While some may be quick to dismiss these and other questions, there is a significant difference between Hispanics from Spain and those who were born and raised in the territories as colonial subjects of the Spanish authorities,

relationships best understood by the framework proposed by postcolonial studies.[13] We should not forget that Spain was an imperial power that colonized the
Americas, and these emerging nations, inspired by the slave rebellion of Saint
Domingo of 1791, sought to liberate their territories, significantly, without abol-
ishing slavery. Be that as it may, I am perplexed why some scholars look for an
origin of Latino discourse among the works produced by Spanish conquerors
and explorers who roamed what is now considered to be the southern part of
the United States. If we accept that Latinos are the descendants of Hispanics
who lived in colonies once under Spanish domain, which after independence
came under the influence of a neocolonial power, is it possible for Spaniards
to occupy the same postcolonial condition as other Latinos or Hispanics? How
can Latinos be descendants of these conquerors and colonizers, especially since
there was then no territory known as the United States, a geographic space
that has given the term Latino its present significance? Are these scholars inadvertently attempting to equate a colonial power with a postcolonial condition?
Or would it be more appropriate to compare Spain with other European and
Western powers, including the United States, even though Spain had ceased to
be a superpower when it lost its last remaining colonies? My objective in raising
these questions is not to homogenize the Spanish condition but to problematize
it. I am conscious that Spain is made up of different provinces and cultures, some
of which continue to resist Castilian central control of the Iberian Peninsula.
Such is the case with the Basque Provinces, whose citizens continue to fight
for regional, national, and linguistic sovereignty. Though this may be the case,
many Spaniards of the nineteenth century, regardless of class, language, and
geographic origin, when traveling to the colony of Cuba, considered themselves
to be superior to even the wealthiest creoles. In the twentieth century, Barcelona
entrepreneurs—from a Catalonia with a cherished language and culture—partici-
pated in the exploitation of Equatorial Guinea.[14] Certainly other Spaniards, like
those fleeing Franco Spain (1936–39), traveled to and resided in Spanish-speaking
countries and contributed to the development of Spanish American national,
cultural, literary, and artistic expressions; some, like Américo Castro, even lived
in the United States and taught at leading institutions. Are these Spaniards, however, Hispanics or Latinos in the same way Spaniards living in the Southwest
and Florida are Hispanics or Latinos; that is, the same as those who became so
when the US government annexed these territories to form a larger and growing continental nation? Are the descendents of these and more recent Spaniards
Latinos as other groups, especially if they make the Latino cause their own? The
desiring-machine links them to the linguistic displacement of Latino, as these
boundaries are also erased.

Notes
1. I am indebted to Antonio Benítez Rojo for bringing to my attention this work. In *The
Repeating Island*, Benítez Rojo relies on chaos theory and the the desiring-machine to offer
a different and more convincing understanding of the Caribbean. In particular, he shows
how the sugar plantation is repeated in this heterogeneous geographic space.

2. Though some may consider Puerto Rican American to be a redundancy, I use the term here to distinguish these Puerto Ricans from those who reside on the island. For this and other terms, see *Dance Between Two Cultures*. In a subsequent study, I included Chicano literature as an indispensable aspect of the Latino machine ("Latino Literature").

3. This chapter developed into *Dance Between Two Cultures*.

4. Reinaldo Arenas's famed autobiography, *Antes que anochezca* Trans. (Before Night Falls), begins in Holguín, located in the eastern part of Cuba, continues in Havana, and ends in New York, where he dies from the HIV/AIDS virus. And *El portero* Trans.(The Doorman) takes place exclusively in New York. Similarly, René Marqués's *La carreta* Trans. (The Oxcart) commences in Puerto Rico and, like Arenas's autobiography, concludes in New York. Many of Pedro Juan Soto's characters outlined in *Spiks* respond to a hostile North American environment.

5. While it may be too early to discuss the idea of a Latino canon, the mentioned works will play an important role in this discussion.

6. Álvarez and Días, for example, have contributed enormously to understanding events in the Dominican Republic, in ways national writers have not been able to do. Their works have been translated into Spanish, but also many other languages.

7. See, for example, Julio Marzan's study of William Carlos Williams and David García's of Jesús Colón.

8. Some Cuban Americans have a strong aversion to the term Latino. In his poem, when asked if he is Latino, the speaker responds "tu madre" (your mama).

9. Tato Laviera has a series of poems that end in "ao," which becomes the concern of Juan Flores, who begins his essay in the following manner: "Tato Laviera calls his new book *Mixturao*. It makes me think of other lively words, like asopao, or encebollao, or cansao, or jabao, or some of Tato's own poem titles like asimilao, craqueao, and melao. That final —ao puts a charge into any word, old or new, everyday or highfalutin, a resonance of street, of blackness, and *afrocaribeñismo*. In Tato's case, we are talking about Afro-Spanglish, the ultimate *mixturao."*

10. Pietri's poem first appeared in *Palante: Young Lords Party* and later in *Puerto Rican Obituary*.

11. It is possible that race may allude to José Vasconcelos's *La raza cósmica* Trans. (The Cosmic Race, 1925) or to race relations in the United States. For additional information about the changing subtitles, see *Dance Between Two Cultures*, 108–10.

12. *Gráfico* and Marcantonio are present in Bernardo Vega's *Memories of Bernardo Vega*. Also see *Dance Between Two Cultures*.

13. See, for example, *The Empire Writes Back*.

14. Jordi Sant Gisbert's "El modelo económico colonial y sus congradicciones," Fernando Poo (1900–1936).

Bibliography

Arenas, Reinaldo. *Before Night Falls*. Trans. Dolores M. Koch. New York: Viking, 1993.

———. *The Doorman*. New York: Grove Press, 1994.

Ashcroft, Bill, Gareth Griffiths, and Helen Tiffin. *The Empire Writes Back: Theory and Practice in Post-Colonial Literatures*. London: Routledge, 2002.

Benítez Rojo, Antonio. *The Repeating Island: The Caribbean and the Postmodern Perspective*. Trans. James E. Maraniss. Durham: Duke University Press, 1997.

Deleuze and Guatarri. *Anti-Oedipus: Capitalism and Schizophrenia*. Trans. Robert Hurley, Mark Seem, and Helen R. Lane. London and New York: Continuum, 2004.

———. *A Thousand Plateaus*. Trans. Brian Massumi. London and New York: Continuum, 2004.

Flores, Juan. "Tato's —ao: The Poetics of Eye Dialect," in *Nideaquínideallá: Collected Essays on the Work of Tato Laviera*. Ed. Stephanie Álvarez and William Luis. Unpublished.

Fuguet, Alberto. *Missing (una investigación)/Missing (My Uncle's Story)*. Santiago de Chile: Alfaguara, 2010.

García, David. "Between Myth, Race and Marginality: Jesús Colón and the Afro-Latino Condition." PhD diss., Vanderbilt University, 2004.

Laviera, Tato. *Mixturao and Other Poems*. Houston: Arte Público Press, 2008.

Luis, William. *Dance Between Two Cultures: Latino Caribbean Literature Written in the United States*. Nashville: Vanderbilt University Press, 1997.

——— "Latin American (Hispanic Caribbean) Literature Written in the United States," in *The Cambridge History of Latin American Literature*. Vol. 2. Ed. Roberto González Echevarría and Enrique Pupo-Walker 526–56. Cambridge: Cambridge University Press, 1996.

———. "Latino US Literature," in *The Companion to Latin American Studies*. Ed. Philip Swanson. Arnold Publication, 2003.

Marqués, René. *The Oxcart*. New York: Scribner, 2000.

Marzan, Julio. *The Spanish American Roots of William Carlos Williams*. Austin: University of Texas Press, 1994.

Pietri, Pedro. "Puerto Rican Obituary," in *Palante: Young Lords Party*, by Michael Abramson. New York: McGraw-Hill, 1971.

———. *Puerto Rican Obituary*. New York: Monthly Review Press, 1974.

Sant Gisbert, Jordi. "El modelo económico colonial y sus congradicciones: Fernando Poo (1900–1936). *Afro-Hispanic Review* 28.2 (Fall 2009): 57–80.

Soto, Pedro Juan. *Spiks*. San Juan: Editorial Cultural, 1989.

Vega, Bernardo. *Memoirs of Bernardo Vega: A Contribution to the History of the Puerto Rican Community in New York*. Ed. César A. Iglesias. Trans. Juan Flores. New York: Monthly Review Press, 1984.

About the Contributors

Joy Castro's first book, *The Truth Book: A Memoir* (New York: Arcade, 2005), was named a Book Sense Notable Book by the American Booksellers Association and was adapted and excerpted in the *New York Times Magazine*. Her short fiction, poetry, and creative nonfiction have appeared in several anthologies and in journals such as *Afro-Hispanic Review*, *North American Review*, *Cream City Review*, *Chelsea*, *Quarterly West*, and *Puerto del Sol*.

Daniel Chacón is author of three books, including the novel *and the shadows took him* and the short story collection *Unending Rooms*. He received his BA and MA from California State University, Fresno, and his MFA from the University of Oregon. He teaches Fiction Writing, Kafka, and Xican@ literature in the Bilingual Program in Creative Writing at the University of Texas, El Paso.

Lisa D. Chávez was born in Los Angeles and raised in Fairbanks, Alaska. She has published two books of poetry: *Destruction Bay* and *In an Angry Season* (published by the University of Arizona Press), and has been included in such anthologies as *Floricanto Si! A Collection of Latina Poetry*, *The Floating Borderlands: 25 Years of U.S. Hispanic Literature*, and *American Poetry: The Next Generation*. Her creative nonfiction has been published in *Fourth Genre*, *The Clackamas Literary Review*, and elsewhere. She is an associate professor of English at the University of New Mexico.

Judith Ortiz Cofer was born in Hormigueros, Puerto Rico. Her books include: *A Love Story Beginning in Spanish*; *The Meaning of Consuelo*; *The Line of the Sun*; *Silent Dancing*; *Woman in Front of the Sun*; *The Year of Our Revolution: New and Selected Stories and Poems*, winner of the Paterson Book Prize given by the Poetry Center at Passaic County Community College; *The Latin Deli: Prose & Poetry* (1993), winner of the Anisfield Wolf Book Award; *Terms of Survival* (1989), *Reaching for the Mainland* (1987), and *Latin Women Pray* (1980). Cofer is also the author of essays, fiction, and prose, and her work has been published in numerous anthologies. Cofer's awards and honors include grants from the Georgia Council for the Arts and the Witter Bynner Foundation, and fellowships from the National Endowment for the Arts for poetry, the University of Georgia Humanities Center, the Bread Loaf Writers' Conference, the Florida Fine Arts Council, and the Janet Rice Memorial Fellowship from Florida Atlantic University. She is currently the Franklin Professor of English and Creative Writing at the University of Georgia, and an associate staff member of the Bread Loaf Writers' Conference.

Steven Cordova was born and grew up in San Antonio, Texas and has lived in New York City for almost twenty-five years. His poems have appeared in numerous journals and anthologies, including *Barrow Street, Calalloo, The Journal, Northwest Review, Ravishing DisUnities: Real Ghazals in English* (Wesleyan University Press, 2000) and *The Wind Shifts: New Latino Poetry* (University of Arizona Press, 2007). His full-length collection, *Long Distance,* was published by Bilingual Press in 2009, and a chapbook, *Slow Dissolve,* was published by Momotombo Press in 2003. He also has an essay in *Diva Complex: Gay Men on Their Divas* (University of Wisconsin Press, 2009).

Lucha Corpi is a poet, novelist, and children's book author. She has written four mystery novels featuring Gloria Damasco, including the most recent in the collection, *Death at Solstice: A Gloria Damasco Mystery,* released in 2009 by Arte Público Press. She was a tenured teacher in the Oakland Public Schools Neighborhood Centers Program for over 30 years.

Teresa Dovalpage was born in Havana, Cuba in 1966. She is the author of *A Girl Like Che Guevara* (Soho Press, 2004), *Posesas de La Habana* (PurePlay Press, 2004), and *Habanera* (Floricanto Press, 2011). Inspired by New Mexican traditions, she wrote the play *La hija de La Llorona* (The Wailing Woman's Daughter), staged by Aguijon Theater in Chicago in 2006. Her novel, *Muerte de un murciano en La Habana* (Death of a Murcian in Havana), was a runner-up for the prestigious Herralde Award and published by Anagrama in Spain in 2006. Her articles and short stories have appeared in *Rosebud, Hispanic Magazine, Latina Style, Latino Today, Puerto del Sol, El Nuevo Herald, Caribe,* and *Revista Baquíana.* Her website is http://www.dovalpage.com

Alex Espinoza was born in Tijuana, Baja California, Mexico, to parents from Michoacán and raised in suburban Los Angeles. He earned his MFA from UC–Irvine. His first novel *Still Water Saints* (Random House, 2007) appeared simultaneously in English and Spanish and was selected for Barnes & Noble Discover Great New Writers. His nonfiction and reviews have appeared in the *Los Angeles Times,* the *New York Times Sunday Magazine,* and *Salon.* He was a 2009 Fellow in Fiction at Bread Loaf Writers' Conference and is also a frequent participant in Sandra Cisneros' Macondo Writers' Workshop. He currently teaches English and Creative Writing at Fresno State and has just completed his second novel, tentatively titled "The Other Stranger," about a Mexican actor in Hollywood's Golden Age.

Blas Falconer is an associate professor at Austin Peay State University, where he serves as the poetry editor of *Zone 3: A Literary Journal* and Zone 3 Press. A recipient of an NEA Fellowship, an Individual Artist Grant for the State of Tennessee, and the Maureen Egen Writers Exchange, he is the author of *A Question of Gravity and Light* (University of Arizona Press, 2007), and a co-editor of *Mentor and Muse: Essays from Poets to Poets* (Southern Illinois University Press, 2010).

Gina Franco's collection of poems, *The Keepsake Storm*, was published by the University of Arizona Press in the Camino del Sol series in 2004. Her work appears in numerous journals and anthologies, including *Fence, Black Warrior Review, The Georgia Review, Prairie Schooner, Seneca Review, Crazyhorse*, and *The Wind Shifts: New Latino Poetry* (University of Arizona Press, 2007). She received an Academy of American Poets Prize, the Robert Chasen Poetry Prize, the Corson-Bishop Poetry Prize, and the 2006 Bread Loaf Meralmikjen Fellowship in Poetry. She divides her time between Galesburg, Illinois, where she is an assistant professor of English and Creative Writing at Knox College, and the Arizona desert where she grew up.

Carmen Giménez Smith is an assistant professor of creative writing at New Mexico State University, publisher for Noemi Press, and Editor-in-Chief of the journal *Puerto del Sol*. She is the author of *Odalisque in Pieces* and the memoir *Bring Down the Little Birds* (both published by the University of Arizona Press). Her forthcoming collection *Trees Outside the Academy* will be published by the Center for Literary Publishing.

Gabe Gomez is a poet, playwright, editor, and journalist. He received a BA in creative writing from the College of Santa Fe and an MFA in creative writing from Saint Mary's College of California. He has taught English at the University of New Orleans, Tulane University, the College of Santa Fe and the Institute of American Indian Arts. He is the cofounder and coeditor of Breach Press and a freelance writer. His first book of poetry *The Outer Bands* won the Andres Montoya Poetry Prize and was published in 2007 by the University of Notre Dame Press. Gabe is also the host of a weekly live music radio show called *The Junk Drawer.*

Stephanie Elizondo Griest has mingled with the Russian "Mafiya," polished Chinese propaganda, and belly danced with Cuban rumba queens. These adventures inspired her award-winning memoirs *Mexican Enough: My Life Between the Borderlines*; *Around the Bloc: My Life in Moscow, Beijing, and Havana*; and the guidebook *100 Places Every Woman Should Go*. As a national correspondent for *The Odyssey*, she once drove 45,000 miles across America in a Honda hatchback named Bertha. She has won a Henry Luce Scholarship to China, a Hodder Fellowship to Princeton, a Richard Margolis Award for Social Justice Reporting, and a Lowell Thomas Travel Journalism Gold Prize. Visit her website at www.MexicanEnough.com.

Erasmo Guerra was born in the Rio Grande Valley of the Texas-Mexico border. His debut novel, *Between Dances*, was awarded the Lambda Literary Award, and his personal essays have appeared in the *New York Times, Texas Monthly*, the *Texas Observer, ColorLines* magazine, and a number of anthologies, including *Hecho en Tejas,* edited by Dagoberto Gilb, and *Fifteen Candles* edited by Adriana Lopez. Guerra has received writing fellowships from the Vermont Studio Center, the Fine Arts Work Center in Provincetown, and the Virginia Center for the Creative Arts. He is a member of the Macondo Writers' Workshop and lives in New York City.

Lorraine M. López is an associate professor of English, teaching in the Master of Fine Arts Creative Writing Program at Vanderbilt University. Her short story collection, *Soy la Avon Lady and Other Stories* (Curbstone Press, 2002), won the inaugural Miguel Marmól prize for fiction. Her second book, *Call Me Henri* (Curbstone Press 2006), was awarded the Paterson Prize for Young Adult Literature, and her novel, *The Gifted Gabaldón Sisters*, released in October of 2008 from Grand Central Press, was a Borders/Las Comadres Selection for the month of November. López's short story collection *Homicide Survivors Picnic and Other Stories* was named as a finalist for the PEN/Faulkner Prize in Fiction in 2010, and she edited a collection of essays titled *An Angle of Vision: Women Writers on Their Poor and Working-Class Roots* published by the University of Michigan Press. She has recently released a novel titled *The Realm of Hungry Spirits*, from Hachette/Grand Central Publishing.

William Luis is the Chancellor's Professor of Spanish at Vanderbilt University. He has published twelve books and numerous scholarly articles. His authored books include *Literary Bondage: Slavery in Cuban Narrative* (1990), *Dance Between Two Cultures: Latino Caribbean Literature Written in the United States* (1997), *Culture and Customs of Cuba* (2001), *Lunes de Revolución: Literatura y cultura en los primeros años de la Revolución Cubana* (2003), and *Juan Francisco Manzano: Autobiografía del esclavo poeta y otros escritos* (2007). Also, Luis is the editor of the *Afro-Hispanic Review*. Born and raised in New York City, Luis is widely regarded as a leading authority on Latin American, Caribbean, Afro-Hispanic, and Latino US literatures.

Maria Melendez lives in Pueblo, Colorado, where she publishes *Pilgrimage*, a literary magazine serving a far-flung community of writers, artists, naturalists, activists, seekers, and other adventurers in and beyond the Greater Southwest (www.pilgrimagepress.org). The University of Arizona Press has published two of her poetry collections: *How Long She'll Last in This World* and *Flexible Bones*, and her essays appear in *Sojourns Magazine: Natural & Cultural History of the Colorado Plateau* and *Isotope: A Journal of Literary Nature and Science Writing*. She serves as contributing editor for *Latino Poetry Review* and acquisitions editor for Momotombo Press, a chapbook publisher featuring prose and poetry by emerging Latino writers.

Helena Mesa was born and raised in Pittsburgh, Pennsylvania. Her first book of poems, *Horse Dance Underwater,* was released from Cleveland State University Press in 2009. She is a co-editor for *Mentor and Muse: Essays from Poets to Poets,* and her poems have appeared in various literary journals, including *Barrow Street, Indiana Review,* and *Third Coast.* Mesa is an associate professor of English at Albion College.

Urayoán Noel was born in San Juan, Puerto Rico. His works include the books of poetry *Hi-Density Politics* (Blazevox Books), *Boringkén* (Ediciones Callejón), and *Kool Logic/La Lógica Kool* (Bilingual Press), and the performance DVD *Kool Logic Sessions* (Bilingual Press). An assistant professor of English at the University at Albany (SUNY) and a contributing editor of *Mandorla*, Noel is currently completing a book on Nuyorican poetry from the 1960s to the present.

Peter Ramos's poems have appeared or will appear in *Painted Bride Quarterly*, *Indiana Review, Mississippi Review, elimae* and *Puerto del Sol*. He is the author of one book of poetry, *Please Do Not Feed the Ghost* (BlazeVox Books, 2008), and two chapbooks: *Watching Late-Night Hitchcock & Other Poems* (handwritten press, 2004), and *Short Waves* (White Eagle Coffee Store Press, 2003).

Carla Trujillo was born in New Mexico and grew up in Northern California. She has lived in the San Francisco Bay Area for the past twenty-six years. She received her BS in Human Development from UC Davis and her MS and PhD in Educational Psychology from the University of Wisconsin, Madison. She is the editor of *Living Chicana Theory* (Third Woman Press) and *Chicana Lesbians: The Girls Our Mothers Warned Us About* (Third Woman Press); winner of a LAMBDA Book Award and the Out/Write Vanguard Award. Her novel, *What Night Brings* (Curbstone Press), won the Miguel Marmól Prize for fiction that focuses on human rights. *What Night Brings* also won the Paterson Fiction Prize, the Latino Literary Foundation Latino Book Award, Bronze Medal from *ForeWord* magazine, Honorable Mention for the Gustavus Meyers Book Award, and was a LAMBDA Book Award finalist. Carla works as the director of the Graduate Diversity Program at UC Berkeley and has focused some of her recent activities on improving the work and classroom climate using interactive theater.